T0323039

Building a New Economy

Building a New Economy

Japan's Digital and Green Transformation

D. Hugh Whittaker

OXFORD
UNIVERSITY PRESS

OXFORD
UNIVERSITY PRESS

Great Clarendon Street, Oxford, OX2 6DP,
United Kingdom

Oxford University Press is a department of the University of Oxford.
It furthers the University's objective of excellence in research, scholarship,
and education by publishing worldwide. Oxford is a registered trade mark of
Oxford University Press in the UK and in certain other countries

Published in the United States of America by Oxford University Press
198 Madison Avenue, New York, NY 10016, United States of America

British Library Cataloguing in Publication Data

Data available

Library of Congress Control Number: 2023946075

ISBN 9780198893394

DOI: 10.1093/oso/9780198893394.001.0001

Printed and bound by
CPI Group (UK) Ltd, Croydon, CR0 4YY

Links to third party websites are provided by Oxford in good faith and
for information only. Oxford disclaims any responsibility for the materials
contained in any third party website referenced in this work.

Acknowledgements

Although this book focuses on Japan since 2015, the perspectives brought to the task are the result of several decades of living and researching in Japan, and more importantly, of countless people who have generously given their time and shared their insights with me over that time. To them I express my deep appreciation for their generous sharing of knowledge, wisdom, and company.

More immediately, I benefited from extended fieldwork in Japan in 2021, and shorter periods in 2022 and 2023. 2021 was, of course, a year of the Covid-19 pandemic. Some interviews and meetings could be done in person, often through masks, while others had to be done online. Altogether, I did about 60 interviews, across central and local government departments, businesses and business organizations, NPOs, consultancies, and fellow academics. I also benefited from many less formal conversations. The interviews and conversations helped with sensemaking, and triangulation of a large amount of material published in Japanese, and increasingly in English.

In particular I appreciated the chance to interact with officers of Keidanren (Japan Business Federation), especially President Masakazu Kubota, as well as Atsushi Yamakoshi, and senior managers of affiliated companies. As well, Yoshifumi Nakata of Doshisha University, my institutional host in 2021, was generous in sharing his insights on labour markets, and developments in the field of STEM. I further benefitted from time with researchers at EHESS and Fondation France-Japon in Paris, especially Sébastien Lechevalier and Robert Boyer, and insights from the *Régulation* approach to economic and institutional change. And I wish to acknowledge the benefits of daily conversations with colleagues at the Nissan Institute of Japanese Studies, Oxford.

At the risk of offending those many omitted by name, I would additionally like to thank Yoshitaka Kurosawa, Tim Sturgeon, Fangmiao Zou, and participants of the 'Reforming Capitalism, Going Digital and Green: Does Japan Hold Answers?' conference in Oxford in February 2023. My appreciation also to anonymous reviewers and Adam Swallow of Oxford University Press. And my special appreciation to Toshie Okita, who encouraged me to write this book.

In terms of financial assistance, a Japan Foundation Fellowship enabled me to be in Japan in the first half of 2021, and an Oxford Sasakawa Fund grant during the second half of 2021. A Banque de France Fellowship supported my time in Paris in spring 2022.

Writing about unfolding events and policies demands frequent updates to a manuscript, and sometimes reframing. Hopefully the interpretations offered in this book will stand the test of time, and not be de-railed by tomorrow's surprises, which there will surely be.

Contents

List of Figures

List of Tables

Acronyms and Organizations

3.11	Earthquake, tsunami, and nuclear disasters of 11 March 2011
3E+S	Energy security, economic efficiency, environmental protection, safety
ANRE	Agency for Natural Resources and Energy
API	Application programming interface
BoJ	Bank of Japan
CSTI	Council for Science, Technology, and Innovation
DBJ	Development Bank of Japan
DX	Digital transformation
ESG	Environment, social, and governance
FDI	Foreign direct investment
GFC	Global Financial Crisis
GGS	Green Growth Strategy
GHG	Greenhouse gas
GPIF	Government Pension Investment Fund
GX	Green transformation
IPA	Information Technology Promotion Agency
Kantei	Metonym for Prime Minister's residence and administration, but more expansively includes the Cabinet Secretariat and Cabinet Office. Here referred to as Office of the Prime Minister and Cabinet (OPMC).
Keidanren	Japan Business Federation
LDP	Liberal Democratic Party
METI	Ministry of Economy, Trade, and Industry
MHLW	Ministry of Health, Labour, and Welfare
MIC	Ministry of Internal Affairs and Communications
MITI	Ministry of International Trade and Industry (now METI)
MLIT	Ministry of Land, Infrastructure, Transport, and Tourism
MoE	Ministry of the Environment
MOIP	Mission-oriented innovation policy
NEDO	New Energy and Industrial Technology Development Organization
NISC	National Centre of Incident Readiness and Strategy for Cybersecurity
ODA	Official Development Assistance
OPMC	Office of the Prime Minister and Cabinet; Kantei
Rengo	Japanese Trade Union Confederation
SDGs	Sustainable Development Goals (UN)
SIP	Strategic Innovation Programme
SSE	Social and solidarity economy
STI	Science, technology, and Innovation
TCFD	Task Force on Climate-Related Financial Disclosures
TSE	Tokyo Stock Exchange

Introduction

Can Japan Rise Again?

Japan is attempting to build a new economy, by 2030—or alternatively the 2030s. It goes by various names, such as 'Society 5.0', 'sustainable capitalism', and 'new form of capitalism'. It is to be constructed through digital and green transformation, and a 'virtuous cycle of growth and distribution'. The effort faces strong headwinds, including demographic decline and ageing, Japan's external energy dependence and geopolitical turbulence, and legacies of what some have termed Japan's lost decades. Past attempts have fallen short; Prime Minister Abe's 2013 catch cry 'Japan is back!' may have applied to the diplomatic stage, but not the economy. Abenomics may have helped Japan to arrest deflation, but it did not establish a new growth model. Will this time be any different?

The answer to this question matters not just for Japan, but arguably for other countries facing similar challenges. The challenges extend beyond digital and green transformation to the reform of financialized capitalism, which even stalwarts such as the US Business Roundtable concede needs reform. Countries like the UK and US which have confidently led the way over the past decades are themselves divided or stumbling, while the authoritarianism of emerging giant China does not present an attractive alternative. Japan is seeking to steer a path between market and state over-reach respectively, a new balance of state–market–civil society relations, and socially constructive rather than destructive forms of innovation. This may not be as dazzling as its postwar manufacturing-centred model, but it might offer hints on how to move beyond neoliberalism into a new era.

The scale of the task should not be under-estimated. Japan is frequently castigated as a digital and green laggard, and inhospitable to start-up entrepreneurs. Its current dysfunctional economic model can be seen in the Bank of Japan holding the largest number of listed company shares, banks amassing stocks of government bonds and deposits at the central bank, companies building up massive internal reserves, and using them to repurchase

Building a New Economy. D. Hugh Whittaker, Oxford University Press. © D. Hugh Whittaker (2024).
DOI: 10.1093/oso/9780198893394.003.0001

their own shares, while workers struggle to meet their daily needs and face an uncertain future. Turning this around will not be easy. If anything, however, this is all the more reason to be interested in what Japan is doing. Like its accelerated demographic ageing, the severity brings the nature of the challenges, and the responses, into sharp relief.

It is possible that the responses will be inadequate, as they are often deemed to have been in the past. Indeed, it is possible to envisage a number of future scenarios, with different measures of optimism and pessimism. Focusing on institutions and their coherence, an optimistic one would look something like this:

Scenario 1: Renewal

Japan lost its institutional and ideational coherence in the 1990s to be sure, but there is now a concerted effort to construct a new coherence through digital transformation (DX) and green transformation (GX), expressed at the macro level as 'Society 5.0' and complemented by 'new capitalism',[1] that offers a very different vision of the future than the market-led transformations which have thus far characterized the US, or state domination in the case of China. At company level DX, GX, and corporate governance reform may be creatively reconciled, and a new model of employment relations more compatible with social sustainability and diversity established. This would create a new macro-micro coherence. Japan may not be at the forefront of DX and GX, but this may ultimately be to its advantage in steering a more balanced approach between market and state excesses.

Scenario 2: Maturity

Japan's postwar institutional and ideational coherence was the result of particular circumstances, including social levelling from war, rebuilding and new growth opportunities, and a drive for a better future. As Japan matured interests diverged, productionist national(ist) regulations had to be adjusted to accommodate consumer, financial, and trading partner interests. Social tensions may not be as acute as in some countries, but maturity brings diversity and social division. Institutional coherence through digital and green transformation will be elusive. Japan will continue to muddle along.

Scenario 3: Conversion and imitation

Overlapping with Scenario 2, a combination of external pressure and temptation led Japan to dismantle its postwar model in favour of neoliberal policies, including

---

[1] 'New form of capitalism' is the Japanese government's preferred but somewhat awkward English translation of *atarashii shihonshugi*. 'New capitalism' will generally be used in this book.

financialization, which were partially adopted. The result was institutional dissonance, a rupture of the postwar social contract and a precipitous rise in inequality.[2]
Digital and green transformation may present an opportunity to forge a new institutional configuration, but once the neoliberal cat is released, it will not be put into
a bag called 'new capitalism'. Continued institutional borrowing and inconsistency
is likely; social divisions may intensify.

Scenario 4: Decline

In the most pessimistic prognosis Japan has already peaked; the question is merely
its rate of decline.[3] Politically and institutionally, vested interests impede change
at every turn. Japan excelled at manufacturing, but with diminishing returns, and
it has struggled to grasp the power of software and digital technologies. Fiscal
health will be unattainable. Ageing and population decline will sap the country's
resources and vitality. DX, GX, and new capitalism won't change this.

This book is concerned with the plausibility of the first scenario, tempered
by the less optimistic ones. As these scenarios suggest, the focus of the
book is on institutional and ideational (ideological, motivational) change
and whether or not these are coming together to form a new 'growth'
model, although the term may be misleading as Japan has other objectives
besides growth, such as coping with societal ageing, reduction of inequality, sustainability, and resilience. Growth rates are thus not necessarily
a reliable indicator of transformation, nor as it turns out is institutional
coherence per se. What Japan appears to be aiming at is a new cycle of
growth and distribution compatible with social and environmental sustainability, built with different technologies and social relations than its postwar
model.

The 'builders' of this new economy we will encounter range from central
and city governments to large and small businesses and business organizations, as well as civil society organizations. And the subject matter
addressed spans the changing nature of the Japanese state and state–market
relations, corporate governance, management and employment, education
and training, innovation and entrepreneurship, with cross-cutting themes
of digital and green transformation. It would be quite possible to write
a book on any one of these actors, subjects, or themes, but to assess
whether a new economy is being built, or not, we must see how they come
together.

---

[2] Cf. Dore, 2009; Lechevalier, 2014.
[3] Cf. Glosserman, 2019.

The remainder of this Introduction is divided into three sections. The first offers a very brief introduction to 'Society 5.0', Keidanren's 'sustainable capitalism' and Prime Minister Kishida's 'new capitalism'.[4] The second introduces the conceptual framework which underpins this book, situating Japan in a historical and comparative context, and pointing to the wider significance of the changes Japan is pursuing. This may be skipped if the reader is simply interested in knowing what is happening in the Japanese political economy. The third gives a brief introduction to the chapters which follow.

Re-forming Japan: From Society 5.0 to 'New Capitalism'

In 2015 the Council for Science, Technology and Innovation (CSTI) published the 5th STI Basic Plan (2016–2020), which introduced the concept of 'Society 5.0'. To some this was just an empty slogan, or an attempt to go one better than Germany's 'Industrie 4.0' by claiming its vision was greater than the transformation of industry. In fact, it was significant in three respects. First, it proposed a shift from a technology-driven STI policy approach to 'a more society-centred and challenge-driven innovation policy', one which following the traumatic 2011 earthquake, tsunami, and nuclear triple disaster recognized the need to prepare for an 'unpredictable and unforeseeable near future' as the most fundamental challenge to be addressed (Carraz and Harayama, 2019: 40). Second, it provided a forward-looking focal point for debate and policies about digital transformation which was taken up by government ministries, Keidanren and individual companies. And third, it offered an alternative to a market-led approach to digital transformation, and a state-dominated one, potentially harnessing and balancing both.

The UN's Strategic Development Goals (SDGs) were also announced in 2015, with a target date of 2030 for their realization. As Society 5.0 began to incorporate green transformation, and as the SDGs spread in Japan, 2030—or at least the 2030s—implicitly became the target date for the realization of Society 5.0 as well. A simple definition of Society 5.0 is 'a human-centered society that achieves both economic development and solutions to social issues through a system that highly integrates cyberspace and physical space'.[5] Or as it was originally expressed, less succinctly, in the 5th STI Basic Plan:

---

[4] Keidanren is the Japan Business Federation, the largest peak business organization in Japan.

[5] https://www.openaccessgovernment.org/japans-6th-science-technology-and-innovation-basic-plan/120486/ accessed 14 June 2022. Society 5.0 follows hunting and gathering (1.0), agricultural (2.0), industrial (3.0) and information (4.0) societies.

Through an initiative merging the physical space (real world) and cyberspace by leveraging ICT to its fullest, we are proposing an ideal form of our future society: a 'super smart society' that will bring wealth to the people. The series of initiatives geared toward realizing this ideal society are now being further deepened and intensively promoted as 'Society 5.0'.

A super smart society is … a society where the various needs of society are finely differentiated and met by providing the necessary products and services in the required amounts to the people who need them when they need them, and in which all the people can receive high-quality services and live a comfortable, vigorous life that makes allowances for their various differences such as age, sex, region, or language.

(CSTI, 2015: 13)

The idea had staying power. It was still central in the 6th STI Basic Plan (2021–2025), in which social sciences and humanities started to feature more prominently.[6] The staying power may have had something to do with the original proposers. An influential member—Nakanishi Hiroaki—was the chairman of Keidanren (Japan Business Federation), which took up the concept and proposed a roadmap to 2030 in a report titled 'Revitalizing Japan by Realizing Society 5.0: Action Plan for Creating the Society of the Future'.[7] Nakanishi was also Chairman of the Hitachi group, and together with another influential member of the CSTI, Tokyo University President Gonokami Makoto, established the Hitachi-UTokyo Laboratory in 2016 to create a comprehensive university–industry collaboration, and to advance the agenda.[8] Keidanren, the University of Tokyo and the Government Pension Investment Fund (GPIF), also co-authored a report in 2020 called 'The Evolution of ESG Investment, Realization of Society 5.0, and Achievement of SDGs'.[9] This set out an economic case for investment in 'Society 5.0 technologies', and floated the possibility of a Society 5.0 Index which would combine ESG and DX (digital transformation).

Japan's *GX* (green transformation) took on a new urgency and focus in 2021 when then Prime Minister Suga committed Japan to reducing its greenhouse gas emissions by at least 46 per cent (relative to 2013 levels) by 2030, causing hasty revisions to be made to the recently released Green Growth Strategy, as well as the 6th Strategic Energy Plan. An over-arching ten-year

---

[6] https://www.openaccessgovernment.org/japans-6th-science-technology-and-innovation-basic-plan/120486/ accessed 14 June 2022.
[7] Except in the Acknowledgements, Japanese names are given with the surname first.
[8] The Hitachi-UTokyo Lab produced a book on Society 5.0 in 2018, with an English translation in 2020.
[9] ESG: environment, social, governance—see Chapter 5.

GX Realization Basic Plan and roadmap was released in February 2023. DX and GX became the two driving wheels of Japan's new economic cart.

If DX and GX are the driving wheels, capitalism is the cart itself. Responding to the growing clamour for the reform of capitalism outside and inside Japan, in 2020 Keidanren proposed 'sustainable capitalism' with a New Growth Strategy which would 'bring together the wisdom of diverse stakeholders and establish sustainable capitalism with Society 5.0, which creates diverse value through DX'. This was followed by 'new capitalism', proposed by Kishida Fumio in his bid to become president of the Liberal Democratic Party and hence Prime Minister in 2021. Despite its rocky reception by financial markets, the mantra of a 'virtuous cycle of growth and distribution' spread, most noticeably in lead-up to the 2023 wage bargaining round. 'New capitalism' had four priorities—people (first and foremost); science, technology, and innovation (STI); startups; and DX and GX. Kishida also proposed a Vision for a Digital Garden City Nation to address regional disparities.

Although Japan is frequently branded a laggard when it comes to DX and GX, in some respects the country was at the forefront of both two decades earlier. The Kyoto Protocol (1997) temporarily propelled Japan to the forefront of efforts to combat climate change, and in the early 2000s e-Japan strategies under an IT Strategic Headquarters aimed to make Japan the 'world leader in IT' by 2005. But then Prime Minister Koizumi's neoliberal priorities lay in dismantling the postwar institutions of industrial policy rather than re-directing them.[10] Japan hesitated to extend its own commitment to the Kyoto Protocol beyond 2012, and the central element of e-government, the Network System for Basic Resident Registers (commonly called Juki-net), was quietly abandoned in the face of widespread opposition. Two decades on, Japan is now in many respects a follower rather than a pioneer. In this more familiar positioning, with a better idea of what it wants to change, and avoid, and with more extensive buy-in to its transformation programmes, Japan is arguably better placed to achieve what previously proved elusive.

Conceptual Framework

Underlying much of the criticism of Japan as immobile, lagging, or deviant is an assumption that the structural and policy changes introduced in Anglophone countries—principally the US and UK—are normal, and that Japan, despite dragging its feet, will eventually have to conform to these. These

---

[10] Koizumi was Prime Minister from 2001 to 2006.

assumptions have persisted even in the midst of a growing sense of crisis about the environmental and social costs of neoliberalism and financialized capitalism in those same countries. The conceptual framework for this book tries to avoid such assumptions and dichotomous comparisons by situating Japan in a broader historical and geopolitical context, which encompasses states and markets, organization and technology and production systems, with institutions at its core. Sketching it will show the rationale for the questions which motivate the book, and how Japan's experience is relevant more widely. It consists of two parts: (1) 'dyads' of state–market and organization–technology relations, which constitute the frame, and (2) institutions, which provide the cladding on that frame. Let us look at these in turn.

Co-evolutionary Dyads

Figure 0.1 is a visual aid, consisting of two dyads set in an international economic and geopolitical context.[11] The upper dyad broadly corresponds to the macro, policy level, and state–market relations to the political economy of capitalism. The lower dyad broadly corresponds to the micro, management level, and organization–technology dynamics to innovation. The figure will help to visualize the coherence of Japan's postwar high growth system or model, and how this coherence was eroded from the 1980s (Chapter 1). It will also help to visualize how Japan has been building a new economy through evolving relations within and between the dyads (subsequent chapters). That Society 5.0 became a guiding motif for DX and GX may be attributed to the beacon it offers for the recovery of institutional coherence, or at least a direction for institutional change, at both macro and micro levels. Finally, the figure helps to visualize the influence of geopolitics and Japan's external dependencies (Chapter 9).

The upper dyad of 'states' and 'markets' is a combination familiar to political economy, with the caveats that states are complex entities, and 'markets' is something of a misnomer, as it includes big business and finance, which Braudel famously referred to as the great predators of the *anti-market* because they concentrate power and excel in extra- (anti-)market manoeuvres.[12] Nonetheless, the labels are convenient. Historically speaking, modern nation states and capitalism emerged together in an interactive, co-evolutionary

---

[11] This framework draws on Whittaker et al., 2020, in which a fuller explanation can be found.

[12] Braudel (1982: 229–230) depicted the economy in three tiers; a self-sufficient base tier, a middle, market tier, and above this 'the zone of the anti-market, where the great predators roam and the law of the jungle operates. This—today as in the past, before and after the industrial revolution—is the real home of capitalism.'

process, and they continue to evolve. Polanyi (1944) portrayed this as a dialectical process, or 'double movement', in which the state plays an active role in the creation of new markets by 'dis-embedding' them from social relations (the liberalizing phase in Figure 0.1), and a counterbalancing reaction to 're-embed' those markets (the regulating phase), which also involves the state.[13]

Polanyi's insights have been extended to the post-World War II period. Postwar 'embedded liberalism' was a historical compromise intended to ameliorate the extremes of the double movement: '(U)nlike the economic nationalism of the thirties [embedded liberalism] would be multilateral in character; unlike the liberalism of the gold standard and free trade, its multilateralism would be predicated upon domestic interventionism' (Ruggie, 1982: 393). Significantly, it was in the age of postwar embedded liberalism that Japan's 'developmental state' flourished which, according to Johnson (1982), created a distinctive state–market balance. However, postwar embedded liberalism was rejected in the dominant geopolitical power (the US, also the UK), setting in train a new cycle, this time of neoliberalism, and signs of a recent double movement push-back. It is in this context that Japan's partial neoliberal conversion and nascent 'new capitalism' respectively should be seen.

The lower dyad expresses a relationship between organization and technology which is also co-evolutionary. Major new technologies are typically diffused in new forms of organization. Here the co-evolutionary dynamic draws on Bodrožić and Adler (2017), whose revolutionizing and balancing sequence is similar to Polanyi's double movement, but at the micro-level.[14] In their model, which is based on US experience, the 'Fordist corporation' associated with autos and oil which spread after World War II went through 'strategy and structure' (revolutionizing) and 'quality management' (balancing) phases. It was in this context that Japan's postwar large-firm manufacturing-centric model was created. Japan rapidly learned mass production and productivity lessons from the US, and was instrumental in the balancing, quality management phase. However, it has struggled in the subsequent waves of information and communications technology (ICT) and the digital economy, and (global) network and platform forms of organization, in which software has assumed an increasingly important role. It

---

[13] Strictly speaking, markets are always socially, institutionally and ideologically embedded, as the dyad suggests, hence 'dis-embedded', like 'de-regulated' is a misnomer: cf. Block and Somers, 2014; Vogel, 2018.
[14] Bodrožić and Adler in turn draw on and simplify Perez's (2002) neo-Schumpeterian model of long techno-economic cycles.

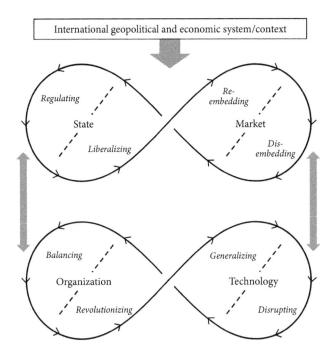

Figure 0.1 State–market and organization–technology dyads
Source: Adapted from Whittaker et al., 2020.

appears that Japan does not excel in 'revolutionizing' phases of new techno-economic paradigms—Schumpeter's 'creative destruction'—but does better in 'balancing' phases. If so, Japan's laggard status (justified or not) in digital technologies is not necessarily a handicap to its digital and green transformation; it could yet produce another balancing model, as it did with quality management.

Interactions *between* the dyads of Figure 0.1 are indicated by the vertical arrows. Although in practice they are difficult to separate, roughly speaking, the lower dyad represents the 'engine' of economic growth, and the upper dyad the enabling and regulatory mechanisms. And importantly, shown at the top of the figure is the international geopolitical and economic system which is shaped by the dominant power(s), which has a strong influence on institutional development in countries incorporated into the international system. This too can change so it matters when a country is integrated into the world economy. Japan's first integration in the late nineteenth century was in the context of imperialism and the international gold standard regime constructed by Britain. After World War II it was under US-led embedded liberalism. Japan's institutional development was strongly, but differently, influenced in both these eras (Chapter 1). Once formed, institutions often become resistant to change. Britain failed to fully utilize the emerging technologies and organizational forms of the late nineteenth century, while Japan has struggled to adapt to those of the late twentieth century.

This framework puts Japan in a historical and geopolitical context without resorting to dichotomous comparisons. It suggests that we are in a period of major historical flux, in which a double movement inflection point in state–market relations overlaps with a similar inflection in organization-technology dynamics, and third, with profound changes in the international geopolitical and economic system marked by the rise of China and severe tensions with the US. It is in this three level perspective that we should understand Japan's attempts to reform its capitalist institutions, and DX and GX.

Institutions and Institutional Complementarity

The 'cladding' on the conceptual framework comes from institutional analysis, which has been concerned not just with individual institutions, but also how institutions fit together in patterned configurations, as well as how they change. 'Varieties of capitalism' writing has emphasized stable, systemic preferences for non-market and market-based coordination, often presented dichotomously.[15] As Thelen (2004: 2) writes: 'These authors all point to more or less the same set of institutional arrangements that have traditionally been defined as central to the functioning of these political economies—financial institutions, industrial relations institutions, vocational training systems, bank–industry links, and more recently, welfare state institutions and policies.... For all their differences, these authors make very similar distinctions across countries, and draw an especially sharp line between "organized" (or "embedded") capitalist economies on the one hand, and "liberal" market economies such as the United States and United Kingdom on the other.'

Institutions and institutional configurations change over time, however, and dichotomies can be misleading. Japan has almost invariably been assigned to the camp of organized capitalism, whose stability was already under question in the late 1980s and early 1990s. Albert (1993: 195) worried

---

[15] For example, socially embedded and liberal market political economies (Streeck, 2001), coordinated and liberal market economies (Hall and Soskice, 2001), Rhineland and Anglo-Saxon capitalism (Albert, [1991] 1993), welfare and stock market capitalism (Dore, 2000). Exceptions include Amable (2003), whose five models also extend to Asia.

that despite being more equitable, Rhineland (organized) capitalism was losing an 'ideological beauty contest', so that 'even the good grey burghers of Zurich and Frankfurt are beginning to wonder what it feels like to win the jackpot with one spin of the roulette wheel'. From stability, institutional writing began to explore change, with Streeck and Thelen (2005) proposing five mechanisms; displacement, layering, drift, conversion, and exhaustion. Examples of each may be found in Japan, but layering and conversion are especially common, with new institutions frequently layered onto old ones, or inhabiting old institutions rather than displacing them. Past and present, tradition and transformation, co-exist. It is important to keep this in mind when we consider Japan's 'new' economy.

When it comes to relations between institutions, Boyer argues that both change and *lack* of institutional coherence are natural. Co-evolution may produce temporary coherent or complementary institutional configurations, but these are typically bookended by structural crises.

> Co-evolution is the process of trial and error through which a series of institutional forms that are initially disconnected and formally independent (since they result from institutionalized compromises among diverse agents in different fields) adjust to one another until a viable institutional configuration emerges. The economic adjustments then become part of a mode of regulation and retrospectively appear as coherent. This extends to institutional analysis a concept developed by neo-Schumpeterian theories for the joint evolution of technologies and organizations.
>
> **(Boyer, 2005: 367)**

Even 'viable institutional configurations' may contain contradictions, and coherence may be a matter of appearance. The Régulation school, of which Boyer has been a leading figure, started out by analysing the breakdown of the US Fordist system at the macro and micro levels in the 1970s, and institutional changes in France which brought about an end to the postwar *trente glorieuses*.[16] Importantly, as well as complementarities—or their lack—the Régulation approach identifies hierarchical relations between institutions— some institutions are more critical or dominant, and impose their logic on other institutions. The *wage–labour nexus* was central to postwar Fordism, but was replaced by a new configuration in which the *monetary and financial*

---

[16] *Les trente glorieuses* refers to the three decades following 1945 which saw high levels of economic growth and stability in France, and many other capitalist/industrialized countries. Sometimes referred to as the 'golden age of capitalism,' it was also an age of 'embedded liberalism,' as referred to above.

regime became most influential, creating pressures for labour market de-regulation and peripheralization of the wage–labour nexus.[17]

Many of these insights apply to Japan as well. The wage-labour nexus—'Japanese-style management/ employment'—which was central to its post-war productionist model, began to come under pressure in the mid 1970s. Tensions between this nexus and a (partial) monetary and finance-centred configuration emerged and persist, as we shall see (Chapters 1, 6, 7). Address-ing these tensions is a task of 'new capitalism'.

Institutional perspectives augment the dyad constructs, and raise impor-tant questions, such as the following. Will a new institutional configuration emerge under the banners of Society 5.0, DX, GX, and new capitalism? What will be the core institutions, and will they achieve institutional and ideational (ideological, motivational) coherence? Finance is vital for economic transfor-mation, but will the transformations steer Japan away from financialization, or more deeply into it?[18] Will the wage–labour nexus again be elevated and a new upskilling–productivity enhancement loop emerge which enables inclu-sive growth and a new social (and environmental) contract, as envisaged by 'new capitalism'? How much will Japan's new economy be the result of con-scious design and state coordination—a new 'developmental state'—and how much will be from trial and error, or market processes?

Organization of the Book

Addressing such questions, the book is organized as follows. Chapter 1 sets the baseline for assessing institutional change with the rise and fall of Japan's postwar economic model. The model was a combination of pre-war and wartime continuities, and postwar Occupation reforms, coming together around manufacturing with a high degree of macro- and micro-level institutional and ideational congruence. Not everyone benefited from this, however, and its very success brought tensions and pressures for change in the 1980s. Currency appreciation and bursting of the asset bubble instigated changes which undermined the model's coherence, with reform contested between advocates of incremental change, and advocates of more radical

---

[17] This occurred through financialization, or, together with the relaxation of competition policy and capital-favouring international trade and investment agreements, empowerment of the 'anti-market' zone in Braudel's terms.

[18] There are many definitions of financialization. Krippner (2005: 12) sees it as 'a pattern of accu-mulation in which profits accrue primarily through financial channels rather than through trade and commodity production'. There is a political side as well, 'characterized by the domination of the macro economy and economic policy by financial interests' (Palley, 2013: 1).

transformation. Neoliberal influences peaked in the early 2000s; their allure diminished with the dot.com bubble burst, Enron, growing domestic wealth disparities and ultimately the Global Financial Crisis. Amidst a flurry of changes in the early 2000s was an initial attempt at digital and green transformation, which faded through a lack of an integrating vision, as well as being caught up in conflicting cross-currents. Abenomics countered Japan's deflationary tide, but did not itself provide a new growth model. Out of the limelight of Abe's policies, however, the buds of Japan's current digital and green transformation were forming.

Chapter 2 takes up the first of these—digital transformation (DX)—at a macro-level which focuses on different modes of intervention by the government to effect change, or as it warns, risk getting left behind. A METI-sponsored report visualized this as a Digital Cliff, looming large by 2025, requiring urgent attention by companies from board to shop-floor level.[19] It especially placed the onus on senior managers to take responsibility for DX, with guidelines, indicators, and a Digital Governance Code. The chapter then turns to the government itself, and the creation of the Digital Agency, in what its first director described as Japan's last chance to reverse 'digital defeat'. Byzantine procedures, incompatible systems and turf protecting which stymied past attempts at e-government were finally to be addressed. Japan has also been chasing a rapidly moving target when it comes to cybersecurity, and embedding it in government, business, and society. This is addressed in the third section, while the fourth section considers the revival of industrial and innovation policy, introducing the Strategic Innovation Programme under the CSTI and METI's Connected Industries. Finally, we look at an attempt to figure out how governance will work in Society 5.0, given the spread of cyber-physical systems in which algorithms are influential, risks are many and complex, and locus of responsibility ambiguous. 'Governance innovation' is necessary to ensure that ultimate values like happiness and liberty are enhanced rather than threatened.

Chapter 3 turns to the second—green transformation (GX)—beginning with electric power generation. Despite the investments and technological gains from the Sunshine and Moonlight projects dating back to the 1970s, here too Japan has gained the reputation of being a laggard in the turn to renewable energy, notably because of its continuing reliance on coal, which increased after the closure of its nuclear reactors following the Fukushima nuclear disaster in 2011 (so-called '3:11'). Although the renewable energy

---

[19] METI is short for Ministry of Economy, Trade and Industry. See the glossary of Acronyms and Organizations.

share of power generation has climbed steadily since, a considerable step-up is needed if Japan is to meet its Paris Agreement and subsequent obligations. When it comes to recycling and the circular economy, Japan's record is more impressive, with substantial gains made over the past two decades, in contrast to many OECD countries. In disaster preparedness and resilience, moreover, a series of natural disasters beginning with the Hanshin-Awaji earthquake of 1995 and including the triple disaster of 2011 ('3:11') have pushed Japan to adopt advanced measures and technologies. Finally in the chapter we consider the 'Green Growth Strategy' (GGS), a set of industrial policies which the government is implementing to meet its climate obligations *and* rejuvenate the economy, as well as the 2023 GX Realization Basic Plan, which sets out more comprehensively Japan's path to a green economy in the coming decade.

Cities have emerged as a critical stage for digital and green transformation. A wave of smart city projects has swept both the global North and South, and Japan is no exception. Chapter 4 looks at the emergence and characteristics of smart city projects in Japan, from disparate energy and compact city projects in the 2000s, to eco cities, future cities, smart cities and eventually 'super cities' which address multiple services on an integrated data platform. The Cabinet Office and related ministries have produced a detailed, stage-by-stage Smart City Guidebook to diffuse lessons within Japan, and, they hope, abroad. Four diverse smart city cases are introduced—Higashi Matsushima in earthquake and tsunami-devastated Tohoku; Kashiwa-no-ha, a land development project on the express train line between Tokyo and Tsukuba; castle town Aizuwakamatsu's City-Accenture-University collaboration; and Toyota's purpose-built Woven City at the base of Mount Fuji. The link with Society 5.0 and the preceding chapters is explicit in another Cabinet Office publication: 'Japan's Smart Cities: Solving Global Issues Such as the SDGs, etc. through Japan's Society 5.0'. The chapter also introduces Japanese MaaS (mobility as a service) initiatives, as well as Kishida's Vision for a Digital Garden City Nation, which seeks to diffuse digital transformation in rural Japan so that 'no one is left behind'.

The next two chapters turn to industry- and company-level transformation. In Chapter 4 the focus is on innovation, and the second dyad. It begins with electronics and IT, a critical sector in which Japanese incumbents have struggled with changing business models and competition. Some like Hitachi have re-invented themselves, others have disappeared. Hitachi's re-invention has been achieved by combining manufacturing with an IT platform, as envisaged by Society 5.0. We also look at the rise of specialist manufacturers which have successfully integrated into global value chains (GVCs) and global platforms. The second section turns to automobiles, Japan's leading industrial sector, which is undergoing multiple upheavals depicted as CASE (connected, autonomous, shared, electric). Like Hitachi, Toyota seeks to combine manufacturing and IT, albeit in a different way. And it has entered into a bewildering array of alliances and capital tie-ups. The third section turns to finance, from banks to fintech startups and digital currencies. While hardly 'gales of destruction', the winds of change and innovation are clearly penetrating this previously staid sector. A digital currency initiative is considered as a distinctively Japanese approach to change. The final section is about startups, hailed as the future of Japan, and SMEs, conversely dismissed as a drag on change. Together, the sections build a picture of 'DX with Japanese characteristics'.

Complementing Chapter 5, Chapter 6 focuses on corporate governance as a critical stage for corporate transformation, and for determining the future of Japanese capitalism. It was also the nerve point of Abe's attempts to make Japan more attractive to overseas investors through the Stewardship and Corporate Governance Codes, which as the first section shows have progressively been strengthened. The second section looks at the influence of the giant Government Pension Investment Fund (GPIF), first in implementing the Stewardship Code, and second in the spread of ESG in Japan. There is a presumption in the corporate governance reforms that shareholders and managers will work together in the pursuit of medium to long term 'corporate value', as well as sustainability, but do their interests really align that well? The third section offers sobering reflections on this from the turmoil which engulfed Toshiba from 2017. These reflections set the scene for the final section, which begins to look at reforming Japanese capitalism, starting with Keidanren's 'sustainable capitalism' and subsequently in Kishida's 'new (form of) capitalism'. Overall we see investor relations emerging as the core institutional nexus of Japanese capitalism, as distinct from employment relations (the wage–labour nexus) in the postwar decades, but it is not yet clear how compatible this will be with new capitalism's emphasis on growth with distribution, investment in human capital, and rebuilding the middle class, which are taken up in Chapter 7.

'People' are alleged to be at the heart of Society 5.0 and 'new capitalism', but that has not been reflected in investment, either by the government, or by companies. There is much to be done if this aspiration is to be brought into reality, as we shall see in Chapter 7. We begin with efforts to expand the workforce in an age of population decline. Attracting more women, elderly, and non-Japanese into the workforce, however, poses significant challenges. It also requires improvements to the allocative efficiency of labour markets through intermediaries. The second section looks at the corollary of increasing labour market diversity, namely reforming 'Japanese style employment'. Abe's work-style reforms made a start but did not change the underlying institutional foundations. The 'new trinity' reforms (2023) of reskilling, mobility, and job-based wages and employment potentially go further, reaching the postwar institutional foundations of employment stability. A fourth element—'respect for diversity and addressing disparity'—is also considered. The next section briefly considers Covid-19 and telework, and the final section focuses on 'investing in people'. First it looks at Keidanren's proposal to rebuild the middle class, and the question of who will make the necessary investments. Then it looks at government investment in reskilling, and in preparing the education system for Society 5.0.

It is often said that capitalism needs non-capitalist ethics and institutions for its survival, and that in the Anglophone heartlands of neoliberalism these have been eroded. Japan, by contrast, has a historical reluctance to separate morals and economy, which may account for the limited impact of neoliberalism. Chapter 8 explores this from three perspectives. First it considers Japan's 'social and solidarity economy' (SSE), including the role of cooperatives—some of the world's largest are in Japan—as well as labour organizations, and their prospects for re-vitalization. Second, it turns to NPOs, taking up the cases of the Asaza Project, which seeks to restore Lake Kasumigaura, Japan's second largest lake, as well as *Mori wa Umi no Koibito* (The Sea is Longing for the Forest), an NPO based in Kesennuma, which was hit by the Tohoku earthquake and tsunami in 2011. It also considers the networks which were formed in the wake of the disaster, including some focused on digital transformation. Finally, returning to capitalism, it looks at corporations as social enterprise, taking up the case of Benesse Corporation and the Setouchi International Art Triennale, as well as alternative visions of capitalism within Japan. The chapter highlights Japan's 'horizontal' economy or SSE, which is typically overlooked in both top-down developmental state and mainstream economic writing. Its significance will become clear in the concluding chapter.

Japan's path to Society 5.0 through digital and green transformation will not be entirely of its own making. Chapter 9 gives an overview of Japan's external geopolitical and economic relations and dependencies, which are influencing its transformation. Starting with its key trading and investment partners, and GVC participation, it notes how these interdependencies are increasingly subject to 'weaponization', raising the strategic importance of economic security, and of proactive economic statecraft. In the midst of an

escalating trade and technology war between its two biggest trading partners and the world's two biggest economies—the US and China—Japan has
managed to steer a proactive path with its 'free and open Indo-Pacific', and
its digital counterpart 'data free flow with trust'. But it has other dependencies as well—most notably in energy and food—which have been exposed
by Russia's invasion of Ukraine. Characteristically, Japan is actively trying to
turn defence into offence, and domestic transformation into export capability, through new overseas development initiatives, especially with ASEAN
countries. And Japan's relations with the EU have deepened markedly in
recent years, with the signing of trade, strategic partnership, and infrastructure agreements, and significantly for DX and GX, mutual recognition of data
privacy and a Green Alliance. Despite choppy geopolitical waters, to date
Japan has been able to create a degree of synergy between its external relations and dependencies on the one hand, and its economic transformation
on the other. Sterner challenges are likely to lie ahead.

The concluding chapter attempts to make sense of the diverse currents of
change identified in the preceding chapters. It identifies three undercurrents
of change, and associates each with a 'spirit' of capitalism, namely financialized capitalism, the new, adaptive developmental state (in preference to 'state
capitalism'), and communitarian capitalism. These tug in different directions, and may be seen as tensions, or even contradictions, in Japan's DX, GX,
Society 5.0, and new capitalism. Optimistically, they can also be seen as being
played off each other to create 'controlled dis-equilibrium' as a counter to
institutional stasis. There are also tensions in innovation and innovation policy, between focusing on large firms and startups, between technology-driven
and social needs-oriented innovation, and ultimately between a reversion
to a 'catch-up' stance (especially with DX) and forging a post-catch-up path
(especially with GX). Perhaps Japan will solve these tensions creatively as
well. The chapter then considers the claim that Society 5.0 will be 'people-
centred', first in terms of becoming a 'social investment state', then in terms
of an 'anthropogenic' mode of development, and finally as a 'digital democracy'. The chapter, and the book, conclude with prospects of Japan developing
a new socio-economic model, and whether there is still a case for optimism
over Japan's future.

1

The Rise and Fall of the Postwar Economy

To many people Japan is a wealthy, developed country which has nonetheless been mired in low growth and rising public debt for as long as they can remember. Those with longer memories may recall the postwar 'miracle' economy, which was transformed in the span of three decades from exporting cheap plastic products and textiles to high-tech machinery, provoking intense controversy about its trading practices and industrial policy before its asset bubble burst in 1989–1990. It is a struggle to reconcile these two pictures of anaemic and innovative Japan, separated by a sliver of time from 1989 to 1992. Before we consider Japan in the present and where it is heading, we need to consider where it has come from, to see if we can resolve this apparent paradox.[1]

This chapter applies the framework presented in the Introduction to show that Japan's challenge was a *combination* of changing state–market relations, which is what most commentators focus on, *and* changes in the organization–technology dyad, including the organization of production which corporate Japan struggled to respond to. As well, the geopolitical environment changed dramatically with the simultaneous end of the Cold War, forceful assertion of US economic interests abroad, and the rise of Asia, especially China.

These new challenges compounded a growing sense in the 1980s that a reorientation was needed to Japan's 'catch-up' growth model, whose aims had largely been achieved, and whose very success was causing intense friction with trading partners. Unsurprisingly, opinions about the best way forward diverged. Policy—and management—responses were not always consistent. There was an oscillation between conservative instincts and interests, which favoured modest change, and those favouring more radical reform, which drew on neoliberal ideas and institutions. By and large manufacturing

---

[1] Arguably it is not a paradox at all, but a series of self-imposed missteps, mixed with shocks and disasters over which Japan had little control. Yet this also contrasts with the sure-footedness of Japan's postwar rise.

Building a New Economy. D. Hugh Whittaker, Oxford University Press. © D. Hugh Whittaker (2024).
DOI: 10.1093/oso/9780198893394.003.0002

interests aligned with the former, and those of Japanese finance, like policy makers, were split.

The institutional dissonance of the 'lost decades' resulted less in a longing for the dynamic postwar years than for a narrative for the future, going beyond crisis management to identify something to pull together towards, like Society 5.0, and digital and green transformation. These have their own challenges, but they are challenges to work towards solving, collectively.

The chapter is organized as follows. The first section looks very briefly at the evolution of the Japanese economy up to 1945, focusing on the question of change and continuity. The postwar economy, which is taken up in the second section, was the product of prewar and wartime continuities and radical postwar institutional change. These were melded into a distinctive institutionally and ideationally coherent model, which was nonetheless recognizable as a variant of embedded liberalism (or developmentalism, with a 'developmental' state) and Fordism (or Toyotism). Whereas the 'golden age' of postwar capitalism began to break down in many countries in the 1970s, Japan's success sustained it into the 1980s, and in some aspects beyond.

The success of the model generated intense trade and investment friction with the US and Europe, as well as a domestic 'post-catch-up' debate. As we shall see in the third section, institutional coherence impeded change, while also necessitating it. This is followed in the fourth section by fallout from the bubble economy in the 1990s. As the name suggests, the 'lost decades' are often seen as a period of immobilism, stumbling, and fumbling, but they can equally be seen as a period of upheaval and change, contestation, and adaptation. Ironically perhaps *too much* change was attempted at this time. The period was marked by a financial and economic crisis, with recovery hampered by deflation. The final section considers Abe's return to power in 2012, and his attempts to rebuild the economy through Abenomics, with mixed results. Yet out of the spotlight, the buds of a new growth model were quietly growing in the form of digital and green transformation, as we shall see in the following chapters.

Change and Continuity in the Japanese Economy

New economy is always a contentious term when it comes to Japan. The Meiji Restoration of 1868 is widely considered a turning point marking the beginning of Japan's modern era, but in the preceding Tokugawa era (1603–1867) the market economy expanded both in towns and in the countryside. Productivity rose and income sources diversified, with the widespread use of money.

Instead of capital, Japan made use of plentiful labour; it had an *industrious* revolution instead of an *industrial* one (Hayami, 2015). The 'great divergence' between Europe and China brought about by the industrial revolution was muted when it comes to Japan.[2] Complementing this view, Dore (1965) showed that literacy rates rose among all classes in Tokugawa Japan, and that at the end of the Tokugawa era, literacy rates in Japan were broadly similar to Britain at the same time. Much of Meiji Japan's early economic growth took place in the countryside, moreover, and in small factories and workshops. Politically, the Meiji Restoration was followed by civil war, which absorbed much of the fledgling government's budget, along with paying off the previous regimes' debts and meeting financial obligations to former samurai. If 1868 was a turning point, it was not an instant one.

Yet out of the upheaval emerged a centralized nation state, and much institutional innovation. Joining the late nineteenth century geopolitical and economic order led by Britain, Japan established a national currency in 1871, the Bank of Japan in 1872, the Tokyo Stock Exchange in 1878, and national banks, including the Yokohama Specie Bank to service growing foreign trade. It switched from the silver standard, adopted in 1885, to the gold standard in 1898, aided by the massive reparation from China following the first Sino-Japanese War (1894–1895).[3]

An industrial economy began to grow. In the half century between 1888 and 1938 manufacturing's share in the Japanese economy rose from 14 per cent to 51 per cent, while the share of agriculture declined from 42 per cent to just 16 per cent. Japan doubled its industrial output between 1913 and 1919 alone, and between 1913 and 1938 Japan's growth rate averaged almost 4 per cent, which was double that of the other major powers.[4] Japan rapidly absorbed new technologies and organization forms associated with the first and second industrial revolutions in a compressed form, aided by the spread of compulsory education (starting from 1872, just four years after the Meiji Restoration, and two years after the first English Education Act), as well as elite higher education (Amano, 2011). Selection by education and the professionalization of management took root faster than in Britain. Railways, as in other countries, provided a vehicle for the diffusion of modern administration and management practices, and 'when accounts of the Taylor System first

---

[2] Pomeranz, 2000; Francks, 2016.
[3] Mitchener, Shizume, and Weidenmeir, 2010; Bytheway and Metzler, 2016. For Japan becoming part of the international order also meant aspiring to great power status through imperialist expansion: Iriye, 1989.
[4] Nakamura, 1988: 453; Minami et al., 1995: 3–4.

began to appear in Japan in 1911—the same year as the publication of *The Principles of Scientific Management*—a receptive audience already existed.'[5]

The path was far from smooth, however. Rapid urbanization and industrialization saw the birth of a labour movement, which in the wake of Russia's revolution and riots caused by rising rice prices, fanned fears over social stability. Not all capitalists were like Shibusawa Eiichi, who helped to legitimize capitalism in Japan through his advocacy of *gapponshugi*, or bringing capital, labour, and management together to serve the public interest. Indeed, resentment simmered over 'avaricious' capitalists who 'keep the employees in a miserable state and endanger the basis of the existence of the company'.[6] The deflationary effects of trying to return Japan to the gold standard in the 1920s did not help. With the Showa Financial Crisis (1927), the Wall Street crash (1929), and the 'Manchurian Incident' (1931) staged by the Japanese army in Mukden (Shenyang), Japan's hitherto relatively liberal capitalism took a drastic turn towards 'military Keynesianism' (Samuels, 1994), signalling Japan's Polanyian 'double movement'. When Japan plunged into the second Sino-Japanese War in 1936 and the Pacific War in 1941, government control over the economy became virtually absolute.

The result of war was industrial and economic devastation, including the loss of Japan's colonies, but not the loss of its accumulated knowledge of building a new economy, which henceforth would be focused on commercial ends. From a state of chaos, Japan also entered the postwar period with an opportunity to rebuild state-market relations suited for the new era of embedded liberalism, and business organizations suited for the emerging technologies of mass production.

The Rise of the Postwar Economy

Whether this was a *new* economy is again debatable. Some have emphasized institutional continuities, including the regulation of financial markets and wartime controls on dividends, which pushed Japan decisively towards a system of indirect financing, as well as elements of the employment system such as wages which emphasized age, years of service, and family living costs over the job actually done. Wartime 'patriotic industrial associations' (*sanpō*) played a role in shaping postwar enterprise unions, and wartime control

---

[5] Ericson, 1989; Tsutsui, 1998: 18.
[6] These are the comments of a manager of a major spinning company, cited in Morikawa, 1989: 42. Cf. also Takahashi, 1930. With views similar to Veblen in the US, Riken director Okochi Masatoshi denounced 'capitalistic industry' and advocated instead 'science-based industry' (Cusumano, 1989).

associations became postwar industry associations. Government direction of the economy continued in many forms, including most famously industrial policy and policy financing through the Fiscal Investment and Loan Programme (FILP) and its associated institutions. The developmental state had postwar features, but its roots were in the prewar political economy.[7]

On the other hand, the US-led Occupation reforms reshaped Japan in important ways, including a new Constitution, land reform, (partial) dissolution of the *zaibatsu*, education reform, and legal recognition of workers' rights to organize, bargain collectively, and strike—which they exercised. These reforms relied to a considerable extent on the Japanese bureaucracy for implementation, but they also bore the imprint of US New Deal thinking about state-market relations, regulation of capital, and class compromise. The newly formed Keizai Doyukai (Japan Association of Corporate Executives) called it 'modified capitalism' (*shūsei shihonshugi*).

There was intense conflict over policy; should production recovery or monetary stabilization be prioritized, for example? The US banker Dodge enforced the latter in 1949, with unanticipated consequences:

> Dodge's restriction of credit induced another systemic transformation.... In fact, it did not end the Japanese government's policy of subsidized priority investment. Rather, it displaced it into private banking channels, which Dodge left unregulated. In this, the Dodge Line set in place the final piece of the integrated state-bank mechanism that would form the financial core of the High-Speed Growth system. The sources and control of capital thus assumed the distinctive forms of the classical age of Japanese capitalism.
>
> (Metzler, 2013: 136)

The architects, Metzler claims, were Schumpeter's Japanese students, who innovatively saw entrepreneurship as a *national* function, financed by a massive expansion of credit organized through tiered institutions. This credit expansion *preceded* high levels of savings and was necessitated by the impoverished state of the nation and its citizens at that time.

US military procurements for the Korean War (1950–1953) offered a fresh wind for struggling Japanese manufacturers, but the specifications were demanding, forcing them to quickly improve standardized parts manufacture, testing, and quality control (Samuels, 1994). Productivity missions were sent to the US to narrow the productivity gap, and Deming's quality management message fell on particularly fertile ground in Japan. Thus, US organization and management ideas associated with the 'Fordist corporation'

---

[7] Johnson, 1982. Noguchi (1998) called it the '1940 system'. Cf. also Okazaki and Okuno-Fujiwara eds, 1999. Gordon (1985) shows that postwar industrial relations were the result of pre-war management initiatives, wartime controls, *and* postwar labour initiatives, which were later reshaped by management.

were absorbed, modified, and embedded in Japanese industry as it moved into its high growth period (1955–1970).[8]

Key to postwar Fordism from the *Régulation* perspective was the wage–labour nexus, a 'socio-technical system covering all aspects of the capital-labour relation' (Guttman, 2002: 57). After a timultuous period of labour militancy and a government-backed management counter-offensive, managers largely accepted the workers' demands for job security, living wages and an end to sharp blue collar-white collar status and pay differences, laying the foundations for the 'three pillars of Japanese-style management/employment'—lifetime (long-term) employment, *nenkō* (seniority plus merit) wages and promotion and enterprise unionism. An implicit social contract—job security in return for dedication to company— was buttressed by pro-employment government policy. This was distinct from the prewar institutional configuration, but a recognizable variant of class compromise politics seen in other industrialized countries. It was also a male breadwinner model, based on a gendered social division of labour.

Based on this implicit contract, technical skills were nurtured through in-house job rotation and on-job training. New promotion paths were opened up for blue-collar workers, who also became eligible for company welfare provision, which ranged from subsidized housing and loans to company pensions and share ownership.[9] Stabilized industrial relations created a basis for shop-floor-based quality control circles. Just-in-time management was pioneered by Toyota and diffused through supply chains. The increasing synchronization of inputs and production processes, pioneered by Ford and extended by Toyota, was eventually expanded into product development as product cycle times were shortened into 'time-based competition'. This was a period of considerable social and (process) technological innovation.[10]

Numerous other features of the postwar model created a sense of institutional coherence. The tripartite Japan Productivity Centre was established in 1955 with three core principles—employment security, joint consultation, and a 'fair distribution' of the fruits of productivity increases between managers (company), workers and consumers. (This was an age of managerial capitalism; shareholders were not mentioned.) The 'spring wage offensive' (*Shuntō*) was also formalized in 1955, creating a mechanism in which powerful unions bargained first to secure an annual wage increase that would set the goal for other unions. *Shuntō* became an unofficial mechanism to spread

---

[8] Between 1955 and 1970 the primary sector share of GDP dropped from 17% to 6%, while mining, manufacturing, and public utilities rose from 29% to 48%. The share of heavy and chemical industries (including machinery) within manufacturing surged from 39% to 60%, all the while with high overall growth; Minami et al., 1995: 4.

[9] Dore, 1973; Koike, 1981; Inagami and Whittaker, 2005; Miura, 2012.

[10] Abegglen and Stalk, 1985; Stalk, 1988; Best, 1990; Odagiri and Goto, 1996.

the fruits of productivity increases and was extended to the public sector in 1964 (Ogino, 2021). It underpinned Ikeda's income doubling policy, which was a source of inspiration for Kishida's 'new capitalism'.

At the intermediate, meso level, many of the former *zaibatsu* and supplier groups were re-formed as *keiretsu*. 'Horizontal *keiretsu*' came together around banks, which fed their members' voracious appetite for capital, while reciprocal shareholding freed managers from investor (and speculator) pressure, creating a distinctive form of 'patient capital'. Relationships between large firm assemblers and their subcontractor suppliers were also stabilized as 'vertical *keiretsu*'. Wartime control associations were resurrected as industry associations. *Keiretsu*, industry associations, cooperatives, and other forms of intermediate organization, often with close links to the government and ministries, ensured a high degree of coordination in the economy which went by various names, including 'relational contracting', 'corporate capitalism', 'alliance capitalism', and because of its restrictive trade and investment tendencies, 'Japan Inc.'[11]

In brief, postwar Japan built a new economy with manufacturing at its core which was both coordinated and achieved a high degree of institutional and ideational coherence. Manufacturing employed over 30 per cent of the workforce until the late 1970s, and over 20 per cent until the early 2000s. Prewar inequalities were reduced, and technological and economic upgrading supported a rising middle class. At the same time there were many individuals and groups that were marginalized in these patterned relationships, including small firm employees—which is notable because the proportion workers in small firms was higher than in most other industrialized countries—and women, as male breadwinner norms were deeply inbuilt.[12]

Tensions and Emerging Contradictions

Rapid reconstruction and high growth brought a new set of challenges, including friction with trading partners, especially the US. The 'Nixon shocks' (1971), which raised tariffs on Japanese exports and started a process

[11] Dore, 1983; Okumura, 1984; Gerlach, 1992; Witt, 2006; Sasada, 2013. Cooperatives and cooperative associations became a pervasive part of the postwar economy, ranging from savings, loans, insurance, funerals and mutual aid to joint purchasing, production, and R&D in small businesses, to consumption and agriculture; see Chapter 8.

[12] Even these norms suppressed household income inequality, as spouses of higher income earners became full-time housewives, while those of lower income earners worked to supplement family income: Chiavacci and Hommerich, 2017.

of yen appreciation, were quickly followed by 'oil shocks' (1973, 1979), triggered by war and revolution in the Middle East, bringing an end to the post-war era of stable oil prices, and sending inflationary shock waves throughout the world. Japan responded with a combination of structural adjustment, innovation, and an expansion of exports in the machine industries, whose competitiveness was heightened through the taming of inflationary pressures as *Shuntō* became a mechanism of wage increase *moderation*.[13] This intensified trade friction.

At the same time there was a growing sense within Japan that the postwar economic objectives had been achieved, and that a new course had to be charted, beyond 'catching up' with the West. A blue-ribbon council opined in 1980:

> In order to 'catch up' as speedily as possible with the advanced nations of the West, Japan has proactively pushed forward with modernization, industrialization and westernization since the Meiji Restoration. As a result, Japan succeeded in reaching the stage of a mature, highly industrial society, and everyone has come to enjoy freedom and equality, progress and prosperity, economic wealth and the convenience of modern life, high education and high welfare standards, as well as advanced scientific technology. These are all qualities we can be proud of in the world.
>
> **(Age of Culture Research Group, 1980: 2, cited in Kariya, 2020)**

Henceforth, the report argued, Japan would have to find its own path, one which caused less friction with its trading partners. It would also mean a greater international role for the yen, with a progressive de-regulation of financial markets and relaxation of capital controls. In 1983 a Yen-Dollar Committee was established jointly with the US, and in 1985, following the Plaza Accord, the yen underwent a dramatic appreciation, from ¥240: $1 to ¥160: $1 less than a year later.[14] Collateral rules for issuing corporate bonds, in place since the early 1930s, were relaxed, and outstanding bond issues rose fivefold during the 1980s. Financial dis-intermediation—a shift from financing through banks to direct market finance—became a catch-cry, and Japan was on the way to establishing a market-based financial system. Or so it appeared.

Japan's new path and appreciation of the yen had other implications as well. On the one hand, as envisaged by the Maekawa Report (1986), Japan needed

---

[13] This was a case of institutional conversion: Sako, 2007.
[14] ¥240: $1 was already a significant appreciation from the pre-1971 fixed exchange rate era's ¥360: $1. The yen continued to climb, reaching ¥79: $1 in 1994, well after the bursting of the asset bubble in 1990.

to become a 'giant in living' as well as in production, through a structural shift towards domestic demand. Combined with a loosening of monetary policy to counteract recessionary effects of the yen appreciation, it stoked a massive rise in land and stock prices. In mid 1985 the market value of residential land in Tokyo was about half of Japan's GDP; by late 1987 it had reached one and a half times. Companies raised the equivalent of $600 billion in equity markets between 1985 and 1990, and while some of this went into capital investment, much went into assets unrelated to corporate activities. Losing business from their blue-chip customers, banks turned to small firms and property invest-ment, as did non-bank financial institutions. The financial authorities were slow to deflate the growing bubble because consumer prices were steady, and because fears of recession from the yen's appreciation persisted.[15]

Trade friction and the yen appreciation prompted a rise in Japanese foreign direct investment (FDI) in North America, Europe, and Southeast Asia.[16] The looming spectre of 'hollowing out' de-industrialization in the late 1980s gave urgency to the search for a new, possibly post-industrial, future, an economy driven by innovation rather than volume manufacturing, and a greater role for the financial sector. In education the quest for a new, individual-centred pedagogy to produce creative thinkers—and Nobel Prize winners—led to successive reforms and the implementation of *yutori* (de-stressed, relaxed) education (Kariya, 2012).

On top of all this, and despite 'voluntary' export restraints, Japan's trade surpluses stubbornly persisted. Outbound FDI dwarfed inbound FDI. US trade negotiators deemed that Japanese capitalism operated under differ-ent rules (while US rules by implication were fair and proper) and initiated the 'Structural Impediments Initiative' (SII) in 1989 to bring about a 'level playing field'. The SII report, backed by the threat of trade sanctions, cov-ered fiscal policy, savings and investments, land policy, the distribution system, exclusionary business practices, *keiretsu* relationships, prices and public expenditure.[17]

In sum, Japan's very success in its high growth era generated a sense of pride—hubris even—but it also set in train external and internal pressures for change, and discordant currents and ideological contradictions in the quest

---

[15] Noguchi, 1992. Some $220 billion in new loans for property were issued between 1985 and 1990, which was more than the total of previous outstanding loans. An estimated $75 billion came from the soon-to-be-infamous *jūsen* housing loan companies (Whittaker and Kurosawa, 1998).

[16] Asia was, in the words of Hatch and Yamamura (1996), in 'Japan's embrace', at least temporarily. The authors noted that by 1994 there were almost twice as many Japanese affiliates in the electric industries in Southeast Asia as US and Europe affiliates combined.

[17] Matsushita, 1990. Since this was supposedly a *bilateral* trade agreement, some rather general mea-sures were recommended for the US government, reflecting the Japanese view that the US should put its own house in order.

for a new path. The 1980s began a shift in the relationship between industry and finance; from serving as facilitator for industrialization, Japanese finance was partially set free in an attempt to establish Japan as a major global financial centre. A combination of factors resulted in a massive bubble in land and share prices, which was belatedly popped in 1990 by the raising of interest rates. Still, it was far from clear that this marked a turning point for the Japanese economy, as trade surpluses persisted, and Japanese manufacturing prowess was at its peak.

The 'Lost Decades'

From a high of almost ¥40,000 in late 1989, the Nikkei Index of Tokyo Stock Exchange (TSE) shares dropped by 40 per cent in 1990, held in 1991, and fell to just over one third of its peak in 1992. Land prices began to fall in 1990 and plunged in 1991. The asset price spiral went into reverse, creating a surge in bad debts. Accounting standards of the time, how to apportion losses, and hope for a recovery all led to prevarication in dealing with them. A backlash against the use of public money to rescue failing housing loan *jūsen* in 1992–1993 made subsequent public rescues more difficult. The 'convoy system' of stronger financial institutions supporting weaker ones began to fray. A recovery in 1996 was undone by a rise in the consumption tax in 1997, and by late 1997 a full-blown financial crisis had emerged, with the failure of the first major 'city bank', followed by the fourth largest securities company.

Stung by criticism that it failed to raise interests rates earlier in the asset bubble, the Bank of Japan deepened the post-bubble slump by keeping them too high. Simmering public anger over political scandals was vented in the 1993 election, causing the ruling Liberal Democratic Party (LDP) to lose its single party majority and ushering in an era of political uncertainty. Pessimism replaced hubris. In bureaucrat-turned-critic Sakaiya's 'Japan 2018', serialized in the *Asahi* newspaper, economic growth 20 years hence averaged zero per cent, the consumption tax and average income tax rates had risen to 20 per cent and 40 per cent respectively, meagre pensions started at age 67, and the yen-dollar exchange rate had fallen to ¥230:$1.

'Big Bang' financial reforms in 1998, intended to re-ignite the movement towards a market-based system, diverted the attention of banks from dealing with non-performing loans, and caused the financial authorities to hesitate to intervene. The Bank of Japan and financial supervisory functions were separated from the Ministry of Finance, which was also tainted by scandals.

Public funds were eventually injected into major banks, but by this time the banking crisis had become an economic crisis (Nakano, 2016).

Japan's travails of the 1990s deepened disillusionment with the postwar model. At the same time a resurgent US appeared to be pointing the way forward. US credit rating agencies became more influential than their newly established Japanese counterparts, and the tide of US and UK corporate governance reform reached Japan's shores. Foreign investors bought up shares from banks unwinding their relational stocks—a feature of the postwar system—and began to exercise their voice. Investor relations occupied the attention of senior managers as they sought to rebuild their balance sheets.

A flurry of legislation starting in 1997 was designed to facilitate corporate restructuring, change accounting practices, and shift the focus of labour regulation from employment security to employment flexibility, which employers were seeking even as they were hiring more part-time and temporary workers. Amendments to the Commercial Code implemented in 2002 gave companies the option of adopting a new US/UK-inspired 'company with committees' corporate governance system. Now Japan appeared to be well on the way towards dismantling its postwar system in favour of neoliberal market solutions.[18]

The legislation on corporate governance was contested, however, and the dotcom bubble burst and Enron scandal took some of the lustre off the new US model. While Prime Minister Koizumi (2001–2006) pursued his neoliberal reform agenda, the public became increasingly alarmed at growing social divisions and inequality. With the fall of flamboyant financial entrepreneur Horie Takafumi along with activist investor Murakami Yoshiaki in 2006, legislation reining in consumer credit interest, and the 'Lehman Shock' of 2007–2008, the *visible* tide of neoliberalism turned as conservative forces led by Keidanren and LDP politicians regained control of the reform agenda.[19]

Emerging Organization and Technology Challenges

Meanwhile, Japan's manufacturing champions were facing other challenges, which the organization–technology dyad helps to bring into focus. These challenges originated from the US, and from emerging Asia, with Japan's

---

[18] The growing allure of Silicon Valley was also seen in an overhaul of the SME Basic Law in 1999, measures to promote technology transfer and commercialization from universities, and the fostering of entrepreneurship.

[19] Gotoh (2020) depicts a struggle between neo-classical economists, Keizai Doyukai (Japan Association of Corporate Executives), non-Japanese firms and US credit rating agencies, ascendant from the 1990s until the early 2000s, and interventionist bureaucrats, anti-free market politicians, Keidanren, banks, legal elites, and Japanese credit rating agencies, who regained ascendance in the mid 2000s.

manufacturing champions caught in between. Competition from Japan and Germany in the 1980s had eroded US manufacturing companies' profits at the same time that shareholders were demanding higher returns, and incentivizing managers to deliver them. One response was to 'learn from Japan', through the quality movement, total supply chain management and just-in-time. Another was outsourcing, initially inspired by 'lean' and 'just-in-time' production but taking a very different path. To restore their profits, US manufacturers began to outsource production—sometimes all of it—to domestic contract manufacturers, to emerging Korea and Taiwan, and subsequently to mainland China. Vertically integrated Fordist corporations were 're-engineered'; they became vertically specialized with the creation of global value chains (GVCs), creating a 'new American model'.[20]

The information and communication technology (ICT) industries were simultaneously being transformed. Just when Japanese competitors were within reach of IBM's technological leadership in mainframe computers, which were built on closed product architecture, there was a shift towards smaller computers using open or modular architecture. This accelerated outsourcing and also enabled a proliferation of new, specialized entrants. The industry was radically changed from being a virtual monopoly to a very large modular cluster (Baldwin and Clark, 2000) centred in Silicon Valley, geographically and symbolically separated from previously dominant East Coast and Midwest manufacturers. Silicon Valley startups were fuelled with venture capital, and attracted talent from around the world.[21] The pace of change increased after the dotcom bubble burst, and China's WTO accession in 2001.

Japan's manufacturers were caught by this combination of outsourcing and offshoring through GVCs, emerging technologies, new network organization forms, and venture capital. Once-nimble lead companies had now become large and slow, a victim of their own success in what Porter once described as a 'wealth driven' stage of development.[22] They were reluctant to break their implicit social contract with their employees—job security in return for dedication to the company—preferring instead to buttress it by 'loaning' surplus workers or hiring non-regular employees. At first doubling down on what

---

[20] Champy and Hammer, 1993; Sturgeon, 2002; Milberg, 2008.

[21] Saxenian, 1996, 2007; Norton, 2001. As Minsky (1988: 3) observed: 'Those who finance a Schumpeterian innovator always have novel problems in structuring the financing. Two new sets of combinations, in production and in finance, drive the evolution of the economy.' Venture capital and startups were a potent combination for the emerging technologies of Silicon Valley, with their disruptive organization forms.

[22] In this stage: 'Stewards ascend to senior management positions in the place of entrepreneurs and company builders. Belief in competition falls not only in companies but in unions, which both lose the taste for risk-taking. The compulsion to innovate diminishes and the willingness to violate norms and bear disapproval fails': Porter, 1990: 556. Cf. also Greiner, 1998.

they did best, they found their profits nonetheless diminishing at a time when they were trying to rebuild their balance sheets. Many scaled back on R&D investment.

Corporate Japan's spectacular rise and subsequent stumble in the face of a changing external environment is dramatically illustrated by semiconductors. The technological foundations for Japan's rise in this industry—through giants Hitachi, Toshiba, NEC, and Fujitsu—were laid in the government's very large-scale integration (VLSI) project in the 1970s. A decade later Japanese manufacturers had risen to dominate the global dynamic random-access memory (DRAM) market, so much so that US trade negotiators forced Japan in 1986 to sign an agreement limiting their 'dumping' on world markets, and promising to open up Japan to semiconductor imports.

A further decade later, the semiconductor divisions of these companies were making huge losses, and ceding market share to Micron Technology of the US and emerging Asian competitors, notably Samsung. The fall came less from the semiconductor agreement than a failure to switch their orientation from DRAM production designed for mainframes to personal computers, which could be produced more cheaply. They also failed to respond to the new outsourcing and Taiwanese foundry model, and to the rapid diversification of semiconductor types required to support the multiplication of functions users were performing on computers. A succession of government projects and consortia did nothing to reverse the decline and may even have accelerated it.[23]

Japanese companies lost ground across the ICT sector as a whole, struggling to adapt to the (again less quality-stringent) TCP/IP internet protocol, the growing importance of software in product and organization design, and the winner-takes-most nature of the emerging platform business model. From 2000 to 2011 Japan's production of electronics products declined by 50 per cent, and exports by 37 per cent.[24]

In photovoltaic (PV) solar panels, pioneer Sharp was the world's largest producer in the early 2000s, just as China's PV industry was starting out; by 2010 it had ceded the top spot to China's Suntech, and in 2016 Sharp itself was acquired by Taiwan's Hon Hai Precision Industry (Foxconn). Japan did, to be sure, remain dominant in automobiles, where its manufacturing (*monozukuri*) strengths were still critical, but this industry, which became ever more crucial to the Japanese economy, is now being challenged by the

---

[23] Yunogami, 2006, 2021; Sturgeon, 2007; Brown and Linden, 2009.
[24] Cole, 2006; Cole and Nakata, 2014.

modularization and digitization that transformed the electric and electronic industries (Chapter 5).

Overall, the response of Japanese companies to organization and technology challenges was mixed. On the one hand, as Schaede (2020) details, many repositioned, established strategic niches in advanced equipment and materials, and underwent organizational renewal. But in the globalizing economy with rapidly changing industry contours and competition, others failed to do so. Performance diverged within sectors, and the industry and inter-firm cohesion which had been characteristic of the postwar model was weakened.[25]

Mixed Progress, Institutional Clashes, and Crises

The years leading up to the 2007–2008 Global Financial Crisis defy simple categorization. The non-performing loan problem was largely settled, profits were restored in (many) large firms, and Japan entered its longest postwar spell of continuous monthly expansion (75 months from January 2002), albeit with much reduced growth. Capital investment remained largely flat, however, even with unconventional monetary policy—zero interest rates and quantitative easing. From relying on banks to finance growth in the postwar decades, large companies now reduced their loans, and after restoring their balance sheets, built up their internal reserves. Meanwhile small firms struggled to get loans. Households continued to keep half of their assets in banks (earning virtually no interest), which bought government bonds and built up reserves at the Bank of Japan (BoJ). The BoJ also purchased government bonds, as well as corporate stocks from banks in 'price keeping operations'.

Labour's share of value added and national income declined, particularly sharply in the case of large companies, while the proportion of 'non-regular' workers continued to climb—from around a quarter of the workforce in 2000 to over a third by 2008. The number of dispatched workers rose particularly sharply, from 360,000 to 1.4 million over the same period. Household budgets were squeezed, while returns to shareholders increased (Table 6.1).

Corporate governance became an arena for debate about how the economy and businesses should be run. Even though only a small minority of companies opted for the new 'company-with-committees' system, managers still faced pressure to improve shareholder returns, and to explain their future plans. Activist shareholders appeared on the scene and began to test the

---

[25] Lincoln and Gerlach, 2004; Lechevalier and Monfort, 2018.

market for corporate control. The 'Livedoor shock' of 2005 was less about the flamboyant T-shirted Horie Takafumi's audacious attempt to take over Nippon Broadcasting System (NBS, part of the Fuji Sankei group), shocking though it was, than about the injunction from the Tokyo District Court preventing NBS from using a warrant issue to fend off the attack, a decision upheld by the Tokyo High Court shortly after.[26] Horie was chosen by Koizumi to stand against an opponent of his neoliberal reforms in the House of Representative election that year, a symbol of the new Japan Koizumi wished to build. Within months Horie was not only defeated in the election, but arrested for financial irregularities, a reversal which some saw as a re-assertion of power by the defenders of Japan Inc. Activist shareholders were forced to change their tactics, but the debate about corporate governance was later re-ignited under the second Abe government.

Japanese direct financial exposure to the US subprime mortgage crisis was limited—the least among the G7 countries, in fact—but Japan suffered the largest GDP decline from 2007 to 2009 because severe conditions in the US and Europe suppressed Japanese exports, especially of vehicles, which had knock-on effects in the domestic economy. As well, the yen underwent a sharp appreciation due to massive monetary easing in the US and Europe. This caused a rise in unemployment as dispatched and other non-regular workers were laid off.[27]

It was not just the market side of the state-market dyad that underwent change during this period; the state was also being reshaped. Mogaki (2019) characterizes it as a shift from direct provision of services and intervention in the economy by a developmental state to a rules-based, regulatory orientation. Electoral reform in 1994 had a number of effects, including enhancing the power of party heads, which in the case of the ruling party meant the Prime Minister. Administrative reforms in the late 1990s further enhanced this power, which was used by Koizumi to force through his deregulation and privatization agenda. Bureaucrats retreated from strategy into rules, ironically because in theory at least, MITI's remit was expanded when it became METI in early 2001.

In 2009 the DPJ sealed its rise with victory in the lower house election, seemingly realizing another goal of the 1994 reforms—the creation of a two party (or coalition) system capable of alternation of power. But the DPJ was a very diverse grouping, inexperienced in government, forced to deal with the aftermath of the Global Financial Crisis, and before long with the

---

[26] Hayakawa and Whittaker, 2009; Jacoby, 2009; Buchanan, Chai, and Deakin, 2012.
[27] Ito and Hoshi, 2020: 545. The yen rose from ¥120: $1 in July 2007 to ¥90: $1 in October 2009.

triple earthquake, tsunami, and nuclear disaster of 2011. Promising to 'put peoples' livelihoods first', its very public assault on bureaucracy and wasteful government spending provided few solutions, and when its third leader in as many years indicated a rise in the consumption tax the DPJ's fate was sealed, and with it the promise of alternating government. The LDP returned to power in 2012 under Abe, who further strengthened the offices of the Prime Minister (*Kantei*) by extending control over key bureaucratic appointments.[28]

Abenomics

The 2011 triple disaster had huge repercussions, many visible and immediate, some less visible but long term. It had a profound impact on energy policy, and on thinking about resilience, but not necessary on Japanese politics, or the economy, at least directly (Kingston ed., 2012; Samuels, 2013). Abe returned to power with a passion for strategic diplomacy and constitutional revision, but he also realized the importance of a sound and stable economy. He set about building it with 'three arrows', namely qualitative and quantitative easing ('bold monetary policy'), fiscal expansion then consolidation ('flexible fiscal policy') and growth through structural reforms ('growth strategy to promote private investment'). Some aspects were past or current policies recycled; but what *was* distinctive was his attempt to create a coherence between them, and to move beyond a laundry list of policy proposals through concrete targets and timelines.

The first two arrows attracted most attention. Whatever else may be said about them in terms of hitting their targets, Japan was (almost) able to exit deflation, and the economy was stabilized. In the eyes of many economists, the third arrow barely left the quiver. Yet Abe brought Japan into the TPP over vehement opposition from the agriculture sector whose votes were still very important for his party, and he shifted the debates around agriculture itself, from a budget-sapping declining sector to one with a potentially bright future—'agriculture on the front foot' (*seme no nōgyō*). He also furthered reforms in corporate governance, which will be discussed in more detail in Chapter 6. On the other hand, while Abe hoped to increase inward investment, in fact it was far eclipsed by outbound foreign direct investment (FDI). The official figures—$40 billion inward FDI versus $258 outward

[28] *Kantei* is a metonym for Prime Minister's residence and administration, but more extensively can include the Cabinet Secretariat and Cabinet Office. Referred to here as Office of the Prime Minister and Cabinet (OPMC).

FDI in 2019—do not portray the real imbalance according to Katz (2021a), and Japan languishes near the bottom of UNCTAD's country rankings of cumulative inbound FDI as a share of GDP.[29]

Abe was more pragmatist than neoliberal. In order to refresh his agenda in the context of population decline and a rapidly tightening labour market in 2015, he unveiled three more arrows, aiming to ease supply side labour constraints and create a 'dynamic society of 100 million people', and 'a society in which all women can shine'.[30] He set up a Council for the Realization of Work Style Reform, and a bundle of bills was passed in the Diet in 2018.[31] At the end of the day, Abenomics did not bequeath Japan a new growth model (Lechevalier and Monfort, 2018), but ironically, underneath all the 'Japan is back' fanfare and the flurry of arrows, the buds of a new growth model were quietly growing, in the form of digital and green transformation.

Concluding Comments

This chapter began by considering continuity and change in Japan's modern economic history. In the two great periods of upheaval—the Meiji Restoration, and the end of World War II—there was continuity in the midst of far-reaching institutional change. Despite a degree of upheaval, in post-1990 Japan institutional change has been less extreme. Moreover, the double movements described in the Introduction—the shift from postwar embedded liberalism to neoliberalism in state–market relations, and from the Fordist (or Toyotist) corporation to the networks and platforms with the rise of digital technologies—have been relatively muted compared to Anglophone countries.

This may be the result of (a) the absence of a threat or reality of direct foreign intervention; (b) ambivalence as to the best way forward; or (c) scepticism over the alleged benefits of neoliberalism, financialized capitalism, and

---

[29] FDI figures are from https://www.jetro.go.jp/en/reports/statistics.html (accessed 21 March 2023). It is worth noting in this context that income derived from outbound FDI and portfolio investment almost trebled in the decade to 2022 to ¥50 trillion ($378 billion), an amount equivalent to almost 10 per cent of Japan's GDP. In terms of net overseas assets and primary income surplus, Japan ranks highest in the world: *Nikkei Asia*, 24 December 2022 ('Investment Powerhouse Japan Earns 10% of GDP From Overseas Income'). This investment mainly contributes to the GDP of other countries, however, not Japan.

[30] The arrows were a 'robust economy that creates hope', 'child care support that fosters dreams', and 'social security that fosters a sense of safety'. The package was often referred to as Womenomics.

[31] Over his second term in office (2012–2020) the female labour force participation rate did indeed rise, to almost 70 per cent, but the proportion of 'non-regular' female employees remained stubbornly high at 56 per cent, while the proportion of female managers remained stubbornly low, at less than 15 per cent, with the goal of 30 per cent of 'leading positions' held by women remaining a distant dream. Cf. Emmott, 2020.

Schumpeterian 'creative destruction'. Although Adam Smith has been widely read in Japan, market fundamentalists are few.[32] Advocacy of neoliberal policy solutions is typically more a matter of overcoming inertia than ideological conviction. Politicians' election campaigns were peppered with pledges of *anshin-anzen* (peace of mind, security) after 2006 in the midst of growing inequality.

Japan may have avoided extremes of political and social upheaval, but the institutional coherence of the postwar high growth decades was lost during the 'lost decades'. The developmental state gave way to a regulatory state, and bureaucrat autonomy over policy making gave way to subservience to politicians—but not fully. Bank-centred finance did not turn into a market-based financial system. 'Japanese-style management/employment' frayed, but was not abandoned. A question we will need to address in the following chapters is whether the pursuit of DX, GX, and 'new capitalism'—the building of Society 5.0—will lead to a new institutional and ideational coherence, or something else.

Finally concerning continuity and change, of Streeck and Thelen's (2005) five types of institutional change—displacement, layering, drift, conversion, and exhaustion—conversion and layering have especially featured in this chapter. This is not surprising given that the past is frequently invoked to justify change in Japan. *Shuntō* was converted to a mechanism of wage moderation, then declared moribund through deflation, but it may be resurrected in a new form to serve 'new capitalism'. As we shall see in Chapter 5, an IT startup ecosystem with a distinctive institutional logic has been layered onto institutions built around large firms in Tokyo, although 'partitioning' may be a more appropriate term than layering in this case. Indeed, Japan has a long history of creative borrowing, partitioning and selective mixing to overcome institutional stasis and bring about change.

We can expect no less with the digital and green transformation. We can expect, for example, attempts to maintain manufacturing or *monozukuri* centred on large firms at the core of the economy, *and* transformation through IT startups. But when it comes to the role of the state, or finance, will such inclusivity prove helpful, or dysfunctional in the building of Japan's new economy? We will return to this question later in the book.

---

[32] Dore, 1987; Morris-Suzuki, 1989.

2

Building and Governing the Digital Economy

Japanese companies are heading for a '2025 digital cliff'. That was the stark warning issued by a METI-sponsored report in 2018 exhorting Japanese companies to seriously confront and engage in 'DX', or digital transformation. At the same time, it was an implicit admission that years of exhortation through METI's own IT Promotion Agency (IPA) had had little impact; Japan was sleepwalking into the future chained by legacy systems. Whether the cliff pointed down, towards financial ruin, or upwards, to a climb that would become so steep as to become virtually impossible to scale, was unclear, as both were implied by the report.

From the giddy heights of the early IT economy in the 1980s, when Japan controlled much of the world's semiconductor production and appeared ready to challenge US technological leadership in mainframe computers, to the dismal 2025 vision, Japan had already fallen a long way.[1] We have already touched on why this happened in the context of the 1990s and 2000s in Chapter 1; in this chapter we focus on contemporary and prospective 'DX', and the government's role in this. If nothing else, the cliff imagery and the understanding that 'DX' is about more than using IT to do current business more efficiently became widely recognized as a result of the report. And needless to say, DX is a precondition for the attainment of Society 5.0.

The first section of this chapter briefly outlines the background to the 'DX Report', the report's content, and ongoing follow-up measures by METI. It is not just companies that have been deemed laggards in this transformation; the government itself has been accused of foot-dragging. This was highlighted when it came to disbursing the ¥100,000 it promised each resident in 2020 to cope with the Covid-19 pandemic. Stung by the ensuing criticism, the government rushed to create a Digital Agency, which would

---

[1] The penchant for self-castigation now extends into Japan's core ministries. In fact, Japan has a mix of leading, lagging, and fast changing 'going digital indicators' according to the OECD: https://goingdigital. oecd.org/countries/jpn (accessed 25 March 2023); Lechevalier, forthcoming.

Building a New Economy. D. Hugh Whittaker, Oxford University Press. © D. Hugh Whittaker (2024).
DOI: 10.1093/oso/9780198893394.003.0003

rationalize and upgrade fragmented government IT systems and create a path for e-government. This is covered in the second section.

The emerging digital economy raises a host of new concerns, one being cybersecurity, which is crucial on many levels, and requires those levels to be joined up in new ways. This is taken up in the third section. Japan has been building a framework and new institutions for cybersecurity, within government, government contractors—especially defence contractors—and companies in general, but new vulnerabilities are constantly emerging. Cybersecurity increasingly overlaps with defence, as well as economic security, and these with geopolitics. The third section probes Japan's approach to cybersecurity, both in terms of its incorporation into the national security structures, and in terms of its application to the emerging Internet of Things (IoT) and Industrial Internet of Things (IIoT). This leads to initial comments on the return of industrial policy, which has become increasingly oriented to the building of Society 5.0, or at least is presented as such.

The final section extends this to a discussion of governance in and of Society 5.0, which is seen to be quite different from that of Society 4.0. Two reports set out the case for 'agile governance' in view of the quickening pace of innovation, increasing prevalence of cyber/physical systems, interlocking of stakeholder interests, and ambiguities about the locus of responsibility and increasing risks.

The chapter is paired with Chapter 3, which looks at green transformation (GX), also from a mainly macro perspective. There is a contrast in which DX is broadly cast as a threat—as in the cliff metaphor, using strong rhetoric—while GX is presented more as an opportunity, and carrots are used instead of sticks in government policy. Despite an asymmetry, DX and GX are considered the two driving wheels of Japan's economic transformation, heading towards Society 5.0. This chapter is also complemented by Chapter 4, which looks at smart cities, and Chapter 5 on DX at the company and industry levels.

Confronting the '2025 Digital Cliff'

Chapter 1 touched on the competitive problems of Japan's ICT sector, of which software is an important part. We will start with the software industry, as it is germane to the DX Report and the 2025 digital cliff. It, too, is the story of a remarkable reversal from the late 1980s, when many thought that software would be the next industry to fall under Japanese domination (Cusumano, 1991). Already in the 1990s, however, it was clear that the software industry was dominated by spinoffs from large firms (including eight of the top ten information service companies), that most of their business was customized for these large firms (75 per cent of their orders), and that the industry was more reminiscent of the construction industry in its hierarchical nature than a high-tech industry populated by dynamic independent startups. The chairman of a SME software association lamented that 'MITI's policy of thinking that if it nurtured computer makers, software would automatically develop was a mistake.'[2]

From 2000 to 2011 Japan's production of electronics products—which contain embedded software—declined by 50 per cent, exports by 37 per cent, and the market capitalization of electronics manufacturers by more than half, compared with an average Tokyo Stock Exchange decline of 16 per cent (Cole and Nakata, 2014), setting the tone for the software industry. Spinning out software operations from these large companies was less about setting them free to flourish than cost-cutting; a reflection of the subordinate role of software relative to hardware, which dominated the mindset of senior managers and boardrooms; and indeed which dominated the minds of METI officials, as a campaign was launched to revive 'making things' or productionism—*monozukuri*. A law to promote *monozukuri* was passed in 1999, an annual white paper published, and a '*monozukuri* university' (Institute of Technologists) set up.[3] Again, software was seen to be more about cost cutting and raising efficiency for manufacturing than a product, or something which could fundamentally transform business.

It is worth citing Cole and Nakata's assessment of what went wrong in the software industry, as much of it is echoed in METI's DX Report:

- *University computer science education*: Redundant faculty were 'offloaded' onto newly established informatics departments in a context of fiscal and enrolment constraints; many other staff were 'retirees' from electronics companies whose expertise was in mainframe hardware and software; computer software was not strongly established as a discipline; student numbers were fixed; and those earning advanced degrees (especially Ph.Ds) generally stayed in academia.
- *Corporate career incentives*: With senior management positions dominated by an older generation steeped in *monozukuri*, and with a bias towards production of hardware and subcontracting of software development, career incentives for software engineers within leading companies were weak, creating a vicious cycle.

---

[2] Cited in Whittaker, 1997: 209. The Ministry of International Trade and Industry (MITI) became the Ministry of Economy, Trade and Industry (METI) in 2001.

[3] For a critical view of the *monozukuri* vogue, see Tsai, 2005.

- *Customized software*: 70 per cent of investment went to outsourced, customized software, 20 per cent to in-house customized software, and only 10 per cent to packaged products (versus 34 per cent, 37 per cent, and 29 per cent respectively in the US), creating among other things a high reliance on service providers, high maintenance costs, and a lack of strategic in-house expertise.
- *Longevity of business application systems*: Because of high costs, systems were kept for an average of 17 years, much longer than the US, again reflecting an emphasis on cost containment rather than investment.
- *Chief Information Officers*: In 2008 only 30–40 per cent of Japanese large firms had a full-time CIO, whereas most large US firms had one; there was a lack of understanding of software's potential among senior management, reflected in the slow implementation of agile (iterative) software, as well as state-of-the art enterprise software.
- *Start-ups*: Fewer start-ups, fewer funded by venture capital, and of these, only 9 per cent in software versus 24 per cent in the US.

The DX Report defined DX broadly, as 'a situation where a company takes advantage of data and digital technologies to deal with dramatic changes in business environments, change its products, services and business models to meet the demands of customers and society and change its business itself, organizations, processes, corporate culture, and corporate climate, so that it can establish a competitive advantage'.[4] This sees DX as about building dynamic capabilities through digital means (Teece et al., 1997; Teece, 2018). The Report credited CEOs with an awareness of the need for, and value of, DX. They know the difference between using IT to make existing processes more efficient and using it for transformation, but there are obstacles standing in the way of undertaking the latter. If unaddressed, the report ventured, they will cost Japan ¥12 trillion a year from 2025, but if addressed, they will boost Japan's GDP by ¥130 trillion by 2030.

The first obstacle was legacy systems, which 80 per cent of companies cited by the Report had, and which 70 per cent recognized as an obstacle. Systems put in place in the 2000s were coming to the end of their usable life. But this was just the tip of the iceberg. Often these systems were created by external parties—vendors or subsidiaries—and to most managers and employees within user companies, they were a 'black box'. Those who *did* know what was inside were retiring. Companies were spending more and more of their

---

[4] This is in fact METI's English translation in a later document: https://www.meti.go.jp/english/press/2020/0825_004.html (accessed 17 August 2021).

IT budgets to maintain these systems, with little left to invest in new or upgraded systems which might create more value—the average ratio was 8:2, but ratios of 9:1 were common. In fact, these systems would be creating a long-term 'technical debt', costing more money to maintain than the value they generated.

Next, there was a people problem. As the most senior managers didn't have a strategic view of these systems, they had been implemented in an ad hoc manner, making it difficult to integrate them. Even CIOs tended to leave details to vendors and were unable to objectively measure the value they were getting, relying instead on vendor reputation. Chronic shortages of in-house specialist IT staff were expected to reach half a million by 2025. Competition to recruit such staff was fierce, and given the rapid pace of technological change, it was not easy to nurture them in-house under lifetime employment. The result was outsourcing to vendors or consultants. But this created a communication gap, a question of where responsibility ultimately lies, and of designing contracts which could cope with agile development, or iterative upgrades. Even vendors had the same issues of staff shortages and coping with rapidly changing technologies. In sum, going forward would be difficult, but maintaining the status quo was not an option.

The second half of the DX Report discussed what may be done. This was fleshed out in more detail with a follow-up report in 2019 called 'DX Promotion Indicators and Guidance'. First, companies were urged to establish metrics which could objectify their current frameworks, systems, and associated costs and issues in a way which could be shared. They were encouraged to draw up DX promotion guidelines as to how to upgrade existing systems. These should be a resource for managers, directors, and shareholders, and not just operational procedures. The guidelines should also allow the company to respond to changes in the environment and technological changes. Costs and risks should be clearly identified. Outdated and redundant systems should be removed. New partnerships with vendors should enable agile upgrading and joint development, with dispute resolution clauses. For this, more investment should be made in human resources, both in IT and operations departments.

The follow-up report set out quantitative measures for five levels of implementation, similar to the schemes that have been developed for ESG (environment, social, governance: Chapter 6) implementation. It also had a separate questionnaire for Boards of Directors, starting with them confirming the necessary expertise does exist within the Board, and following up with questions about the vision, commitment of top managers, supportive company culture, budget allocation, human resources, and roadmap for implementation. The questionnaire was designed to stimulate a high-level discussion and commitment to change.

That was not all. A 'Digital Governance Code' followed in 2020 which was intended to sit alongside the Corporate Governance Code (Figure 6.1). This placed the onus on Boards to ensure various DX-related measures are carried out. It also hinted at the implications of DX for corporate governance itself, suggesting that DX creates an imperative for managers to engage with a wider range of stakeholders, including 'customers, investors, financial institutions, human resources such as engineers, business partners, partners who collaborate to create value by linking systems and data, local communities, and the like'. We will consider this further later in the chapter.

Finally, METI set up a certification system. Businesses which passed the specified criteria would be deemed 'DX-Ready' and were entitled to use a special logo announcing their certification, which would be valid for two years. By the end of March 2021, 69 companies had received it, and a DX Promotion Portal was set up to provide examples for others. METI also launched a scheme with the Tokyo Stock Exchange to select 'DX Stocks' for a particular year, and 'Noteworthy DX Companies' 'that are not only introducing exceptional information systems and utilizing data, but also boldly taking efforts to change business models and management practices in a continuous manner based on digital technologies. They are also expected to play leadership roles in their various industries'.[5] In 2020, 35 DX Stocks and 21 Noteworthy DX Companies were selected, and in 2022, 33 stocks and 15 companies respectively were chosen. Komatsu and Trusco Nakayama Corporation were singled out as winners of the 'DX Grand Prix 2020', and Chugai Pharmaceutical and Nippon Gas as winners of the 'DX Grand Prix 2022'.

DX was taken up in the mass media and ushered in a minor publishing boom. DX proved very profitable for consulting companies as well. In 2022 the Digital Governance Code was revised, placing greater weight on 'digital human resources', incorporating the Indicators and Guidelines, and linking with GX. The expanding agenda of corporate governance is a subject we will return to.

E-government and the Digital Agency

For residents of Japan in 2020 digital transformation was probably first and foremost something the government should do to itself. Many official

---

[5] https://www.meti.go.jp/english/press/2020/0825_004.html (accessed 17 August 2021).

procedures were impossible to do online, or they were very cumbersome.[6] Government data bases were not joined up, making it necessary to present the same information multiple times to different offices. Instead of accelerating the move to online services, Covid-19 had highlighted their inadequacies. In April the government decided to implement a cash transfer of ¥100,000 to each resident. Notifications were sent out manually, and applications had to be made manually. Queues to photocopy documents formed outside convenience stores. Call centres were set up to answer questions. First payments were received in June, and some not until August. In the midst of the pandemic, when people were being told to work online, the impossibility of doing this for official procedures jarred. Suga Yoshihide became Prime Minister, promising to have a Digital Agency up and running by September 2021.

This was not the first push for e-government in Japan. In the early 2000s a series of e-Japan strategies was drawn up under the IT Strategic Headquarters, designed to make Japan the world leader in IT by 2005. At its core was e-government, based on a resident registration system commonly called Juki-net. As its project manager for systems integration lamented, Juki-net was dogged by controversy before and after its launch (Kita, 2006). Opponents such as the Anti-National ID Forum considered it Orwellian because it *did* join up government departments and central and local governments. They were concerned about data security, as well as the right to control their own information. Against such headwinds, the attempt was quietly abandoned.

A new attempt was made in January 2016, with the implementation of the My Number Act, and revision of the Personal Information Protection Act (originally passed in 2003). This time opposition was more muted. Under the My Number Act, each resident was assigned a 12-digit number, which the government was authorized to use for social security, tax, and disaster relief only. Residents were able to see how their data was used. Lack of opposition, however, did not equate with active use. At the beginning of the Covid-19 outbreak, only 15 per cent of residents had acquired their card, and as the outbreak worsened, it became difficult to even apply for one. By March 2021 the proportion had risen to almost a quarter, but having a card—or number— did not equate with usefulness.

This is where the Digital Agency came in, to remove the barriers to e-government and to provide public digital services that the public need and want. The newly appointed Digitalization Minister characterized past efforts to create e-government as 'digital defeat', and the new agency as Japan's 'last

---

[6] According to the Japan Research Institute, it was only possible to do 7.5 per cent of 55,765 procedures online in 2019: *Nikkei Asia*, 15 June 2021 ('COVID Gives Japan "Last Chance" to Reverse Digital Defeat').

chance' to recover. The Digital Agency was to have a much bigger role than the existing IT Strategic Headquarters, with authority to draft new laws, and an expanding budget, starting at ¥300 billion in its first year.[7] Unlike most government agencies, which are under a ministry, it was positioned directly under the Prime Minister, and started on schedule with a staff of roughly 500, including 150 recruited from the private sector.

Envisaged as a 'control tower', the Digital Agency assumed sole responsibility for 30 key government IT systems, and for developing 70 others. The systems would draw on 'base registries' of key data, relating to individuals, corporations (with a unique Corporation Number), land, buildings, infrastructure, traffic, etc. And a Gov-Cloud, or 'co-creation platform' would allow central and local governments to develop their services. A goal was set to have most people using My Number by the end of 2023, and 98 per cent of government procedures online by 2025. Indeed, the ultimate goal was to develop an infrastructure for services that could be accessed anytime and anywhere, within 60 seconds on a mobile phone. Thus the Agency had an inward facing mission to bring disparate government services and IT systems into an integrated structure which can be continually upgraded, and an outward facing mission to ensure that the structure can efficiently deliver services that people actually want.

The inward mission faced some hoary obstacles, including fax. machines and personal seals (*hanko*). Held up as a symbol of small business resistance to digitalization, fax machines have been equally entrenched in government offices. In June 2021 Kono Taro, the Minister responsible for administrative reform, sent a notice to all central ministries and their agencies instructing them to stop using faxes by the end of the month, or to provide a good reason why they could not do so. An official was quoted as saying they received some 400 responses, with reasons ranging from providing documentation to courts, to ease of use for press clipping services.[8] Meanwhile, the *hanko*, which forced many people onto trains during Japan's Covid-19 emergency measures, may yet survive—by going digital. Shares in companies producing digital *hanko* surged after the passage of a law in April 2021, which officially abolished the need for physical hanko in most of the 15,000 official procedures hitherto requiring one.[9]

The public-facing mission began with good intentions. Ideas were solicited from the public through a 'digital reform idea box', which attracted over

---

[7] The total government IT budget in 2021 was ¥800 billion. Information below draws on an interview with a Digital Agency preparation officer, 12 July 2021, and material supplied for the interview.

[8] *The Japan Times*, 9 August 2021 ('Phasing out Faxes Faces Fierce Resistance from Japan's Bureaucrats')

[9] *Nikkei Asia*, 6 April 2021 ('Japan Investors Swoop for "Digital Hanko" Stocks').

6000 ideas. A year after the ¥100,000 cash transfer debacle, however, similar chaotic scenes were played out in the setting up of the national vaccination programme. Frustration that such programmes could not be delivered more efficiently with online systems was ironically directed at Suga, whose tenure as prime minister was short. And while 77 per cent of the population had allegedly been issued with a My Number card, and 44 per cent had used it by mid 2023, well-publicized glitches and a growing resistance to merging health insurance cards and My Number cards cast a shadow over prospects for universal take-up.[10]

Trust over data privacy and security is crucial. This time around public resistance seems to be more about implementation than underlying principles. The government is probably helped by *not* being a pioneer, and by having the public debates which led to revision of the Personal Information Protection Act in 2016. Data protection is sufficiently close to the EU's General Data Protection Regulation (GDPR) for an adequacy agreement to be signed in 2018, creating the 'world's largest area of safe data flows'. Japan is seen to be aligning with best, or better, practice regarding the protection of data, and the right to privacy.[11]

The minister in charge of setting up the Digital Agency used the catchphrase 'government as a startup'. In some respects the Digital Agency *was* a startup. Its founding team was generally young and energetic, and spoke at startup forums. They were attempting to reform Japan from 'below' in terms of their age group. But the scale of the Agency's task is very large, and larger still if the health and education sectors are considered, while data security concerns persist.

Cybersecurity

Digital systems have penetrated most sectors of society with a rapidity that has left cybersecurity struggling to keep pace, creating new vulnerabilities and risks hitherto undreamed of. Almost daily one can read about cyber-attacks on companies or infrastructure, state-encouraged ransomware attacks, as well as spoofing, phishing, and similar incidents which run into the millions, even billions every year. Not surprisingly, Japan has struggled

---

[10] Figures come from the Ministry of Internal Affairs and Communications (MIC). *The Japan Times*, 9 June 2023 ('My Number Glitches Undermine Japan's Digital Future').

[11] The Digital Agency itself has ten founding principles, drawn up by a panel which included academics and citizens, the first three of which are transparency and openness; fairness and ethics; and security and safety.

to keep up too. A report by the International Institute for Strategic Studies (IISS, 2021) assessed that:

> Japan has been among the global leaders in the commercial application of information and communications technologies since the early 1980s, but its readiness to deal with the security aspects of cyberspace is a much more recent phenomenon.... Japan's defences in cyberspace are not especially strong, with many corporations unwilling to meet the costs of bolstering them. The country's resilience planning has been rather limited, though this intensified in the run-up to the 2020 Olympic and Paralympic Games.
>
> **(IISS, 2021: 79)**

The report assigned Japan to the bottom tier of three cyber capability tiers, in the company of India, Indonesia, Iran, Malaysia, Vietnam, and North Korea. Indeed, in much of the writing on the digital economy and Society 5.0 in Japan, the issue of cybersecurity seldom arises, despite its increasing importance to the economy, as well as national security. This is a rather broad generalization, however, and in this section we will consider evolving cybersecurity policies from the perspective of the economy.

Extending the discussion of software in the first section, cybersecurity is also assigned a lower priority in Japanese businesses than their US counterparts. Cole and Fushimi (2020) cite a Nomura Research Institute (NRI) study which found that twice as many US businesses assign more than 10 per cent of their IT budget to information security as Japanese businesses: 72 per cent as against 35 per cent. And 71 per cent of US businesses had a Chief Information Security Officer (CISO), as against 36 per cent of Japanese companies.[12] Cole and Fushimi's analysis of *why* this is the case is interesting.

First, they cite Akamai, the largest US content delivery network service provider, which reported that its US customers experienced a billion attacks on their web applications in 2017, compared with 44 million attacks on Japanese customers. As they were attacked less often, Japanese customers have a lower threat consciousness, and have been slower to mobilize against such threats. In the NRI study, 70 per cent of US firms reported fraudulent emails and 32 per cent suffered financial damage, versus 58 per cent and zero respectively. In addition, there was a much lower ratio of insider attacks to outsider attacks in Japan (5 per cent versus 52 per cent), probably reflecting the benefits of long-term employment and organizational cohesion, and possibly wider cultural differences. This leads to the flip side of the software

---

[12] Cole and Fushimi (2020: 200) A different survey produced higher CISO figures but with a similar gap: 86 per cent for US companies and 53 per cent for Japanese companies (ibid., 110).

problems identified earlier. In the US, a lot of software has been produced by startups, which have sought to be first to market and have upgraded security later. In Japan, by contrast, a strong focus on quality first means that problems, including security issues, are expected to be ironed out before software is released. There is evidence that software patches are applied earlier, and more consistently in Japan, the authors add, which is important because a large proportion of breaches happen as a result of delays in applying patches.

On the other hand, the biggest cybersecurity headache in Japan is a lack of technically competent personnel, whereas this is ranked only fourth in the US, with its much bigger pool. Specialized information security is not a recognized career path in Japan, and with an emphasis on quality, and contractual specification completeness, there has been less need. A closed loop is thus created (Cole and Fushimi, 2020), which might explain at least some of the apparent complacency of Japanese companies, and their 'unwillingness' to bolster defences in the eyes of the IISS.

Slowly, however, and with increasing urgency, a national framework is being established which, when placed within the national security, economic security and digital agency frameworks, will force companies to enhance their own cybersecurity measures. Again, the origins go back to 2000, with the establishment of an IT Security Office in the Cabinet Office at the same time as the IT Basic Law was passed. The focus then was on data assurance with the spread of information technology, and despite an evolving institutional structure, and national strategies on information security published from 2006, that essentially remained the case for much of the 2000s. Cybersecurity was not mentioned in any defence white paper in the 2000s (Kallender and Hughes, 2017). In 2009, however, US and South Korean internet services were assailed with large-scale distributed denial of service (DDoS) attacks, and Japan experienced a surge in advanced persistent threats (APTs). Spear-phishing attacks on Japanese technology companies, research institutes, and government departments also rose markedly, with Mitsubishi Heavy Industries, Japan's largest defence contractor, facing a serious attack in 2011 (Kallender and Hughes, 2017).

In the face of such threats, cybersecurity assumed greater prominence, first with the Democratic Party of Japan (DPJ) government in 2009, and then with the return of the Liberal Democratic Party (LDP) in 2012. The National Strategy on Information Security was re-named the Cybersecurity Strategy in 2013, and a new Basic Act on Cybersecurity was passed in 2014. A Cybersecurity Strategic Headquarters was established under the Prime Minister, and the National Information Security Centre (now renamed the National Centre of Incident Readiness and Strategy for Cybersecurity but retaining the acronym NISC) was positioned as the secretariat. This framework remained in place until 2021, when the IT Strategic Headquarters was absorbed into the Digital Agency (Figure 2.1).

Through this reorganization cybersecurity policy and strategy were not only centralized, but more strongly aligned with national security. Kallendar and Hughes go so far as to argue that:

> Cybersecurity's facilitation of 'cross-domain' operations means it is positioned at the leading edge of and helping to drive forward transformation in Japanese policy and capabilities across a full range of land, sea, air, and outer space activities. Japan has thus moved to first securitize its response to challenges in the domain of cyberspace by taking data assurance issues traditionally within the realm of information technology public policy governance and now defining and embedding them as central security issues and thus to be accorded higher national priority and resources, requiring a whole of government approach.
>
> **(Kallender and Hughes, 2017: 120)**

Bartlett (2018) offers a very different assessment. He points out that the secretariat NISC *is* staffed by officials from a variety of ministries, as shown in Figure 2.1, *but* MIC and METI have put aside their differences to work together and, because of their links to networks of cybersecurity specialists, are able to claim key positions, including deputy director, with control over day-to-day operations and agenda setting. As a result, he argues, cybersecurity policy has been developed as *industrial* policy, rather than the other way round, and 'is driven far more by concerns about international economic competition than it is about international security competition' (Bartlett, 2018: 332). Given its lack of competitive advantage in a broad range of cybersecurity products, according to Bartlett's interviewees, it is better for Japan to focus its cybersecurity efforts on industrial sectors such as the Internet of Things (IoT) and autonomous cars. In fact it is doing so, as we shall see.

With some dexterity, it might be possible to accommodate both views, and to offer a slightly different nuance, as follows. The 2021 Cybersecurity Strategy reminds us that the aims of the Cybersecurity Basic Law are 'enhancing socio-economic vitality and sustainable development', 'realizing a digital society where people can live with a sense of safety and security', and 'contributing to the peace and security of the international community and Japan's national security.' It then appeals to the need to advance DX and cybersecurity together—cybersecurity is necessary to build the trust needed for DX, while advancing DX will raise awareness of the need for cybersecurity.

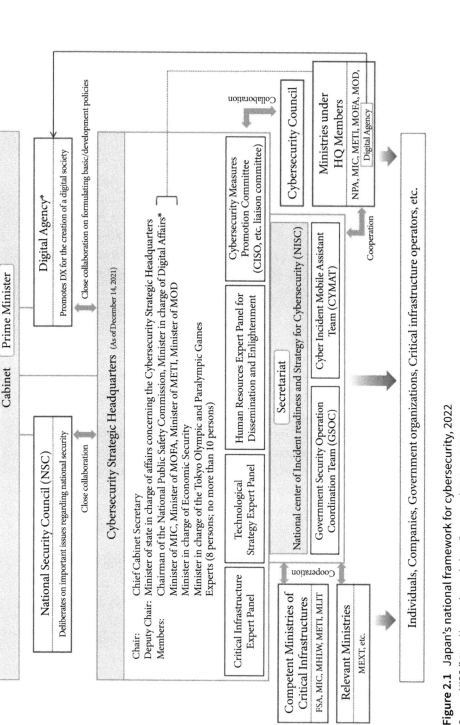

Figure 2.1 Japan's national framework for cybersecurity, 2022

Source: NISC (https://www.nisc.go.jp/eng/) accessed 28 June 2022.

Note: NPA = National Police Agency; MIC = Ministry of Internal Affairs and Communications; METI = Ministry of Economy, Trade and Industry; MOFA = Ministry of Foreign Affairs; MOD = Ministry of Defence; FSA = Financial Services Agency; MHLW = Ministry of Health, Labour and Welfare; MLIT = Ministry of

To build Society 5.0, it continues, it will be necessary for all stakeholders to assume greater awareness of and responsibility for cybersecurity, requiring self-help, mutual help, and public help. With the challenges of cloud infrastructure, complex cross-border value chains, and emerging challenges of IoT, 5G and beyond, the government has a key role to play, but at the same time everyone, not just specialists, needs a 'plus security' attitude. This is essential for a 'people friendly digitalization, with no-one left behind', as well as a 'free, fair and secure' cyberspace.[13] It also emphasizes international cooperation, especially with the US, and suggests that cyberattacks could equate with an armed attack. 'Resolute responses' will include 'political, economic, technological, legal, diplomatic, and all other viable and effective means and capabilities'—leaving scope, it would seem, for stretching its hitherto defensive and deterrent posture towards pre-emptive action.[14]

Cybersecurity in the service of building Society 5.0 is specifically addressed in METI's 2019 'Cyber/physical Security Framework' (CPSF, version 1.0), which sees data flowing differently, and new kinds of value chains, with the IoT and 'Connected Industries', and with the integration of cyberspace and physical space.[15] This will create new types of risk, calling for new types of cybersecurity. Reminiscent of the five levels of DX implementation (and autonomous vehicles: Chapter 5), the CPSF for Factory Systems envisages cybersecurity for five levels of smart factory automation, each with different cybersecurity challenges, as well as distinct challenges for different factory zones.[16] More immediately, METI and IPA have been issuing Cybersecurity Management Guidelines since 2015—version 3.0 was released in 2022—which are supposed to complement the Digital Governance Code (cf. Figure 6.1).

In sum, Japan may not be a cyber power in the terms evaluated by the IISS. It is strengthening its cyber capabilities to address its vulnerabilities—exposed by a persistent attack on, and infiltration of, sensitive defence networks in 2020 and 2021—both for its own security, and in the context of the evolving US–Japan, Quad and other external security relationships. It is also developing cybersecurity for the digital economy, and ultimately for

[13] This echoes Abe's 'data free flow with trust', and 'Free and Open Indo-Pacific' mantras.
[14] The quotations are from a provisional English translation, especially pp. 29–30.
[15] https://www.meti.go.jp/english/press/2019/pdf/0418_001a.pdf (accessed 19 August 2021). Public-private working groups (which we will encounter in a range of settings in this book) were set up to map out the implications for specific sectors, as well as a CPSF for Factory Systems.
[16] https://public-comment.e-gov.go.jp/servlet/PcmFileDownload? seqNo=0000236565 Guidelines for cyber/physical security of smart appliances were released in 2020: https://www.dataguidance.com/news/japan-meti-releases-draft-guidelines-cyberphysical (both accessed 28 June 2022).

Society 5.0. In this respect, it is arguably less a laggard than feeling its way towards an as yet partially imagined future.

New Industrial and Innovation Policy

Industrial policy, once famously associated with MITI and Japan's 'developmental state' (Johnson, 1982), fell out of favour in the 1990s and was replaced—albeit not entirely—by a regulatory approach to governance (Chapter 1). As in other countries, however, it has undergone a revival since the Global Financial Crisis and has been harnessed to promote DX (and GX—Chapter 3), enhance cybersecurity and build Society 5.0.[17] METI still plays a key role, but so too does the Kantei. R&D consortia are still formed, but now there are many study groups and working groups at work on a wide range of projects. Government financing institutions such as the Development Bank of Japan (DBJ, previously Japan Development Bank) still play an important policy financing role, but there are new public–private bodies and funds such as the Japan Investment Corporation (JIC) as well.[18] Codes and guidelines have replaced administrative guidance. Old and new are layered in the 'new (adaptive) developmental state'.

Ironically, whereas once other countries assiduously studied Japanese industrial policy, the reverse is often the case now. The Moonshot R&D programme, for example, which started in 2019 with nine future-oriented social, environmental, and socio-technological themes, was influenced by the EU's Horizon 2020. Its predecessor ImPACT mimicked aspects of the US Defence Advanced Research Projects Agency's (DARPA) programme and project management. In this section we will look briefly at the Strategic Innovation Programme, which like Moonshot (and PRISM—Public/Private R&D Investment Strategic Expansion Programme) is under the CSTI in the OPMC, as well as the Connected Industries Programme, which is under METI.

---

[17] A broad definition of industrial policy is 'any type of intervention of government policy that attempts to improve the business environment or to alter the structure of economic activity towards sectors, technologies or tasks that are expected to offer better prospects for economic growth or social welfare than would occur in the absence of such intervention' (Warwick, 2013: 16).

[18] The Industrial Revitalization Corporation (2003) became the Innovation Network Corporation (2009), before being re-launched as JIC in 2018 as a kind of sovereign wealth fund and structured as a limited time public–private investment fund. Most of its funding comes from the public sector, and many of the companies invested in are startups: cf. https://www.incj.co.jp/performance/data/index.html (accessed 13 June 2023).

Strategic Innovation Programme

The Strategic Innovation Programme was started in 2014 as a cross-ministerial initiative under the CSTI in the OPMC, with a budget of around ¥30 billion per year. Eleven themes that are 'crucial for society and are leading the world that could contribute to the revival of the economy in Japan' were selected for the first five-year round (2014–2018).[19] Some were carried over into the second round (2018–2022), including autonomous driving, and were then linked to Society 5.0. The link was even more explicit in the call for proposals for the third round, starting in 2023, whose themes were:

Comprehensive community platforms
Post Corona study and work platforms
Maritime safety platforms
Smart energy management systems
Circular economy systems
Smart disaster prevention networks
Smart infrastructure management systems
Smart mobility platforms
Basic technologies and rules for safe and secure AI and data use
Social applications for advanced quantum core technologies
Core technologies for material process innovation
Core technologies and rules for the expansion of human interaction robotics
Core technologies and rules for expansion of the virtual economy
Building smart communities, smart cities, smart islands[20]

Projects are supposed to be 'end-to-end', from R&D to application and commercialization, and are led by a high-profile director from industry or academia. In the case of SIP-adus (autonomous driving for universal services) this was a senior manager from Toyota with a background in vehicle safety. Whereas in the first round the autonomous driving project focused on technical issues, including dynamic maps, the second round opened out into issues concerning practical application and social acceptance. Social scientists were recruited to carry out simulations of effects on road transport, traffic safety,

---

[19] https://www.jst.go.jp/sip/k03/sm4i/en/outline/about.html   also   https://www8.cao.go.jp/cstp/panhu/sip_english/sip_en.html (accessed 20 August 2021). The words 'crucial for society and are leading the world that could contribute to the revival of the economy in Japan' express multiple aims of Japan's innovation policy: cf. Conclusions.

[20] https://www8.cao.go.jp/cstp/stmain/pdf/20211224_siryo1.pdf (accessed 28 June 2022).

industry and society, and collaborations were formed with researchers at several institutes and government departments in Germany.

SIP-adus brought together personnel from related ministries, which succeeded in cutting through administrative hurdles to Level 3 autonomous driving. Commented one participant: 'There is a sense of urgency. Regulation used to be used as an excuse for non-action. That's no longer the case. Even the police, who you would expect to be resistant, and not concerned about economic competitiveness, are moving much quicker than before.'[21] SIP-adus has been succeeded by new programmes, including smart mobility platforms, noted above, and 'RoAD to L4' from 2023.

Arimoto (2023) claims that SIP-adus meets all of the criteria of OECD's 'mission-oriented innovation policy' (MOIP) and represents a fourth phase of postwar STI policy in Japan, the predecessors being state-led large-scale technology development, industrial technology development, and the national innovation system.[22] In fact Japan was a pioneer in incorporating new sustainable and resilient society goals into innovation policy, he claims.

Connected Industries and the Digital Architecture Design Centre

Some of SIP's themes reappear in METI's Connected Industries programme, started in 2017 with a vision of 'creating new added value and providing solutions to societal challenges by connecting a variety of data, technologies, people and organizations in the midst of the global rise of the internet of things (IoT) and artificial intelligence (AI)'.[23] Its five priority fields were autonomous driving and mobility services, manufacturing and robotics, plant infrastructure safety management, biotechnologies and materials, and 'smart life'. A METI official gave an example of the challenges addressed in the programme:

Take drones to check pylons. Before, people went out and climbed up pylons, took photos and took them back to look at, then sent people out to fix what was needed. Now a drone can take photos, and send them back to a server for auto analysis....

---

[21] Interview, 7 April 2021.
[22] MOIP is 'a co-ordinated package of policy and regulatory measures tailored specifically to mobilise science, technology and innovation in order to address well-defined objectives related to a societal challenge, in a defined timeframe. These measures possibly span different stages of the innovation cycle from research to demonstration and market deployment, mix supply-push and demand-pull instruments, and cut across various policy fields, sectors and disciplines' (Larrue, 2021: 3).
[23] https://www.meti.go.jp/english/policy/mono_info_service/connected_industries/index.html (accessed 1 May 2021).

But the drones need maps, not only with x and y, but z as well, otherwise they might hit something. So there needs to be another layer which makes the maps. These maps, though, can be used for more than pylon checking—in towns where there are curbs that might trip up robots, or self-driving vehicles, a z (vertical) dimension is needed there as well. Building data might be needed. Various data is held by various people, so what is the most efficient way of gathering and structuring the data?[24]

Such questions led METI to establish a Digital Architecture Design Centre in 2020, locating it in the IPA to make it easier to hire project participants from the private sector. Commissioned by METI, the Digital Agency, and the private sector, projects such as mobility as a system (MaaS), and 'smart safety' focus on the design of cyber-physical systems. Bringing together the data from connected industries to create new value, safely, requires the construction of platforms, designed with flexible architecture. At the level of Society 5.0, it needs a reconceptualization of governance rules and processes.

Governance for Society 5.0

Japan has typically been cast as a DX laggard—by outsiders, by the media, and even by the Japanese government—needing to 'catch up' with front runners, typically the US. To build Society 5.0, however, original thinking is needed; neither path dependence nor catch-up will take Japan there. Changes will need to be made to governance. This was the reasoning of a group of academics, business leaders, lawyers, and others, brought together by METI in 2020 to produce a series of reports on governance for Society 5.0.[25] The first focused on the accelerating pace of innovation, its potential risks, and the need to preserve fundamental values. Not only must innovation be governed, but turning it around, governance must be innovated, the authors reasoned, since industry boundaries are no longer rigid, and promising new innovations, including business models which add value to society, might be blocked by existing regulation, while harmful innovations, including business models, may escape regulation, at least temporarily. Thus the need for 'agile governance'.

---

[24] Interview, 26 July 2021.
[25] The full titles of the reports were 'Governance Innovation: Redesigning Law and Architecture for Society 5.0, Version 1.1' (METI Study Group, 2020), 'Governance Innovation Ver.2: A Guide to Designing and Implementing Agile Governance' (METI Study Group, 2021a) and 'Agile Governance Update: How Governments, Businesses and Society Can Create a Better World by Reimagining Governance' (2022). This section is based on the first two reports.

The second report more systematically set out a vision for agile governance for Society 5.0. Differences with Society 4.0, depicted in Table 2.1, mean that instead of traditional regulation in which the government sets fixed rules, monitors, and enforces them, governance needs to be adaptive, and carried out in a horizontal, multi-stakeholder manner. The widespread use of cyber-physical systems, the authors argued, will mean that rules are incorporated into algorithms which are at the same time constantly updated and adjusted in response to data assessed by AI. Systems will interact with each other through interoperability, with input from multiple stakeholders. They will be difficult to monitor from the outside, and the locus of responsibility will often be difficult to determine. There will be new challenges to ensure fair competition, disclosure, data rights, and dispute resolution. New mechanisms for the participation of individuals and communities in system design, monitoring and adjustment will be needed.

Agile governance will be brought about through a hierarchical structure consisting of ultimate goals (happiness and liberty), core values (human rights and economic growth, with sustainability), and concrete objectives, such as privacy and use of personal data, freedom of expression and access to information, health and safety... (Figure 2.2). Multiple cyber-physical systems will have a similar hierarchical structure, and together will make

Table 2.1 Differences between Society 4.0 and Society 5.0 (METI study group)

	Society 4.0 and earlier	Society 5.0
Daily life and digital technology	Physical space and cyber space are separated	Cyber space is integrated with physical space and becomes an indispensable foundation for lives
Object of trust	Tangible (people, things)	Intangible (data, algorithms)
Acquirable data	Limited	Greater scale, scope, variety
Decision-making actor	Only humans	Humans + AI and systems
System conditions	Stable	Fluid
Predictability and controllability	Relatively predictable and controllable	More areas become unpredictable and uncontrollable
Responsible actor	Easily identified	Not easily identified
Concentration of control/power	Predisposed to concentration	More predisposed to concentration
Geographical relationships	Local OR global	Local AND global

Source: METI Study Group on New Governance Models in Society 5.0, 2021: vii.

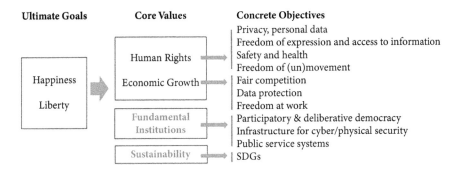

Figure 2.2 'Agile governance': Goals, values, and objectives
Source: METI Study Group on New Governance Models in Society 5.0, 2021: viii.

up Society 5.0. Ultimately, the group proposes a need for participatory 'governance of governance'.

Meanwhile, at the corporate level 'it will be critical for stakeholders to improve disclosure systems and to provide compliance guidelines. It is also important to revise corporate sanction regimes in a way that focuses on risk management and future improvement of systems, rather than mere outcomes' (pp. xi–xii). This view echoes a growing body of research on digital transformation and its impact on corporate governance. Filatotchev and Lanzolla (2023), for example, argue that digital transformation requires companies to shift from 'legacy' corporate governance focused on narrow criteria of financial performance to 'open' corporate governance incorporating effectiveness in satisfying the requirements of multiple stakeholders. It is relevant, too, to the increasingly urgent debates about making AI 'black box' decision making explainable and accountable, with the UK's Royal Society (2019) calling for a stakeholder approach.

Concluding Comments

This chapter has explored DX largely from a policy perspective and has identified a revival of industrial policy in Japan, principally to address the perceived lag relative to other 'advanced countries' and to pave a path towards Society 5.0. Programmes are devised which are 'crucial for society and are leading the world that could contribute to the revival of the economy in Japan'. While Arimoto sees Japan as having entered a fourth phase of postwar STI policy in the form of 'mission-oriented innovation policy', with added features of sustainability and resilience, traces of the former phases are also clearly discernible. The toolbox is diverse, ranging from soft law (such as the Digital Governance Code and various guidelines) to working groups and investment funds. The target of change is both industry and the government itself, which must change in order for Society 5.0 to be built.

Considering all this, it appears that industrial and innovation policy is animated by two underlying orientations, or 'spirits'. The first is a reversion to 'catch-up'—Japan must try harder or it risks getting left behind. Supposedly liberated from it in the 1980s, Japan has slipped back into this orientation, almost by habit. Yet there is a second orientation as well, namely a desire for Japan to plot its own path, guided by the image of Society 5.0, which will be people-centred and address social needs. At one level, these appear to be in contradiction, but at another level, it seems that this duality has become a driving force, like a stick and a carrot.

Within this mix, moreover, one can sense the emergence of a third orientation, or spirit, namely a focus on security and cybersecurity, both in government, and in the economy at large. Emerging technologies which create new risks, as well as emerging geopolitical risks, are propelling it into the foreground. Japan's defence-related R&D has been given an unprecedented boost, while the Self Defence Forces plan to quadruple their cyber specialists over four years from 2023, albeit from a comparatively low base. Japan intends to set up its own version of DARPA. All-in-all, this represents a significant evolution of state-market relations, a re-embedding of the economy which is likely to become more pronounced.

Some of these themes will re-appear when we look at green transformation (GX) in the next chapter. Although Japan is frequently castigated as a green laggard, however, and although green policy is very much approached as industrial policy, these are not symmetrical wheels of the proverbial cart. Green transformation policy has been set out more recently, but it arguably offers greater prospects of mobilizing actors through cooperation rather than competition, which animates DX. Here, too, however, the tension—between GX and DX, cooperation, and competition—could be additive in the long-run.

3

The Green Economy

Russia has used energy supply as a weapon of war. Countries that have seen their peoples' lives severely disrupted by this have begun to pursue a robust 'kill-three-birds-with-one-stone' strategy that simultaneously aims to achieve the three goals of decarbonization, a stable energy supply, and economic growth. Japan's green transformation is also designed to realize these three goals.

So said Prime Minister Kishida in a speech to the opening of a new Diet session in January 2023, restating Japan's energy policy formula—3E+S—in less prosaic language.[1] Just two months earlier Kishida had been criticized for not attending COP27, where Japan had been tarred with a 'Fossil Award of the Day' by Climate Action Network, an award given to countries 'doing their best to achieve the least'. Similarly, the Climate Action Tracker rated Japan's efforts as 'highly insufficient' in 2020, a category which would allow temperatures to rise by up to 4 per cent relative to their pre-industrial level, far above the 2 per cent Paris Agreement pledge level and 1.5 per cent goal.[2] Green Alliance Japan was likewise critical in its 2020 'civil society environmental white paper' *Green Watch*; local governments covering 44 per cent of the population issued net zero declarations in 2019, while the central government continued to procrastinate, insisting on growth, betting on unproved technologies, lacking openness, and addicted to coal, it lamented.

On the other hand, DeWit (2020) argues, critics both inside and outside the country typically cite the low renewable energy share in the power mix, but a more comprehensive set of indicators that include the circular economy, waste reduction, resource efficiency, and resilience would paint the country

[1] https://japan.kantei.go.jp/101_kishida/statement/202301/_00012.html (accessed 29 March 2023). 3E+S is short for energy security, economic efficiency, environmental protection, and safety.
[2] https://climateactiontracker.org/countries/japan/ (accessed 5 August 2021). 'NDCs [nationally determined contributions] with this rating fall outside of a country's "fair share" range and are not at all consistent with holding warming to below 2°C let alone with the Paris Agreement's stronger 1.5°C limit.'

Building a New Economy. D. Hugh Whittaker, Oxford University Press. © D. Hugh Whittaker (2024). DOI: 10.1093/oso/9780198893394.003.0004

in a more favourable light. While many countries fail to meet their pledges, Japan 'has consistently achieved or approached targets over a much wider range of parameters than those set by most other nations' (p. 9). It is able to do this, he suggests, because it has quietly built a network of actors working at multiple levels to achieve policy integration and implementation; the image of siloed ministries and turf wars no longer fits the reality of the Japanese government, or governance. Holroyd (2018: 194), too, argues that Japan is far from exemplary in environmental terms, but its model of 'green growth' and 'techno-environmentalism' offers 'reasons for optimism and important possibilities that link environmental sustainability and continued prosperity'.

Opinions diverge. It is a fact that in 2015 Japan joined almost 200 other countries in signing up to the UN Framework Convention on Climate Change, otherwise known as the Paris Agreement, pledging to reduce its greenhouse gas (GHG) emissions by 26 per cent from their 2013 level by 2030. This would mean an 18 per cent drop from its 1990 level, which was considerably less than the 25 per cent it had pledged in 2010. It was not a simple matter of backsliding, however. In the interim, Japan had faced the devastation of the 3.11 triple disaster, leading to the closure of all its nuclear power plants, which had hitherto generated over 25 per cent of the country's electric power. While campaigners had hoped this would lead to a decisive switch to renewable energy sources, to the contrary, Japan's reliance on fossil fuels increased, with mothballed coal-fired power stations re-opened, and new ones built. As a result, Japan began to acquire a reputation as a foot-dragger on climate change.

In October 2020 Prime Minister Suga committed Japan to carbon neutrality by 2050, and the following April he raised the 2030 GHG reduction target from 26 to 46 per cent (at least). Asserting green to be compatible with growth, government ministries drafted a 'Green Growth Strategy', with five policy tools, and 14 'growth sectors' targeted for investment and transformation. Then Russia invaded Ukraine....

This was the backdrop for Kishida's speech, in which he was about to launch a clutch of bills to enact Japan's 'GX Realization Basic Plan' (referred to as the GX Plan below) with a ten-year roadmap. Finally, Japan had its overarching blueprint for GX, again decried by critics as a lost opportunity, but also an opportunity for the type of coordination and commitment cited by DeWit. Green transformation is complex, and Japan has serious challenges, including its susceptibility to natural disasters.[3] The GX Plan was also complex, and set out roadmaps for over 20 sectors and technologies in terms of strategic goals, finance, regulation, and internationalization.

---

[3] 2023 marked the centenary of the Great Kanto Earthquake, which destroyed much of Tokyo and Yokohama and claimed over 100,000 lives.

The first section of this chapter looks at Japan's electric power mix, energy policy, and changing emphases within its '3E+S'. It focuses on what happened in the decade after the triple disaster, and what changes are envisaged to meet the 2030 target. The second section considers the cautious use of carbon taxes and emissions trading schemes. The third looks at another common target of campaigners' criticism, the use of plastics. It puts this in the context of the circular economy, and this gives a nuanced picture. Given the country's propensity to natural disasters and reliance on imported energy, it is impossible to separate GX from measures to promote resilience and security. Resilience is taken up in the fourth section, which also considers integrated policy making.[4] The final section considers Japan's 'Green Growth Strategy' (GGS) and 'GX Realization Basic Plan'.

This chapter complements Chapter 2 in that DX and GX are considered two wheels of Japan's economic transformation cart, headed for Society 5.0. The emphasis in both is on policy, and more specifically, on industrial and innovation policy. The GGS is explicitly called industrial policy, as well as a *growth* strategy—an assertion that green is compatible with growth. Although it has come slightly later than DX, there is a very strong push to mobilize the public and private sectors around the GGS and GX Plan—this is part of the rationale of combining green and growth—which may make GX more pervasive or consequential than DX in the long run.[5]

Energy and Greenhouse Gas Emissions

An ambitious government project has been announced. As a matter of urgency, government, industry, and academia will work together to develop new energy sources, namely:

- Solar energy
- Geothermal energy
- Coal gasification and liquefaction
- Hydrogen energy

The year? Putting 'coal gasification and liquefaction' aside, one might be tempted to say 2022 or 2023. In fact, it was half a century earlier, in 1974, and these energies were to be developed under the Sunshine Project. Japan rapidly outgrew its domestic supplies of coal in the postwar high growth

---

[4] Energy dependence, and security are addressed in Chapter 9.
[5] There are, of course, other voices and visions, including organizations within mainstream business which believe the Japanese government, and Keidanren, are not moving fast enough on green transformation—such as the Japan Climate Initiative—just as there are on digital transformation, such as the Japan Association for the New Economy (JANE) (Katz, 2021 b, c).

period, and it turned to oil and natural gas, which it had to import. When the Arab–Israeli War broke out in 1973, Saudi Arabia led an oil embargo to countries seen as siding with Israel, which included Japan. Oil prices surged, and Japan was hit hard. It was in this context that MITI created the Sunshine Project, which was joined by the Moonlight Project for energy saving in 1978. The two were merged into the New Sunshine Project in 1992, which lasted until the early 2000s.

Japan's solar industry was born through the Sunshine Project, and battery storage through the Moonlight Project. Until the mid 2000s Japan was the world's largest producer of solar cells, and many citizens installed them on their roof. Under the Koizumi government in 2005, however, government subsidies were dropped. Japan ceded its lead to Germany, as well as China. With their focus on stable energy supply, moreover, Japan's centralized electric power companies were not very interested in unstable wind power, while hot spring owners opposed harnessing of geothermal energy for electric power generation. As a result 'inadequate policies advocating the use of [renewable energy] between the 1990s and 2010 suppressed its share in annual power generation to about 10 percent' (The Green Alliance Japan, 2020: 6).

Instead the nuclear industry grew, from the opening of the first reactor in 1966, to supply over a quarter of Japan's electricity generation in 2010, with ambitious targets and generous support to reduce Japan's reliance on imported fossil fuels. Here, too, Japan's vulnerability was laid bare with the Fukushima nuclear disaster in 2011, which wreaked massive, ongoing human and environmental damage. Under the short-lived Democratic Party of Japan (DPJ) governments, ambitious renewable energy (RE) targets were set. The 'moment of engagement between the public and policymakers' was closed, however, with the return of the Liberal Democratic Party (LDP) under Abe late 2012, whereupon energy and climate policy reverted to pre-Fukushima norms (Ohta, 2020: 14) As the country's nuclear reactors were shut down, the government turned once again to oil, gas, and even to coal.

Figure 3.1 shows the dramatic shift in Japan's electric power mix from 2010 to 2020. Nuclear power plummeted to just 1 per cent in 2012, and zero in 2014, as all reactors were shut down. Some were subsequently re-opened, but they only supplied 4 per cent of electricity in 2020.[6] Although there were

---

[6] In 2010 two-thirds of nuclear capacity was utilized; in 2019 the proportion was one-fifth. Campaigners opposing the re-opening of nuclear plants point to the risks of another Fukushima Daiichi-type disaster, and delays in decommissioning that plant, increased cases of thyroid and similar cancers, and inadequate support for displaced families.

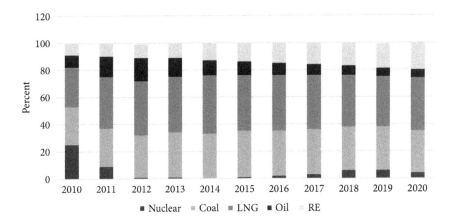

Figure 3.1 Electric power generation mix, 2010–2020

Source: Kankyōshō (MoE) (2021), '2020 nendo no onshitsu kōka gasu haishutsuryō ni tsuite' (About Fiscal 2020 GHG Emissions Volumes).

savings in energy use—Japan produced 13 per cent less electricity in 2020 than in 2010—fossil fuels filled much of the void. Natural gas share rose from 29 per cent in 2010 to 43 per cent in 2014, then dipped to 38 per cent in 2020. RE sources also rose; in fact they more than doubled, from 9 per cent in 2010 to 20 per cent over the decade. Hydro-electric power remained largely flat (7.8 per cent in 2020), while solar power generation surged to eclipse hydro (7.9 per cent), aided by an initially generous feed-in tariff (FIT) in 2012. The balance of RE came from biomass, wind, and geothermal power, in that order. DeWit (2020) observes that Japan's investments in RE capacity from 2010 to 2019 were only surpassed by China and the US; Japan invested over 10 per cent more in RE than Germany during that time.[7]

When it comes to GHG emissions, electricity generation only gives part of the picture (43 per cent of Japan's GHG emissions in 2018), and industrial (28 per cent), transport (19 per cent), residential and commercial sources (10 per cent) must be included. Figure 3.2 shows total GHG emissions from all sources, measured in CO_2 equivalent tonnes. These peaked in 2013 and declined by almost 18 per cent by 2020. Some of the recent drop can be attributed to the restarting of (some) nuclear reactors; other factors include less power generation, increased use of RE, deindustrialization and energy efficiency gains, as well as the spread of hybrid and more fuel-efficient cars.

---

[7] https://www.fs-unep-centre.org/wp-content/uploads/2020/06/GTR_2020.pdf (p. 31, accessed 5 August 2021).

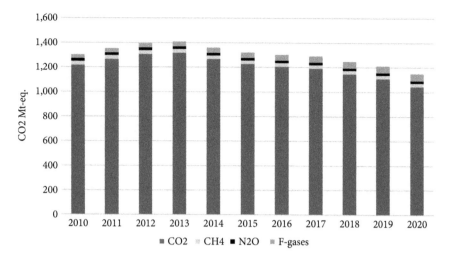

Figure 3.2 Greenhouse gas emissions, 2010–2020

Source: As for Figure 3.1.

The 46+ per cent Target: Feasible or Not?

Japan's Basic Law on Energy was passed in 2002, and a Strategic Energy Plan (SEP) was issued the following year, setting out the 3E+S formula. At COP21 in 2015 Japan pledged a reduction in GHG emissions of 26 per cent relative to 2013 levels by 2030. This pledge framed the targets of the 5th SEP of 2018. In April 2021, however, PM Suga pledged a much more radical reduction target of at least 46 per cent by 2030, inverting the normal decision-making process and throwing the plan, and planners, into confusion. The 6th SEP was hurriedly prepared and released by the Agency of Natural Resources and Energy (ANRE) in July 2021. Building on this, the GX Plan, discussed below, was released in 2023.

Table 3.1 gives a breakdown of the projected power mix in 2030 according to targets of the 5th SEP and the 6th SEP. The difference in ambition between the two is striking. Even more striking is the difference between the actual mix in 2020 and those projected in the 6th SEP. Relative to the 2020 figures, the 6th SEP envisages a decline in overall power generation of about 8 per cent, a major decline in fossil fuel use from 75 per cent to 40–42 per cent, and a countervailing doubling of RE and quintupling of nuclear power. The plan also envisages the development and deployment of carbon capture and storage (CCS) technologies, which are controversial.

How feasible are these new targets? The time frame is potentially problematic, as each of the adjustments raises a host of issues. Normally these

Table 3.1 Projected 2030 electric power mix, 5th and 6th SEP (%)

	2020 (Actual)	2030 (5th SEP)	2030 (6th SEP)
Renewables	20	22–24	36–38*
Nuclear	4	20–22	20–22
LNG	38	27	20
Coal	31	26	19
Oil	6	3	2

Sources: As for Figure 3.1; targets from ANRE, 2018, 2021.
* Specific RE targets are: solar 14–16%, hydro 11%, wind 5%, biomass 5%, geothermal 1%, hydrogen 1%.

would be resolved first, but the top-down 46 per cent target made it difficult for the advisory committee to follow its normal consensus procedures, according to a member of the committee.[8] Japan already has the third largest installed capacity of solar power, after the US and China, and there are limitations to its continued expansion. Restrictions on the use of abandoned farmland are being eased, but local communities have increasingly placed restrictions on solar panel siting. Auctions have been held for offshore wind projects, but given the limited potential for fixed platforms, the greatest potential lies in floating platforms, often in remote prefectures, which makes it an expensive source (Nakamura, 2022; see below).

Although nuclear energy would still be below the pre-3.11 level, even restoring its share to 20–22 per cent raises a host of technical, social, and political issues. Russia's invasion of Ukraine may have swayed public opinion towards supporting nuclear power, but in 2022 only 10 of the country's 33 nuclear reactors had been cleared to restart, and only five were actually in operation. Half were 30 or more years old. Most significantly, after a decade-long hiatus many suppliers had left the industry, and many engineers had also left or retired. Even with heavy investment, it will be years before a new generation of reactors—such as small modular reactors—becomes operational, meaning ways need to be found to extend the life of existing reactors. Nuclear energy is unlikely to provide a magic bullet, and nor are hydrogen, CCS and other new technologies either, at least for 2030. DeWit's observation that Japan meets its international pledges will be tested.

[8] Kikkawa Takeo, https://www.japanpolicyforum.jp/economy/pt2021083013564211429.html (accessed 6 July 2022).

Market Mechanisms: Emissions Trading Schemes and Carbon Taxes

Japan's use of market mechanisms for environmental purposes—especially to reduce GHG emissions—started relatively early, but has been cautious, experimental, and mostly voluntary, possibly reflecting an initial scepticism about solving environmental impacts through their commodification.[9] Both of the main mechanisms—carbon taxes and emissions trading schemes (ETS, including cap-and-trade and baseline-and-credit)—have been tried.[10] In 1997 Keidanren introduced a voluntary cap-and-trade scheme (Voluntary Action Plan on the Environment), in which *industries* were to set their own targets with the aim of stabilizing their GHG emissions at below 1990 levels by 2010. Thirty-five industry associations signed up. While appearing to respond to the Kyoto Protocol, environmental organizations saw the scheme as an attempt to pre-empt compulsory government measures.[11]

The central government started a scheme—also voluntary—in 2005, which almost 400 companies participated in. JVETS (Japan Voluntary Emissions Trading Scheme) covered emissions from industry, offices, and waste management. An offset crediting mechanism J-VER (Japan Verified Emissions Reduction) was added in 2008, as well as a CDM (Clean Development Mechanism).[12] However, with the massive jolt to the economy from the Global Financial Crisis, a change of government, and ebbing enthusiasm for market-based solutions, the scheme atrophied.[13]

Tokyo introduced a compulsory scheme in 2010, covering large commercial office and industrial facilities which produce 40 per cent of the capital's GHG emissions. The reduction targets of the first five-year compliance period were rather lenient—8 per cent for commercial buildings, 6 per cent for manufacturing facilities—and in the second five-year period they were increased to 17 per cent and 15 per cent respectively. Five types of offsets

---

[9] Cf. Chiapello and Engels on 'commodification processes that aim to transform environmental impacts into commodities' (2021: 517).

[10] Cap-and-trade schemes set an upper limit for emissions with the possibility of buying credits from those under the limit, while baseline-and-credit schemes offer credits to those whose emissions fall below the baseline.

[11] E.g. http://www.kikonet.org/english/publication/archive/keidanren-vap.pdf (accessed 14 August 2021).

[12] The Clean Development Mechanism was set up under the Kyoto Protocol to recognize emissions reduction projects in developing countries for certified emission reduction credits.

[13] J-VER and a domestic CDM were brought together in 2013 under the J-Credit Scheme, which remained voluntary. https://www.edf.org/sites/default/files/japan-case-study-may2015.pdf (accessed 14 August 2021).

were created.[14] Then after a successful demonstration project in 2022, the Tokyo Stock Exchange launched a baseline-and-credit ETS scheme in October 2023. This will face competition from another exchange, set up jointly by SBI Holdings and Asuene.

Next, although Japan debated introducing a relatively bold carbon tax as early as 1995, it was not until 2012 and after much wrangling that a modest version was finally introduced, set at a relatively low ¥289/t-CO_2. As there are other taxes on energy production and use, however, a more inclusive measure is the 'effective carbon rate' (ECR), which varies enormously by sector. In 2018 road transport had an ECR of €188.3/t-CO_2, while for the electricity sector it was €10.4/t-CO_2, and for manufacturing just €3.3/t-CO_2. The national average was a modest €34.8/t-CO_2.[15]

In sum, although Japan started to experiment with market mechanisms in the 1990s, and accumulated considerable experience with them, they were mostly cautious and their impact outside the Tokyo metropolitan area was limited. The GX Plan's (2023) ten-year roadmap saw an initially voluntary ETS 'GX League' start in April 2023, to which 600 companies responsible for 40 per cent of GHG emissions signed up. These will be responsible for diffusing knowledge, and the system will be expanded and strengthened in 2026, becoming fully implemented from then on. The carbon price will be gradually lifted, but within upper and lower limits to ensure predictability for investment. From 2028 a new carbon levy targeted at energy importers will be introduced. And an auction mechanism for the power sector, similar to that of the EU, will be introduced in 2033. A new GX Promotion Agency will oversee the schemes.[16] The system has been designed; its effectiveness will depend on implementation, and whether it is ratcheted up, or watered down. In the meantime, market mechanisms for emissions reduction play a relatively modest role in Japan's GX efforts.

Plastics and the Circular Economy

Many of the world's largest oil and gas companies are also the biggest producers of plastic, and one concern is that as demand for oil decreases, they

---

[14] These were: excess credits, small and medium facility credits, renewable energy credits, outside Tokyo credits, and Saitama credits. https://icapcarbonaction.com/en/?option=com_etsmap&task= export&format=pdf&layout=list&systems%5B%5D=51 (accessed 14 August 2021). Saitama created its own scheme similar to that of Tokyo. Kyoto created a less stringent scheme in 2011.

[15] Kojima and Asakawa, 2021: 12–13. Cf. also OECD, 2021.

[16] https://www.cas.go.jp/jp/seisaku/gx_jikkou_kaigi/pdf/kihon.pdf (accessed 28 March 2023).

will pivot to increase plastic production.[17] Plastic, and in particular single use plastic which accounts for a third of production, has become emblematic of waste and environmental destruction. And it is another area in which Japan is often criticized. In 2019 Japan ranked fifth in the per capita use of single use plastic, albeit considerably behind the worst offenders Australia and the US.[18] The same year, Japan drew up a Resource Circulation Strategy for Plastics, and at the Osaka G20 Summit, it proposed the Osaka Blue Ocean Vision to rid the oceans of plastic by 2050. In 2020 charges were introduced on plastic shopping bags in Japan, and the following year a new law was passed to accelerate the recycling of plastic and the development of alternatives.

Plastic encapsulates the contradictions, and aspirations, of the circular economy. It has become indispensable for daily lives, and plastic wrapping and bags in Japan have become deeply embedded in the culture of service and gifts, to the frustration of environmental campaigners. Whereas in 1980 Japan produced just 7518 tonnes of plastic, by 2018 this had risen to 10.7 million tonnes, with 8.6 million tonnes of plastic waste.[19] On the other hand, the 'utilization rate' of waste plastic in Japan has also risen, from 58 per cent in 2005, to 86 per cent in 2020.[20]

As well as production and utilization, however, there is a further, troubling statistic—exports. In 2018 China sent shock waves around the world by banning waste plastic imports, forcing exporters to seek other markets. In 2020 Japan was still exporting an estimated 821,000 tonnes, mostly to Southeast Asian countries.[21] More optimistically, the heightened focus on plastic has stimulated new measures within Japan, from NPOs working with retailers and companies to replace throwaway plastic wrappers, containers, and utensils with environmentally friendly substitutes, to research intensive ventures seeking economical and scalable bio-based alternatives. Commented one chemist, the 3Rs of the circular economy—reduce, reuse, recycle—are being supplemented by a further 3Rs—rethinking, re-inventing, and redesigning.[22]

---

[17] 'They are making big investments in plastic because they are projected to loose oil demand as pushes to decarbonize the economy continue', Odachi Hiroaki, Greenpeace Japan's Plastic Campaign Project Leader, cited in *The Japan Times*, 21 February 2021 ('Can Japan Embrace an Alternative Approach to Plastic?'); also *The Guardian*, 18 May 2021 ('Twenty Firms Produce 55% of the World's Plastic Waste: Report').

[18] *The Japan Times*, and *The Guardian*, ibid.

[19] *The Japan Times*, ibid.

[20] PWMI, 2021; 2022. This was mainly through incineration with heat or electric power capture. The unused 15 per cent was split between incineration without heat or electric power capture, and landfill.

[21] https://www.weforum.org/agenda/2023/03/charted-the-flow-of-global-plastic-waste/ (accessed 1 April 2023).

[22] *Japan Times*, 21 February 2021 ('Can Japan Embrace an Alternative Approach to Plastic?')

The Circular Economy

Geographic constraints and a high population density limit Japan's options for getting rid of waste, especially through landfill. Its limitations have propelled the search for innovative solutions. Japan's postwar high growth created chronic pollution problems, and eventually a legal and practical framework was devised to deal with them. The current framework for the circular economy is built on the Environment Basic Law passed in 1993, and the Basic Law for Establishing a Sound Material-Cycle Society, passed in 2000.[23] They are augmented by a range of subsidiary laws.

In 2018 Japan produced 379 million tons of industrial waste, a drop of almost 10 per cent from the early 2000s.[24] More conspicuous has been the fall in waste going to landfill—by 2018 this was a mere 2.4 per cent of all industrial waste, with over half of the total recycled. Household waste, moreover, fell from roughly 54 million tons in 2003 to 43 million tons in 2018, with just 1 per cent going to landfill and 20 per cent recycled.[25] Municipal waste fell from 430kg/year/person in 2000 to 337kg in 2019, a drop of 22 per cent. This compares with an OECD average reduction of *less than 2 per cent* over the same time period. Japan's average was 63 per cent of the OECD average in 2019, and just 42 per cent of the US average. In fact, in contrast to Japan, many OECD countries showed little or no improvement over the two decades (Figure 3.3).

Over two-thirds of waste incineration facilities in Japan now use residual heat for heating public baths, swimming pools, etc. Over a third are able to generate electric power, sufficient to supply the needs of 3.7 million households. The conversion efficiency of some facilities is low, however, and measures are being implemented to raise the ratio. Incineration problematically generates pollutants, like dioxins, which have long been a source of grievance for people living near the facilities. Standards were introduced in 1997 and a law in 2000 tightened regulations on existing and new facilities. As a result dioxin emissions fell from 6505 g-TEQ in 1997 to 37 in 2019.[26]

Subsidiary laws bolstering the volume and proportion of waste recycled in Japan include the Containers and Packaging Recycling Act (1995), Home Appliance Recycling Act (1998), Food Recycling Act (2000), Construction Recycling Act (2000), Automobile Recycling Act (2002), and Small Home

[23] 'Material-cycle society' has been the government's preferred term for circular economy.
[24] Figures here are from Purasutiku junkan riyō kyōkai (Plastic Waste Management Institute (PWMI)), 2021.
[25] The balance was incinerated. The pressure on landfill sites is intense, and the government carefully monitors how many years of capacity is left, with a goal of maintaining at least 20 years.
[26] PWMI 2021: 24, 26. g-TEQ is weight in grams times a measure of toxicity.

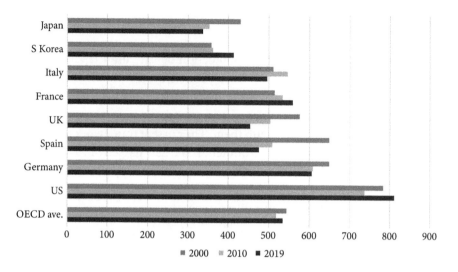

Figure 3.3 Municipal waste per capita (kg/yr)

Source: https://stats.oecd.org/index.aspx?DataSetCode=MUNW (accessed 7 July 2022).
Note: Recent US figure is for 2018.

Appliance Recycling Act (2012). These have created roles for the public—sorting rubbish, especially—and obligations for manufacturers. Consumers are required to return unwanted home appliances to the retailer or municipality, usually for a fee, and the latter relay the products to the manufacturer, importer, or their agent, for recycling. The process is more complicated for vehicles, and has created an industry of dismantlers, shredders, CFC recovery operators, handling agents.... The recycling and recovery industry grew from ¥40 trillion in 2000, dipped after the Global Financial Crisis in 2009, recovered to ¥47 trillion in 2015, and has a government target of 'roughly double' the 2000 figure.[27]

Life-cycle assessment (LCA) has become increasingly important in waste and emission reduction measures. In 1995 the Life Cycle Assessment Society of Japan was formed, and in 2004 an Institute of Life Cycle Assessment was founded. LCA traces resources from the point of extraction to final disposal and has become part of Japan's '3R' armoury. The overall results can be seen in figures from the Fourth Basic Plan for Establishing a Sound Material-Cycle Society, which has assessed progress on a range of measures from the year 2000, and proposed new targets for 2025 (Table 3.2). If 'what gets measured gets managed', then the number of measures used is indicative of an increasingly comprehensive system to manage Japan's resources. The 2025 targets come with roadmaps, shared by central and municipal governments.

---

[27] https://www.env.go.jp/recycle/circul/keikaku/gaiyo_4_2.pdf (accessed 6 August 2021).

Table 3.2 Resource efficiency measures: achievements and targets

	2000	2015	2020	2025 (goal)
Resource productivity (GDP/input of resources, ¥/ton)	240,000	380,000	460,000	490,000
Cyclical use rate—input resource base (cyclical use/cyclical use + resource input, %)	10	16	17	18
Cyclical use rate—waste base (cyclical use/ waste generated, %)	38	44	45	47
Landfill (million tons)	60	14		13
Municipal waste (grams/person/day)	1185	925		850
Household waste (grams/person/day)	653	507		440

Source: https://www.env.go.jp/recycle/circul/keikaku/gaiyo_4_2.pdf (accessed 6 August, 2021).

Urban Mining, Deep Sea Mining, and Rare Earths

An energy system powered by clean energy technologies differs profoundly from one fuelled by traditional hydrocarbon resources. Building solar photovoltaic (PV) plants, wind farms and electric vehicles generally requires more minerals than their fossil fuel-based counterparts. A typical electric car requires six times the mineral inputs of a conventional car, and an offshore wind plant requires nine times more mineral resources than a gas-fired power plant. Since 2010, the average amount of minerals needed for a new unit of power generation capacity has increased by 50% as the share of renewables has risen.... The shift to a clean energy system is set to drive a huge increase in the requirements of these minerals, meaning that the energy sector is emerging as a major force in mineral markets.

(IEA, 2021:5)

In 2010 China rattled Japan by temporarily banning the export of rare earth minerals over a dispute near the Senkaku Islands. These minerals are crucial to modern technology industries, and Japan was reliant on China for 90 per cent of its supply. Consequently, Japan urgently sought to diversify its import sources, to increase stockpiles, and to create alliances and joint ventures abroad. It redoubled its efforts to extract the minerals from electronic waste, to look for new sources in the seabed, and to develop substitute technologies and materials. A decade later, Japan was still reliant on China for almost 60 per cent of its rare earth minerals. Its goal of less than 50 per cent by 2025 will be challenging, as demand is surging.

Japan's processing of discarded electronic devices increased threefold to 370,000 tons in the decade to 2018.[28] 'Urban mining' produced the medals that were awarded in the 2020 Tokyo Olympics. But as DeWit and Shaw (2022) point out, it took 80,000 tons of mobile phone and other e-waste just to extract the two tons of copper that was needed. And this is only a quarter of the copper needed for a single megawatt of offshore wind capacity. Furthermore, rare earth mineral extraction is even more difficult than copper.

Japan's search for new mineral sources has taken it to the muddy 6000 metre depths of its exclusive economic zone waters.[29] Some 1850km southeast of Tokyo, off the coral atoll Minami-Torishima, a veritable treasure trove of rare earths has been discovered, which Japan hopes to exploit from 2024. Doing so is full of technological challenges, not to mention environmental risks, but Japan hopes to emerge as a leader in deep sea mining, as well as substitution technologies and materials to overcome serious bottlenecks for both the digital and green economy.

Resilience

A green economy must be resilient, as the triple disaster of March 2011 ('3.11') which threw Japan back onto reliance on fossil fuels shows. 3.11 highlighted the need for comprehensive resilience planning, as well as setting Japan on a new path for STI policy, and hence Society 5.0. Japan first passed a Disaster Countermeasures Basic Law in 1961 and has published a White Paper on Disaster Management every year since 1963. The law was overhauled in 1995 following the Hanshin-Awaji Earthquake. Government departments and public corporations, prefectural and local governments were required to draw up disaster management continuity plans. Nothing, however, could have prepared them sufficiently for the multiple disasters that struck Iwate, Miyagi, and Fukushima prefectures in 2011, claiming 20,000 lives, rendering hundreds of thousands of people homeless, and causing environmental carnage.

3.11 exposed the limitations of existing continuity plans, and the central government was widely criticized for being slow to act. By contrast, local governments proved more resourceful, and able to improvise. New networks

---

[28] *Nikkei Asia*, 9 June 2020 ('Resource-poor Japan Unearths Metal Riches in Trash')
[29] https://www.nature.com/articles/d42473-020-00524-y (accessed 8 August 2021). It may also take it to the moon, where a public–private–academic consortium launched in August 2021 is hoping to find water and minerals in sufficient quantities to enable commercialization: *Nikkei Asia*, 10 August 2021 ('Japan Consortium to Collaborate on Water on the Moon').

of support and solidarity were formed as local governments near and far rushed to help, as did NPOs and domestic and international civil society organizations. The vulnerabilities of a centralized power grid structure and cosseted regional monopolies were also exposed, with Tokyo Electric Power Company, operator of the Fukushima Daiichi nuclear reactor, becoming a particular target of criticism. Decentralized, smart grids and sustainable energy sources were given a boost.[30]

But resilience entails far more than decentralization, and the central government retains crucial roles. Many of the immediate lessons from 3.11 were set out in the National Resilience Basic Law of 2013, its associated Basic Plan for National Resilience, as well as in the UN's Sendai Framework for Disaster Risk Reduction (2015–2030) as part of the 2030 Agenda. A World Bank report on the tenth anniversary of the disaster cited amongst other things the following:[31]

Resilient infrastructure: Sendai City's water supply was disrupted and its water treatment plant submerged, affecting other emergency services. Hence the need for: retrofitting seismic resilient pipes, enhanced business continuity planning (BCP) for sanitation systems, a GIS-based asset management system, and decentralization of emergency decision making and community training to set up emergency water supplies.

Prior multi-party agreements including public–private partnerships, such as the agreement between Sendai City and a private consortium to operate Sendai International Airport in specified circumstances, and agreements with local construction companies for road clearance and recovery work.

Early warning: Japan's Earthquake Early Warning system, activated in 2007, was developed further after 3.11. It can identify expected damage quickly. Education about such systems is necessary.

Redundancy in infrastructure can be vital. When their factories in Miyagi lost power for two weeks, Toyota and other companies created a back-up energy system, which is also used to improve energy efficiency.

Schools are a critical infrastructure, for education, community and evacuation purposes, and must be made resilient. They generally were in Tohoku, but standards were raised further.

Community engagement, including the elderly, children, community in general and private companies, is crucial. After 3.11, an Ibasho Café was created in Ofunato by elders, for the elderly, strengthening community cohesion.

---

[30] Kingston ed., 2012; Samuels, 2013; Chapter 4.
[31] The report was prepared by Takemoto, Shibuya, and Sakoda, 2021. The World Bank and the government of Japan have produced numerous reports based on Japan's experience.

Cultural heritage documentation is necessary for rebuilding after a disaster. University professors and volunteers started the Kobe Network and Miyagi Shiryo Net and developed procedures for this.

Simulation drills and basic preparedness measures, which were substantially strengthened in Japan after the Hanshin-Awaji earthquake in 1995, helped save lives.

Business continuity planning (BCP) has spread widely in both the public and private sectors. In fact, BCP has entered everyday parlance in the business community in Japan.

Financial contingency measures and keeping financial institutions open after a major disaster are crucial. The report concludes that 90 percent of bankruptcies following 3.11 were due to indirect impacts, such as supply chain disruptions.

Policy Integration and Multi-party, Multi-level Collaboration

Major disasters underline the need for different sectors and levels of society to work together like no other event can. That was certainly the case with 3.11, but this takes time to deliberate and implement, test, and adjust in an ongoing process which almost by definition can never be definitive. DeWit (2019) argues that despite their reputation for turf wars, Japanese ministries and officials have learned to overcome siloed reflexes, and have learned to coordinate policy and engage with stakeholders at multiple levels. Dams are a case in point, with different types of dams historically under the control of different ministries. The Ministry of Land, Infrastructure, and Transport's Dam Revival Vision (2017) envisaged installing turbines at dams not currently producing power, to double the share of hydro-electric power in the national power mix, and conversely extending the number that can be used for flood control purposes—making them multi-functional, as well as an integral part of a predictive and responsive system through the use of advanced technologies (ibid.). This is clearly an ongoing challenge; Suga Yoshihide made the following comment when he was bidding to become Prime Minister in October 2020:

A recent experience that made me keenly aware of the government's 'compartmentalized administration' was the dam issue. It started with typhoon *Hagibis* in October 2019.... We managed to prevent large-scale flooding in Tokyo, but some regions suffered large damages. I instructed the relevant ministries and agencies to look into flood-control measures to consider whether anything can be done in preparation for next year.

Having done this, I was told the following by the bureau director in charge at the Ministry of Land, Infrastructure, and Transport (MLIT): There are 1,470 dams across Japan, but the only ones with flood-control measures in place are the 570 dams under the jurisdiction of MLIT. The other 900 are dams belonging to power companies under the jurisdiction of the Ministry of Economy, Trade and Industry (METI) and dams for agricultural purposes under the jurisdiction of the Ministry of Agriculture, Forestry and Fisheries (MAFF), but such 'water utilization dams' do not have any flood-control measures. A perfect example of the harmful effects of the 'compartmentalized administration'.[32]

New measures allowed MLIT to operate all dams during the typhoon season, doubling the dam capacity that could be used for flood control measures, saving not only downstream communities from the risk of flooding, but according to Suga's reckoning, saving more than ¥25 trillion in taxpayers' money as well. Mr Suga succeeded in becoming Prime Minister, and it is notable that soon into his tenure the Green Growth Strategy was published under the imprimatur of the Cabinet Office and eight ministries and agencies, although it bears the hallmarks of METI's influence with its focus on growth.

Green Growth Strategy and GX Realization Basic Plan

A critical step in the Japanese government's plans to fulfil its climate pledges and build a green economy was the release of the 'Green Growth Strategy' (GGS) in December 2020, tweaked after Suga's 46+ per cent GHG reduction intervention, and subsequently expanded on in the GX Plan.[33] The GGS cited five policy tools, and 14 'growth sectors', summarized in Tables 3.3 and 3.4. As the policy tools in Table 3.3 suggest, it is *industrial policy*: 'The Green Growth Strategy is a set of industrial policies to create a "virtuous cycle of economy and environment"' (p. 1). They came with ¥2 trillion worth of pump priming designed to elicit ¥15 trillion worth of private sector investment: 'The role of the government is to provide full support to private companies in conducting their forward-looking challenges, such as a bold investment to make innovation' (p. 1.). This is how industrial policy operates in Japan; as Samuels (1987) noted in his historical study of energy markets in Japan, industrial policy has never (except in wartime) been about top-down government directives, but

---

[32] Cited in *Discuss Japan: Japan Foreign Policy Forum*, No. 61, 22 October 2020.
[33] Naikaku kanbō (Cabinet Secretariat) plus eight ministries and agencies, 2021. Holroyd, 2018, gives a longer, historical perspective on 'green growth' in Japan.

Table 3.3 Policy tools for Green Growth Strategy

Policy tool	Content (over 10 years)
Grants	¥2 trillion Green Innovation Fund, to stimulate ¥15 trillion private R&D
Tax incentives	Tax incentives to stimulate ¥1.7 trillion in private investment
Finance guidance	Guidelines for transition finance, and interest subsidy scheme to attract global ESG investment
Regulatory reform	Regulatory reform in areas such as hydrogen, offshore wind power and mobility/batteries; consider carbon border adjustment for level playing field
International collaboration	Cooperation with developed and developing countries in innovation policy, joint projects, standardization, and rule making, etc. Promotion of 'Tokyo Beyond Zero Week'

Source: METI, 2021, 'Overview of Japan's Green Growth Strategy Through Achieving Carbon Neutrality in 2050', https://www.mofa.go.jp/files/100153688.pdf (accessed 10 August 2021), and revised report (in Japanese) June 2021.

Table 3.4 Fourteen growth sectors of the Green Growth Strategy

Energy	Offshore wind power Wind turbines, parts, floating wind turbines Fuel ammonia Combustion burner (fuel in transition period to hydrogen) Hydrogen Turbines for power generation, hydrogen-reduction steel making, carrier ships, water electrolyzers Nuclear power Small modular reactors (SMR), nuclear power for hydrogen production
Transport and manufacturing	Mobility and batteries Electric vehicles (EV), fuel cell vehicles (FCV), next generation batteries Semiconductors and ICT Data centres, energy-saving semiconductors Maritime Fuel cell ships, electric propulsion ships, gas-fuelled ships Logistics, people flow, and infrastructure Smart transportation, drones for logistics, fuel cell construction machinery Food, agriculture, forestry, fisheries Smart agriculture, wooden skyscrapers, blue carbon Aviation Hybrid electric, hydrogen powered aircraft Carbon recycling Concrete, biofuel, plastic materials

Home and office	Housing and building next generation PV
	Perovskite solar cells
	Resource circulation
	Biomaterials, recycled materials, waste power generation
	Lifestyle-related industries
	Local decarbonization business

Source: METI, 2021.

about creating and managing 'reciprocal consent'. For this 'the government needs to present a blueprint of energy policies and energy supply/demand structure needed to realize the 2050 Carbon Neutrality, as a reference value in deepening discussions' (GGS, p. 1).

Public and semi-public financing institutions soon announced that they would increase their lending for green and ESG purposes. The DBJ committed to providing loans of ¥5.5 trillion over the next five years for hydrogen-based energy, electric vehicles, emissions cutting technology and similar purposes. The Norinchukin Bank announced a 70 per cent increase on its green and ESG lending to ¥10 trillion over ten years in the agriculture sector, and separately a programme to work with agriculture cooperatives to preserve forests and plant trees. The Bank of Japan announced a new loan facility in which their reserves held at the central bank would be exempt from negative interest rates for up to twice the amount banks loaned to green projects. The private sector 'megabanks', already under pressure from environmental groups and activist shareholders, responded with green loans, and declarations that they would stop funding thermal and coal mining projects, and that they would use funds from the sale of cross-shareholdings to invest in green projects and startups.[34]

The 14 'growth sectors' identified in the GGS were accompanied by action plans and road maps. Several were in the energy sector itself, while others were in transport, industry, agriculture, tertiary, and household sectors. Let us briefly consider offshore wind power and hydrogen, as well as data centres, which overlap with the digital economy.

Offshore Wind Power

It is important to make full-scale efforts to introduce offshore wind power in Japan from both an energy policy and industrial policy perspective while reducing

---

[34] *Nikkei Asia*, 20 May 2021 ('Development Bank of Japan to Boost ESG Funding up to 80% to $50 Billion'); 26 May 2021 ('Japan's Largest Farm Lender to Pour $90 Billion into ESG Projects'); 16 July 2021 ('BOJ to Offer Interest-Free Loans Under New Climate Facility'); 17 February 2023 ('Japan Banks Pivot Loans to Investment in Green, Digital Ventures').

costs by cultivating Japan's offshore wind power industry and strengthening competitiveness. It is also vital for the public and private sectors to work together to build strategies to capture growth markets in Asia in the future. Therefore, firstly, the government commits to creating an attractive domestic offshore wind power market to attract domestic and foreign investment. On top of that, the government and industry will develop a competitive and resilient domestic supply chain by promoting investment through the establishment of business and other infrastructure. In addition, the government and industry will engage in next-generation technology development and international cooperation with an eye to expanding into Asia and create next-generation industries that can compete on the global stage.

(GGS, 17)

The passage captures the essence of contemporary Japanese industrial policy, which seeks to incentivize the development of technologies and industries domestically, then leverage the capabilities for opportunities abroad, especially in emerging Asia.

According to the Global Wind Energy Council (2022) the potential of Japan's offshore wind energy is massive—128GW for fixed-bottom platforms, and 424GW for floating platforms. This compares with less than 5GW for onshore and offshore production combined in 2021, with a mere 0.06GW generated offshore. Despite hopes for wind power growth with the introduction of a feed-in tariff in 2012, regulatory hurdles presented a head wind, with environmental assessments taking up to five years. Gaining approval from local communities took further time, and uncertainties about licence duration, and a weak supplier base were further issues. On top of this, nature poses challenges as well—earthquakes, typhoons, and in the case of offshore wind generation, deep waters. In sum, costs are high, and there is a lot to do even for the 10GW by 2030 and 30–45GW by 2050, ¥8-9/kw-hour by 2035, 60 per cent Japanese content by 2040 targets to be met.

The GGS offered greater certainty in terms of government commitment. A joint public–private sector working group was set up to address regulatory issues, improvement of grid, ports and other infrastructure, and new funds for investment. The GX Plan of 2023 further boosted public support for offshore wind generation in terms of technology development, supply chain and skill development. Critically, the government will take responsibility for seabed and wind surveys. Although Japan has been slow off the mark, the government hopes that overcoming the challenges posed by offshore floating turbines over deep water will provide participating businesses—domestic and non-Japanese—a springboard for offshore projects elsewhere in Asia.

Startups such as Albatross Technology and partners, which use floating axis instead of windmill turbines, are trying to seize this opportunity.[35]

Hydrogen

Hydrogen has long been seen as a promising clean energy and was part of the Sunshine project as far back as the 1970s. It is also attractive because of its range of uses, its range of possible sources, and energy efficiency relative to fossil fuels. Plans for the 2020 Tokyo 'hydrogen Olympics' were scaled back, but the hope of building a 'hydrogen society' lives on. Japan launched the first ship to transport liquified hydrogen, from Australia, in 2021, while on land it boasted the largest number of refuelling stations—over a quarter of the world's total—in 2021.[36] Nonetheless, to become a 'hydrogen society' numerous obstacles also need to be overcome to achieve a significant lowering of costs. The GGS aims to reduce these to one-third (to ¥30/Nm^3) of the current level by 2030, and less than the cost of fossil fuels by 2050.

Hydrogen is not necessarily green. 'Grey hydrogen' is produced from fossil fuels and releases CO_2 into the atmosphere. 'Blue hydrogen' is also produced from fossil fuels but utilizes carbon capture technology, while only 'green hydrogen' is made from renewable energy sources. Although Japan opened the world's largest green (solar-powered) hydrogen plant—the Fukushima Hydrogen Energy Research Field—in 2020, given its limitations in producing RE at scale, hopes for a large boost to hydrogen use are currently pinned mainly on 'blue hydrogen' using carbon capture. Japanese companies are investing in such facilities both domestically, and in the Middle East and Australia. Significant investment is needed to create reliable supply chains, and to progressively greenify them.

In terms of hydrogen utilization, the GGS foresees uptake in the energy (fuel cells, turbines), transport (cars, ships, aircraft, railways) and manufacturing (steel, chemicals, petroleum refining) sectors. It is seen as potentially competitive for commercial vehicles, like long haul trucks, as distances and refuelling times currently place electric cars at a disadvantage. Toyota has invested heavily in hydrogen, but its hydrogen-powered Mirai (meaning 'future') cost over twice Nissan's EV Leaf in 2021, and with relatively few hydrogen stations, its customers were mainly Japanese government fleets and wealthy, environment-conscious individuals. Substantial bets are being

---

[35] *Nikkei Asia*, 24 June 2023 ('Team Japan Bets on Next-generation Wind Turbine to Slash Costs').

[36] Japan aims to launch hydrogen-powered ships in the second half of the 2020s to decarbonize shipping through public–private investment: *Nikkei Asia*, 8 July 2022 ('Japan Aims to Demonstrate Carbon-Neutral Ships in 2026').

placed on hydrogen as a fuel for the future, however. The GX Plan envisages ¥7 trillion in investment over the next decade—¥5 trillion for building a supply chain, ¥1 trillion for infrastructure development and ¥1 trillion for R&D—as well as ¥3 trillion for zero emission ships.

Data Centres

The GGS envisages both 'greening *of* digital' and 'greening *by* digital': 'What upholds the Green Growth Strategy is resilient digital infrastructures; green and digital are [like] the two inseparable wheels of a car' (p. 2). On the one hand, digitalization will contribute to GHG emission reduction 'through the optimization of flows of people, things and money' in society (p. 35). The GGS claims that digital transformation, and specifically switching from enterprise- to cloud-based systems, could slash energy consumption by as much as 80 per cent. Increased use of telework and online conferences will save on commuting and business trips. Investment in power semiconductors, in which Japanese companies currently have a significant global market share, and in next-generation semiconductors and storage batteries, will result in significant energy saving, and enhance competitiveness as the IT sector is forced to become green. Thus a win–win situation is projected for digital and green growth, which is optimistic if constraints such as rare earth metals are taken into account.[37]

On the other hand, the GGS predicts IT-related power consumption to increase 36-fold between 2016 and 2030 (!) and notes that large data centres can consume as much power as a thermal power station can generate. Yet while there are limitations to Japan supplying cheap electricity, for security reasons and the sake of economic efficiency, such centres must be built around Japan, and current centres must be replaced with 'zero emission and enhanced resilience' facilities (p. 37). This will require cooperation between power companies and installation vendors, as well as market mechanisms. And it will need investment in disaggregated computing, photonics-electronic convergence technology and advanced semiconductors, to the tune of ¥12 trillion according to the GX Plan.

GX Implementation Basic Plan

Some elements of the 2023 GX Plan have already been introduced. What is notable about the GX Plan relative to the GGS is the massive scaling up of

---

[37] Needless to say, significant R&D effort is going into rare earth reduction and substitution technologies.

investment envisaged; *from ¥2 trillion of public sector investment to ¥20 trillion, and ¥15 trillion of private sector investment to ¥150 trillion over ten years.* Public money will be raised by GX Economy Transition Bonds and will go into a special government account to be dispensed according to the GX Plan and company uptake. For example, steel companies, which will need ¥3 trillion to meet their target of a 30 per cent CO_2 reduction and production of 10 million tons of 'green steel' by 2030, will be able to access the fund for up-front investments which they could not otherwise afford. The automobile sector is expected to invest ten times this amount, or ¥34 trillion. Almost all sectors of the economy have had a GX roadmap drawn up, from pulp and paper, cement and housing to aviation, shipping, and power networks. Companies which have signed up to the GX League, accounting for over 40 per cent of CO_2 emissions in March 2023, will have preferential access to these funds and other government support. Money raised from new carbon charges for fossil fuel importers (2028) and an auction system for power generators (2033) will be paid into the special government account to repay the transition bonds by 2050.

Finally, in 2023 an Asia Zero Emission Community (AZEC) was inaugurated to promote (Japan's approach to) decarbonization and cooperation in Asia. The three principles agreed on were: advancing cooperation towards carbon neutrality/net-zero emissions while ensuring energy security, promoting energy transition while achieving economic growth; and 'recognizing there are various and practical pathways toward carbon neutrality/net-zero emissions depending on the circumstances of each country'.[38]

The Sunshine and Moonshine Projects had lasting legacies but did not fundamentally transform Japan. Will the GGS and GX Plan be any different? Most probably. Japan now has firm international commitments to honour in the face of the global climate crisis, with many eyes monitoring those commitments, equipped with comparative statistics and rankings. The whole-of-government approach indicated by the signatories to the GGS suggests a new willingness to overcome sectionalism, while the whole-of-economy coverage of the GX Plan provides a new rationale for industrial policy, mission-oriented innovation policy (MOIP), and public–private collaboration. As a former vice minister put it to this author, 'You can argue about dividing a pie, but when there is no pie left to argue over, you need to make it together.'

---

[38] https://www.meti.go.jp/english/press/2023/0306_002.html (accessed 30 April 2023). Other Japanese initiatives relating to climate and energy cooperation are the Asia Energy Transition Initiative (AETI), with a focus on 3E+S, and the Asian Green Growth Partnership Ministerial (AGGPM) public-private forum.

Concluding Comments

Of Japan's twin economic transformations—DX and GX—the latter was later off the mark, but has gained momentum. Japan's initial climate pledges have been raised, with flow-on effects on energy policy, and a Green Growth Strategy. This in turn has been incorporated into a broader and deeper GX Realization Basic Plan, under which a plethora of activities and investments can be located and coordinated. In fact, it may be through GX that the Japanese economy is really rebuilt. Compared to DX, which is like the sword hanging over Damocles—a looming 'cliff' confronting Japan with its 'last chance to reverse digital defeat'—the new energy sources and technologies of GX potentially play to Japan's traditional STI and *monozukuri* strengths, like process engineering, materials science, and chemistry.

GX requires intense public–private sector interaction and the building of new alliances and stakeholder networks. This will be a challenge, as it is not clear how bottom-up participation beyond industry interests will be enlisted. Ohta (2020: 1) criticizes closed policy circles of bureaucrats, industry interests, and experts, whose interaction produces nice platitudes but 'sticks to fixed energy policy institutionalized in the 1970s to promote nuclear energy and coal as oil alternatives. It rarely has interactions between the policymakers and the public and thus lacks a societal (normative) decision about a future energy path to energy transitions to mitigate climate change.' If 'agile governance' is needed for digital transformation and the realization of Society 5.0 (Chapter 2), according to Ohta 'anticipatory governance' is needed for GX, especially energy transition. Public participation is also a critical issue for smart cities, which we will consider in Chapter 4.

Perhaps there is a need to listen to voices of the past as well. The understanding of human society and economy rooted in nature rather than separate from and dominating it forms an undercurrent in Japan which bubbles up at times like 3.11. Hiroi (2019) notes that most of the old local shrines in the Tohoku region—some dating back 1000 years—remained intact after 3:11: 'Roughly speaking, it is very likely that people at that time built those shrines, leaving messages to future generations, like "Because of the risk of tsunami arriving up to this point, be sure to evacuate to this shrine in the event of a disaster", or "Be aware that the area from this point to the coastline is dangerous"' (p. 315). Japan's rush for growth in the twentieth century drowned out this message.

Returning to the present, and the Green Growth Strategy, what are the prospects that the private sector investments will actually be forthcoming? In FY2022–2023, after languishing for many years, corporate Japan's *planned* capital investment made its highest year-on-year jump since 1973, to its highest level since the global financial crisis, and second highest level ever according to a Nikkei survey.[39] Manufacturers planned a 28 per cent increase, and non-manufacturers a 21 per cent increase. Many of the major investment plans were related to electric vehicles, semiconductors, production equipment, and decarbonization. DBJ's annual survey showed similar results, with capital investment planned to rise by 27 per cent overall, and 31 per cent for manufacturers.[40] DBJ's analysis of the survey data, shown in Figure 3.4, implies a robust connection between government policy and company behaviour. From this, it would appear that the wheels of Japan's dual digital and green transformation have started to roll together. A focal point will be the automobile industry, in which DX and GX are converging to produce radical change. This has been Japan's leading industry, and the stakes are high, while the competition is fierce, as we shall see in Chapter 5.

---

[39] *Nikkei Asia*, 21 June 2022 ('Japan's Capital Spending Poised to Roar Back 25 percent').

[40] Nihon setsubi tōshi ginkō (DBJ), 2022. In fact, the actual increase for 2022–2023 was a more modest 11 per cent according to DBJ's 2023 survey. Plans for FY2023–2024 were for an increase of 21 per cent overall and 27 per cent for manufacturing: https://www.dbj.jp/pdf/investigate/equip/national/2023_summary.pdf (accessed 14 August 2023).

Figure 3.4 Planned capital spending by large companies, FY2022

	Carbon neutrality			Digitization		Enhanced resilience
	Renewable energy	Energy conservation	Materials recycling & hydrogen	Next generation cars	Remote/noncontact tech. & e-commerce	Highly-functional factories, cities, & stores
Petroleum	Biomass, wind power	*Reorganized for net zero*		*Reduced spending on refinery maintenance/replacement*		
Transport equipment		Replaced with energy-saving electric equipment		R&D sites for electrification	*Capacity investment in semiconductors and sc materials*	IOT-powered equipment
Iron & steel		Efficient blast & electric furnaces	Electric furnace capacity enhancement	Magnetic Steel sheets / Batteries	Silicon wafers	*Investment for manufacturing process automation*
Chemicals		Power semiconductors	Recycling plants	*EV-related capacity enhancement*	Electronic materials	
Electric machinery					Electronic parts	Introduction of automated equipment
General machinery	*Widespread investment, including small-scale projects*		Demonstration of hydrogen power generation	Production of robots for automation of factories and logistics		
Telecom & Inform.n						5G
Electric power & gas	Biomass, wind power		Hydrogen production		*Resumed or continued investment in urban function enhancement*	Investment in safety measures: power plants, railways
Transportation	Photovoltaic			Introduction of EVs	Labour saving at stores, including self-serve lanes	
Retail	Biomass				Logistics facilities	
Real estate	Photovoltaic, biomass	Zero energy buildings, houses				Redevelopment of Tokyo Metropolitan area
Services						Hotels

Source: Development Bank of Japan, 'Survey on Planned Capital Spending for Fiscal Year 2022', slides p. 13.

4

Eco Cities, Smart Cities, and Super Cities

Spatial Society 5.0

Smart cities are at the heart of the digital economy and will be crucial for the realization of a green economy. They are the site where many of the technological innovations, institutional reconfigurations, and transformation processes we have discussed converge, are contested, shaped, and implemented. Increasingly they are laboratories for digital experimentation. Eco cities and smart cities have proliferated globally, and not surprisingly Japan has embraced them as well, in distinctive ways. If Society 5.0 is to be realized, it will be in and through Japan's smart cities.

A smart city is one in which 'ICT is merged with traditional infrastructures, coordinated and integrated using new digital technologies' (Batty et al., 2012: 481), and is 'seeking to address public issues via ICT-based solutions on the basis of a multi-stakeholder, municipality based partnership' (Manville et al., 2014: 24). Japan was in fact an early pioneer with its briefly famous but now largely forgotten Technopolis cities of the 1980s and 1990s. The projects were ahead of their time in that the technologies and social relations of the twentieth century could not deliver on the vision, and the cities fell victim to the 'lost decades' slump and scaling back of public spending.

Japan's twenty-first century eco cities and smart cities have more humble beginnings, arising from emerging urban challenges, neoliberal reforms, decentralization, renewable energy projects, and more. A patchwork of projects straddling multiple government ministries started to attract more systematic policy attention in the late 2000s, coinciding with the gathering momentum of the smart city movement outside Japan. After 3:11 new imperatives of disaster preparedness and resilience were added. Better inter-ministerial coordination was called for. From the mid 2010s advances in information technology enlarged the scope of what was conceivable, feasible, and increasingly necessary, with e-government, mobility, logistics, built

Building a New Economy. D. Hugh Whittaker, Oxford University Press. © D. Hugh Whittaker (2024).
DOI: 10.1093/oso/9780198893394.003.0005

environment, health, education, and energy becoming integrated through municipal digital platforms.

Such platforms raise new questions about participation, design, governance, data control, and access. Are smart cities to be top-down, 'neo-cybernetic', efficiency-seeking entities, designed and implemented by IT giants, or bottom-up, participatory, and citizen-empowering? Or a combination (Pican, 2015)? This chapter addresses such questions, and the evolution of Japan's smart cities, their growing complexity and connectedness, and the goal of building a sustainable, human-centred, smart 'Society 5.0'.

The chapter has five sections. The first considers the boom in smart cities in general, which will situate Japan in a wider context. The second traces the evolution of policies in Japan which led to and promoted eco cities and smart cities, starting in the early 2000s, as well as consortia promoting them. The range of policies is large, and somewhat confusing, with numerous ministries involved, and frequent name and emphasis changes. Again, however, the OPMC has played an increasingly important coordinating role, with publication in 2021 of a detailed Guidebook, in English as well as Japanese.[1]

The diversity of actual smart city projects is substantial, however. The third section introduces four types: Higashi Matsushima, a city in northeast Japan which was devastated by 3:11; Kashiwa-no-ha, a land and urban development ('area management') project on the express train line between Tokyo and Tsukuba; Aizuwakamatsu, a more orthodox IT-focused smart city project in a historic castle town which has become a model of sorts; and Toyota's purpose-built demonstration Woven City project at the base of Mt Fuji. These cases are illustrative of the range of aims and backgrounds which motivate smart city projects in Japan.

The latest thinking about smart cities has been packaged into the 'super city' initiative, which is the subject of Section 4. Enabling legislation was passed in 2020, and two cities were initially chosen in 2022—Osaka and Tsukuba. More will follow. We will also touch on the 'digital garden city nation' vision, which seeks to ensure that 'no one is left behind' by digital transformation, including those in locations far from the metropolitan centres. Section 5 takes a brief look at MaaS (mobility as a service), which is associated with smart city infrastructure, and its evolution in a Japanese context.

---

[1] A substantial amount of information on Japan's smart cities is available in English. This is because a secondary objective is to export Japan's approach to smart cities, especially to Southeast Asia.

The Smart City Boom

Although its origin is disputed, the term 'smart cities' began to circulate widely in the mid 2000s. IT infrastructure was an important element, but 'smart' initially also referred to research, creativity, and human capital (Caragliu et al., 2009). As with DX and businesses, the application of IT to city environments is not simply about digitalizing individual processes and activities, but it brings about qualitative and interconnected changes: 'Cities are becoming smart not only in terms of the way we can automate routine functions serving individual persons, buildings, and traffic systems but in ways that enable us to monitor, understand, analyse and plan the city to improve the efficiency, equity and quality of life for its citizens in real time' (Batty et al., 2012: 482). The question of who is doing the planning is critical, as decisions are incorporated into algorithms which become embedded and invisible. Meaningful civil society participation is thus a critical issue.

Europe has been especially active in smart city scoping and promotion. According to the European Commission, smart city projects nowadays span and combine elements of:

- sustainable urban mobility
- sustainable districts and built environment
- integrated infrastructures and processes in energy, ICT and transport
- citizen focus
- policy and regulation
- integrated planning and management
- knowledge sharing
- baselines, performance indicators and metrics
- open data governance
- standards
- business models, procurement, and funding.[2]

Increasingly, these elements have been incorporated into software platforms, such as Firware, developed by the (EU) Future Internet Public Private Partnership, and Decidim, open source software originating in Barcelona. The need to structure data and interactions with the Internet of Things (IoT) has also motivated such platforms, which are infrastructures *regulating* access to and flow of data, while *enabling* startups, established businesses, organizations, and citizens to develop new ideas and businesses.

---

[2] European Commission. https://ec.europa.eu/info/eu-regional-and-urban-development/topics/cities-and-urban-development/city-initiatives/smart-cities_en (accessed 15 July 2021).

Smart cities have spread worldwide. There are regional and global networks of smart cities, as well as indexes and rankings. Smart cities are big business. They may be seen in the context of decentralization, often inspired by neolilberal thinking, which both developed and developing countries embarked on in the late twentieth century (Dillinger, 1994). They take on extra significance in developing countries, where they offer the allure not just of solving chronic problems associated with urbanization such as congestion and pollution, but of jumping directly into the digital age, or 'urbanization without industrialization' (Gollin et al., 2016).

'Compressed developer' China has embraced both smart city and eco city projects. Dongtan claims to be the first *purpose-built* 'eco city', designed by the UK-based consultancy Arup in 2005 under contract from the Shanghai Industrial Investment Corporation. Caofeidian and Tianjin Eco-City are other early examples. By 2017 there were almost 300 applications for eco-city designation in China, and almost the same number of smart cities.[3] Impressed by what he saw in China, and not to be outdone, India's future Prime Minister Narendra Modi proposed the construction of Dholera in Gujarat, and subsequently 100 smart cities nation-wide. Dholera's master plan, designed by UK-based Halcrow, envisages a staggering 900km^2 city—twice the size of present-day Mumbai, and larger than Singapore—to be built from scratch by 2040![4] And Ahmedabad-Dholera is itself just one of eight special investment regions and one of 16 'nodes' in the massive Delhi Mumbai Industrial Corridor project!

Not surprisingly, Japanese companies and consortia are involved in some of these smart city projects, where they compete and cooperate with US, European, and Chinese counterparts. Examples listed in a Cabinet Office (2022) publication promoting Japanese expertise abroad include Northern Hanoi (Vietnam), Delta Mas City (Indonesia), Amata Chonburi Smart City (Thailand), Clark City (the Philippines), and more.[5] Interviewed in 2013, the CEO of Delhi-Mumbai Industrial Corridor noted the involvement of Japanese consortia in four cities:

> A consortium led by Hitachi and including Itochu, Tokyo Electric Power Company and Kitakyushu City will study Dahej while a consortium led by Mitsubishi Heavy Industries will supervise Changodar. The Maneswar Bawal region of Haryana will

---

[3] http://www.citymetric.com/skylines/can-hundreds-new-ecocities-solve-chinas-environmental-problems-1306 (accessed 9 August 2017).

[4] Datta and Shaban (2017: 3) call such projects 'fast cities', characterized by 'rhetorics of urgency' in which '(s)peed continues to be a prerequisite to conceptualizing and legitimizing these cities as "solutions" to the crises of urbanization, migration and climate change'.

[5] The Japan Association for Smart Cities in ASEAN (JASCA, launched 2019) promotes such projects.

be looked after by a consortium led by Toshiba with Tokyo Gas as one of the three partners. The Shendra industrial region in Maharastra will be conceptualised by a consortium led by JGC Corp including Mitsubishi Corporation and Yokohama City as partners.[6]

Smart Cities and Smart City Policies in Japan

MITI's 'Vision for the 1980s' proposed a number of model Technopolis projects, which would create 'rural serenity in the city and urban activity in the country'. The rationale offered in government publications for these projects was twofold, observed Morris-Suzuki (1998): with IT it was now possible to separate research functions from headquarters without losing touch with metropolitan market trends; and working hours could be reduced with IT, opportunities for home-based work would expand, and local communities would become more central in peoples' lives. The vision reflected a number of 1980s themes, but the second of these resurfaced during the Covid-19 pandemic (Chapter 7).

Although 26 projects were approved, the Technopolis Act and its associated funding were discontinued in 1998 and have largely been forgotten. In contrast to Caofeidian and Dholera, and its own Technopolis projects, Japan's projects in the 2000s were more modest, but cumulatively began to build a base for a new generation of smart city projects in the 2010s. The downscaling may be attributable to the gulf between the still-buoyant 1980s, when Japan appeared on course to catch up with the US and dominate the emerging IT industries, and the early 2000s, after a recessionary decade in which the US re-asserted its IT dominance, and grand plans for remodelling Japan, including relocating capital city functions, were set aside.

Table 4.1 offers a timeline of eco city and smart city-type initiatives by various ministries from the early 2000s. Initially IT was not a central theme; more notable were the contexts of decentralization, de-regulation, revitalization, and energy saving. 'Smart' initially referred to grids rather than cities.

[6] https://www.business-standard.com/article/companies/hitachi-toshiba-mitsubishi-jgc-corp-led-consortiums-to-give-shape-to-four-smart-cities-in-dmic-110041700024_1.html (accessed 14 July 2021). Whether these specific consortia actually materialized is unclear. Nor is it clear whether the Japanese government's goal of obtaining orders worth ¥30 trillion by 2020 was met. Kitakyushu and Yokohama cities were part of METI's Next Generation Energy and Social Systems Demonstration programme, described below.

Table 4.1 Select central government compact, eco, and smart city initiatives, 2000–2022

	Cabinet Office (A)	Cabinet Office (B)	METI/NEDO	MLIT	MIC
—2007	Structural reform special zones (2003)		Regional power grid & RE demonstration project	Compact cities	
2008		Eco model cities		Low CO_2 footprint urban dev.t (with MOE)	
	Comprehensive special growth & welfare zones			Ecological urban dev.t project	
2010	Strategic economic zones	Future cities Regional revitalization law	Next gen. energy & social systems testbed (Smart Communities)	Future environmental cities Compact city plus network	Council for ICT-based urban dev.t
2015					
2017		SDGs future cities		Smart city models	Data-based smart cities
2020	Super cities				

Source: Various, including Deguchi, 2020: 63.
Note: METI = Ministry of Economy, Trade and Industry; NEDO = New Energy Development Organization; MLIT = Ministry of Land, Infrastructure, Transport and Tourism; MIC = Ministry of Internal Affairs and Communications; MOE = Ministry of the Environment. Excludes cluster programmes.

Decentralization and De-regulation

Decentralization from 1999 to 2006 gave local bodies more authority and responsibility to address emerging problems, and amalgamated cities and towns for fiscal savings. The 'trinity' reforms under Koizumi re-shaped fiscal transfers and tax-raising authority. Structural Reform Special Zones were set up under the Office for the Promotion of Regional Revitalization in the Cabinet Office as part of Koizumi's de-regulation drive. The zones acquired new names and emphases under successive governments—Comprehensive Special Growth and Welfare Zones under the DPJ (2009–2012), and Strategic

Economic Zones under the second Abe administration (2012–2020). The Super City programme belongs to this special—de-regulation—zone lineage (Cabinet Office A in Table 4.1).

The emerging problems just referred to included population outflow and population ageing, factory closures and deindustrialization, and the beginnings of 'shuttered' shopping arcades, which the growing presence of outskirts superstores, enabled by de-regulation, hastened. Contrarily, 'compact cities' gained attention for their potential to revitalize, to save on infrastructure maintenance and allay budget deficits, and to reduce carbon emissions. Toyama was an exemplar. With urban sprawl, it had a very low population density, and a high reliance on cars for transport. In 2003 it drew up a central district revitalization plan and a public transportation revitalization plan, assembled a strong change coalition, and built a light rail transit system, making use of existing railway infrastructure to reduce costs. This was extended to surrounding towns, six of which were merged with Toyama in 2007, creating a 'skewer and dumplings' configuration.[7] Toyama's selection as a Future Environmental City in 2011 funded biomass and small hydro-energy projects.

Energy, Environment, Resilience, and Disaster Prevention

Urban revitalization was linked to energy projects, some supported by NEDO under various names such as the Regional Power Grid with Renewable Energy Demonstration Project.[8] This funded renewable energy for the 2005 Osaka Expo, as well as a project in Hachinohe, in northern Honshu, in which the city, Mitsubishi Research Institute and Mitsubishi Electric built a regional power grid fed by solar, wind, biomass, and batteries, supplying energy to schools, the city office, and office buildings. Despite—and because of—rigidities in the highly regulated national grid system, the number of such projects grew.[9]

The Cabinet Office added a new programme to its special zones in 2008. Twenty 'eco-model cities' were designated to address environmental challenges, ageing, and related social issues, with a further ten cities selected in 2012 and 2013. A Future City Initiative (FCI) was started in 2011, and with

---

[7] Akimoto, 2019; Kriss et al., 2021.

[8] NEDO (New Industry and Industrial Technology Development Organization) was set up in 1980 in the wake of the oil shocks.

[9] Cf. 'The Resilience Programme: Changing Japan's Grid' in *Power Technology*, 19 February 2018 https://www.power-technology.com/features/resilience-programme-changing-japans-grid/ (accessed 19 July 2021).

the triple disaster, six of the 11 cities selected were in the devastated Tohoku region. Resilience and disaster prevention were incorporated into the rationale for Future City promotion, both domestically and abroad. Each year from 2011 the FCI Promotion Council has held an international forum, with themes covering reconstruction, revitalization, resilience, and integration of environment, society, and economy.[10] In 2015 and 2016 the forums were held outside Japan, in Malaysia, and the US. The latest iteration of this lineage is the SDGs Future City Initiative, for which roughly 30 (Japanese) cities have been selected each year since 2018.

Finally, METI began a Next Generation Energy and Social Systems demonstration programme in 2010, in which Yokohama and Kita Kyushu (active in India, as noted above) as well as Keihanna (Kansai Science City) and Toyota were selected from among 20 applicants. Each project was to have at its core a community energy management system (CEMS), integrating house and building energy management systems (HEMS, BEMS). These became known as 'smart community' projects, and a Japan Smart Community Alliance (JSCA) was assembled to foster collaboration between public and private sector participants. It too held annual international conferences from 2015 until 2019. As might be expected from METI, one project selection criterion is marketability overseas.[11]

Inter-ministerial Coordination, Networks and Citizen Participation

The initiatives listed in Table 4.1 are associated with specific ministries. As individual projects may span multiple jurisdictions, however, there is a need for inter-ministerial coordination. While early smart technology initiatives 'were largely led by central agencies of the national government, with limited horizontal collaboration', 'the current paradigm is marked by horizontal and vertical collaboration and co-creation, assessing and addressing community needs within a national regime of inclusive stakeholder collaboration' (Barrett et al., 2021: 84; cf. DeWit, 2019). A turning point, the authors suggest,

---

[10] Future Cities are supposed to create environmental value, social value and economic value, and integrate compact city, traffic system upgrading, residential concerns, renewable energy, and conservation and environmental education: FCI Promotion Council, 2016. http://doc.future-city.go.jp/pdf/pclcc/pamphlet2016_e_no01.pdf (accessed 19 July 2021).

[11] The programme has five objectives: infrastructure to handle large-scale roll-outs of renewable energy; IT-enhanced lifestyles, with energy saving; marketability overseas; standard-setting potential; and management and financing systems for future development: Deguchi, 2020.

was 3.11, which brought home the need for an integrated and collaborative approach.

Smart cities typically involve public private partnerships. The JSCA lists 32 participating organizations in the Yokohama smart community project, of which 28 are from the private sector, including project lead Toshiba.[12] The Toyota City Low-carbon Verification (Smart MeLit) project lists roughly the same number, led by Toyota, and featuring many of its group companies.

The Smart City Public Private Partnership Platform, launched in 2019, listed 453 companies, universities and research institutes, 187 local government bodies, 12 ministries and agencies, two business federations, and 256 observer organizations in July 2022.[13] It has a number of cross-cutting themes such as renewable energy and mobility, transport and health services, and working groups, including mobility and transport, tourism and revitalization, which promote interaction, and match-making. The Smart City Institute, also formed in 2019, is a private sector-led NPO with around 40 corporate members, dozens of local bodies and university institutes and seven supporting ministries, which promotes information gathering and exchange.[14]

There is additionally the expectation of citizen participation. A detailed Smart City Guidebook issued by the supporting ministries and Smart City PPP Platform in 2021 lists 'three basic philosophies'—being resident-(user-) centric; being vision- (challenge-) focused; and attaching importance to collaboration among sectors.[15] It stipulates the need for public participation, and cites Kakogawa City which introduced a 'citizen-participatory consensus-building platform [using Decidim, open source software originating in Barcelona] to solicit a wide range of opinions and ideas from citizens'. It further claims that initiatives to 'create a living laboratory, a place for social experiments in which businesses, government, citizens, and others co-create' are spreading nationwide. Space is allocated to citizen participation in the Guidebook's five stages of preparation and implementation.

---

[12] https://www.smart-japan.org/english/vcms_lf/Resources/JSCApamphlet_eng_web.pdf (accessed 24 July 2021). In July 2022 JSCA's website listed 231 members. Hitachi established a Smart City Business Management Division as a one-stop shop for participation in smart community/city projects as early as 2010.

[13] https://www.mlit.go.jp/scpf/about/index.html (accessed 29 July 2022). The website is hosted by MLIT, but on behalf of the Cabinet Office, MIC, METI, and the Digital Agency.

[14] https://www.sci-japan.or.jp/english/index.html (accessed 29 July 2022).

[15] https://www8.cao.go.jp/cstp/society5_0/smartcity/00_scguide_eng_ol.pdf (accessed 29 July 2022).

Data Free Flow with Trust

The 'people-centric' rhetoric is steadily acquiring the mystique of a distinctive Japanese approach to smart cities. In an OPMC web publication appropriately titled 'Japan's Smart Cities: Solving Global Issues Such as the SDGs, etc. Through Japan's Society 5.0' (2022) the originality of Japan's approach is stated as follows:

> The operating system of Japan's urban cities that embodies this concept [openness and transparency] is an information coordination platform. The platform collects and manages all kinds of urban data on the cities, thoroughly takes into account residents' perspectives, provides complex and personalized services, as well as having data interoperability and distribution capability that can also be extended to other cities…
>
> In this context, Japan's smart cities are oriented toward free, trustworthy and credible norms. Under the norms, major companies are not allowed to monopolize data handling, excessive regulations are not imposed on the usage of data and the state is not allowed to monitor data handling. This is the 'originality of Japan' that complies with the DFFT (Data Free Flow with Trust) presented at the G20 Osaka Summit.[16]

Data Free Flow with Trust has become an integral part of Japan's strategic diplomacy; here it is mobilized as a core smart city principle as well, both within Japan, and in Japan's international infrastructure projects.

Smart City Cases

Japan's smart city policies have evolved from pilot projects in special zones in a context of fiscal restraint and regional and urban regeneration, to programmatic promotion. Resilience was added to the initial focus on energy, environment and compactness, and IT has become central. As the need for sector-specific projects to become joined up has increased, platforms have been created (or licensed). As these raise important questions about the control and use of data, citizen participation needs to be addressed. This fits well with the 'people centric' language of Society 5.0, as well as Japan's strategic diplomacy.

---

[16] https://www.kantei.go.jp/jp/singi/keikyou/pdf/Japan%27s_Smart_Cities-1(Main_Report).pdf (accessed 29 July 2022).

In reality, there are several types of smart city in Japan, with their own developmental trajectories, and different forms of citizen participation. In this section we will look at four specific cases to get a better sense of this diversity, of 'top down' and 'bottom up' dynamics, and how policy meets reality. The cases represent four different types—post-disaster reconstruction; land and urban development ('area management'); IT-focused; and a futuristic demonstration city—which can also be seen as a spectrum in terms of techno-centrism.

Higashi Matsushima

Adjacent to the beautiful Matsushima Bay and islands made famous by poet Matsuo Basho, Higashi Matsushima was formed by the merger of two smaller cities in 2005. In 2011 two-thirds of the city was destroyed and 1110 residents were killed (with 23 missing) by the massive earthquake and tsunami which devastated the Tohoku region. The citizens came together in eight self-governing bodies for mutual assistance, and to agree a plan for collective relocation, and reconstruction.[17] They agreed on four basic development policies: a city made resilient through disaster prevention; a city where people can live without anxiety while supporting each other; a city with restored businesses and jobs; and an economically sustainable city.

Central government financial support began to arrive—belatedly—in December, and a decision was made to create a local micro energy grid. One shared trauma was the loss of power for several days in the local hospital at the very time it was most needed; this the survivors vowed, should never happen again. An NPO called HOPE (Higashi Matsushima Organization for Progress on Economy, Education and Energy) was set up by organizations and companies committed to reconstruction, including Sekisui House and Panasonic, which built a solar-powered community energy management system (CEMS) able to function for three days if national grid power is cut, and otherwise to supply up to a third of the homes. Almost all the debris and rubble was cleared and recycled, agriculture and fisheries were restarted, and new schools were built, including an elementary school designed by the environmentalist C. W. Nicol, with a 'reconstruction forest' behind it.

Drawing on its reconstruction experience, the next phase of economic rehabilitation was to develop 'sustainable and responsible tourism',

---

[17] Presentation materials and interviews, Matsushima City, 27 April 2021. Eighty per cent of 2000 participating residents agreed with the collective relocation plan, which involved moving to seven centres away from the coast.

interpreted broadly to include education, reconstruction, and environment. Higashi Matsushima and public–private destination management organization (DMO) Inoutbound were selected as one of 15 model districts under the Japan Sustainable Tourism Standard for Destinations (JSTS-D) in 2021. The DMO is working towards a Green Destination Standards (GDS) award while collaborating with its counterparts in Kesennuma (one of Japan's first Cittaslow cities) and Kamaishi (Japan's first GDS Bronze awardee). It has hosted exchanges with Indonesia's Banda Aceh. The contrast with neighbouring Matsushima City's traditional big-bus, volume tourism is sharp.[18] Succeeding its Future City designation in 2011, Higashi Matsushima became a SDGs Future City in 2018.

Kashiwa-no-ha

Kashiwa-no-ha is a 273ha development led by Mitsui Fudōsan. It was once a golf course, but when the golf course was dissected by the Tsukuba Express railway line, the real estate company decided to redevelop it, building on local resources which included branch campuses of Chiba and Tokyo Universities, the National Cancer Research Centre East Hospital, and parkland. It began with a microgrid built by Hitachi in 2002 and developed into an area energy management system (AEMS) in 2006, the same year that a shopping facility adjacent to the new station was opened. Apartment buildings were built next, and proved very popular because the price of land was much cheaper than in Tokyo, despite the relatively short commuting distance.[19]

Kashiwa-no-ha's 2008 development plan had three themes: environment, health, and new industry creation, coinciding with the Future City initiative, for which it was also selected in 2011. A health centre was built in the shopping complex, called A-shi-ta (meaning 'tomorrow' but also short for walking, talking, and eating). With 3000 members by 2021, it had established a wellness data platform. As owners, residents could opt into allowing their data to be used for research, for example at the adjacent National Cancer Research Centre.

For new industry, the Kashiwa-no-ha Open Innovation Laboratory (KOIL, opened 2014), has substantial co-working space and an incubator, as well as advice and mentoring from a business angel network. An Asia Entrepreneurship Award competition had 30 applicants from 13 countries in 2020, with only two from Japan. One attraction for overseas entrepreneurs is

---

[18] Interviews with DMO Inoutbound staff, 27–28 April 2021 and 6 January 2022.
[19] Presentation materials and interviews, Urban Design Centre Kashiwa-no-ha (UDCK), 19 April 2021.

the opportunity to test ideas locally, especially in the life sciences and Internet of Things.

After initially using Firware, the public–private–university coordinating body Urban Design Centre Kashiwa-no-ha (UDCK) now uses a platform developed by Mitsui Fudōsan and Nihon Unisys, which will be used in other locations such as Nihonbashi in central Tokyo. As it enters its next phase of development as one of MLIT's Smart City Leading Model projects, Kashiwa-no-ha plans to develop this platform for energy, wellness, public space, and mobility data. Mobility plans include an autonomous shuttle bus service, and a subscription-based MaaS system encompassing buses, taxis, car share, and bicycles.[20]

Kashiwa-no-ha is marketed as a smart, compact, and evolving city. Through consultation and co-management it appears to have secured the support of residents for expansion of its data platform. And its down to earth projects include parks, living spaces, and food stalls and bars under the elevated railway lines.

Aizuwakamatsu

Aizuwakamatsu is a castle town in Fukushima prefecture famous for sake, lacquerware, the early-nineteenth-century Nisshinkan domain academy, and the last battle the Boshin War (1868–1869), which destroyed the academy. It was also one of the centres of the 1880s Freedom and Popular Rights movement, which may have something to do with why its smart city has become known for citizens' participation and 'open by default'.

In the 2000s the city was faced with similar problems to other regional cities in Japan—deindustrialization, demographic ageing, and depopulation. Despite its celebrated local university specializing in computing and IT, there were few jobs for local graduates. Then came 3.11, and in its wake, much concern about saving energy and producing energy locally. Aizuwakamatsu built a biomass (woodchip) energy plant, and an app. for smartphones so that people could keep track of their own energy use. The home energy management system (HEMS) was subsequently commercialized.

One of the core participants is Accenture, which set up a facility in 2011 both to contribute to regional regeneration and Tohoku reconstruction, and to work on digital and smart city projects. It formed a partnership with the City and Aizu University. Said a city official: 'We got government funding

---

[20] Mitsui Fudōsan became an investor and strategic partner of MaaS Global in 2019.

to make a data base. The first challenge was to make visible the data we actually use, and the second was to train people who could do the analysis. Accenture made a donation to the university, and we at the City invited the students, who could work on projects for their study using actual data. So that was important, but what was more important was that residents became interested, and became willing to share their personal data, so that we could develop personalized services.'[21] Other technology companies were attracted to the city, especially after the opening of the Smart City AiCT (Aizuwakamatsu ICT) innovation complex in 2019. By 2021 31 companies had moved there, 23 of them from outside the city, and had begun to provide jobs for Aizu's graduates.[22]

Trencher (2019) gives several examples of the city's platform-based services. In one, residents' addresses were combined with Geospatial Information System (GIS) coordinates and visualization software. This enabled bus operators, residents, and community groups to redesign bus routes prioritizing areas with a high proportion of elderly and school children, stopping the vicious cycle of dwindling users, route closures and fare increases. In another, in an outlying town with a high proportion of elderly residents a digital living support package was developed in which household televisions were converted to smart TVs with a purpose-built on-screen menu, enabling the residents to access on-demand wind-power supplied EV transport, local information and health condition monitoring. The residents can monitor the EV van's position to minimize outdoor waiting times in inclement weather.

Innovation here is as much about governance innovation as technology innovation, in which 'the citizen is framed as a central agent in the smart city transition. This interpretation of the smart city pushes an agenda of bottom-up and people-driven innovation in response to local social and business challenges' with the aim of creating a city 'which can solve its own problems' (Trencher, 2019: 125). Aizuwakamatsu's smart city platform has been adopted by a number of other cities in Japan.

Woven City

At the 2020 Consumer Electronics Show in Las Vegas, Toyota's president Toyoda Akio announced a new undertaking—Woven City, which was to be built on a 70ha site at the base of Mt Fuji, until then occupied by Toyota Motor

---

[21] Interview, 16 November 2021.
[22] https://www.city.aizuwakamatsu.fukushima.jp/docs/2020102000010/files/supercity_teiansyo.pdf (accessed 23 July 2021).

East Japan.[23] The ground-breaking ceremony held a year later also broke new ground for Toyota in several ways. It was a step in Toyota's transition from an auto manufacturer to a mobility company, and towards what Woven Planet Holdings CEO James Kuffner calls a 'software first' company, whilst maintaining Toyota's manufacturing principles of *genchi genbutsu* ('go and see for yourself') and *kaizen* continuous improvement.

It turns defence into attack. The automobile industry is undergoing momentous simultaneous upheavals, summarized as CASE (connected, autonomous, shared/subscription, and electric: Chapter 4). Being connected means cars becoming a part of bigger networks, including MaaS (mobility as a service), and who constructs the networks and controls the data of those networks matters a great deal for profits and even survival. Creating a new city gives Toyota and its partners the opportunity to build and test such networks, or platforms.[24]

At the ground-breaking ceremony, Toyoda pointed to three distinctive features of Woven City: it would be 'human-centred' (of course); a living laboratory; and ever-evolving. In other words, it aspires to be a 'programmable city'. This involves making a 'digital twin', in which data from real life experience can be captured by sensors, and the data fed to the cyber 'twin'—in real time ideally—for modification if necessary. With the help of AI, the cyber twin can run simulations in a fraction of the time taken in the real twin, thus speeding responsiveness. Load-carrying robotic home helpers might be welcomed by some residents but not others; the data can lead to modifications in design, or even their removal. Thus many of the features of the Woven City were not pre-determined, although there was an initial design.

It is envisaged that there will be 360 residents from 2024, a mix of elderly, young families, and others, with the number rising to over 2000. Initial work at Woven Planet's Tokyo headquarters focused on designing an underground logistics system, in which goods will be delivered autonomously to residents, and waste taken away. Above ground there will be no private cars(!); people will be transported by autonomous vehicles, or they can travel by personal mobility scooters or bicycles, or walk along pedestrian paths in green zones. The energy sources will be solar—with panels on all the 'smart homes' and other buildings—geothermal and hydrogen fuel cells, aiming for carbon

---

[23] This account draws on Toyota Times promotion video 'Woven City Project Kicks into Full Gear', https://www.woven-city.global/jpn (accessed 22 July 2021), and K. Warren, 'Toyota just started building a 175-acre smart city at the base of Mount Fuji in Japan', *Business Insider*, 24 February 2021, https://www.businessinsider.com/toyota-city-of-the-future-japan-mt-fuji-2020-1?r=US&IR=T (accessed 22 July 2021).

[24] Core partners as of mid 2021 included designer BIG (Bjarke Ingels Group), telecoms company NTT and energy company Eneos, but a call for collaborators was said to have attracted over 3000 responses.

neutrality. Woven City is intended as a laboratory for creating technology and platforms that can be used for other cities.

From Smart Cities to Super Cities

Smart cities are diverse and evolving. In 2020 the Cabinet Office announced a new initiative, which drew a distinction between smart cities and its new 'super cities'. The main differences were that super cities:

- Use AI and big data to 'fundamentally change current social systems';
- Address more areas—at least five of: transportation, logistics, payment, administration, medical and nursing care, education, energy and water, environment and waste, crime prevention, and disaster control and safety;
- Which are connected through a common data linkage platform that sits between the above areas and data providers, linked on both sides through open APIs;
- And—reflecting their special zone background—require 'drastic regulatory reform' to achieve by 2030, which the cities can request from the government.[25]

The call for proposals required evidence of strong public–private–civil society commitment, with a 'perspective from the eye-level of citizens'. Some illustrative examples of the issues proposals should address were provided. In one, the mobility of elderly people is threatened by declining taxi numbers. The proposed solution is a system of volunteer taxis whose drivers are paid in a local digital currency which can be redeemed for municipal services. The online booking, payment, and transport system is linked to telemedicine to optimize the use of medical facilities and expertise. This would require regulatory and administrative reform. In another example a city's tourist venues compete for customers instead of cooperating, and the industry itself is overshadowed by the manufacturing sector. The proposed solution is an autonomous bus loop which takes in the main sightseeing spots *and* gives

---

[25] Chihō sōsei suishin jimukyoku (Office for the Promotion of Regional Revitalization Office) (2021), 'Sūpā shitei kōsō ni tsuite' (About the Super City Concept), https://www.chisou.go.jp/tiiki/kokusentoc/supercity/supercity.pdf and OPMC (2022), 'Japan's Smart Cities: Solving Global Issues such as the SDGs, etc. through Japan's Society 5.0', https://www.kantei.go.jp/jp/singi/keikyou/pdf/Japan%27s_Smart_Cities-1(Main_Report).pdf (both accessed 31 July 2022). API is the acronym for application programming interface: see Chapter 5.

visitors a chance to experience manufacturing. The autonomous bus would be part of a cashless MaaS system.

Thirty-one applications were received, including one from Aizuwaka-matsu addressing most of the ten areas listed above, and reminding the selection panel its platform had been adopted by five other cities, with a further 12 preparing to adopt it.[26] Nonetheless, much still needed to be done. From the citizens' perspective many of the services offered by the city were for 'average' or standardized categories of family, age group, marital status, employment type.... Through opt-in digitalization two-way communication would be enhanced and personalized services developed, supporting a more diversified society. As this further developed and trust was enhanced, a *digital mutual support society* which links people together would be created.

Just two cities were selected in the first round, namely Osaka, which is planning to introduce flying taxis and an autonomous bus in and around the venue of the 2025 Osaka Kansai Expo, and Tsukuba, which will upgrade its Science City resources, digitalize administration, introduce internet voting, create a MaaS system and … introduce luggage-carrying robots and drones.

No-one Left Behind: Digital Garden City Nation

Some cities have greater resources—including entrepreneurial leadership—than others to undertake DX and GX. This certainly applies to Osaka and Tsukuba. The reality for many of Japan's regional cities is less rosey, and DX threatens to exacerbate differences in wealth and living standards rather than reduce them. This concern prompted Kishida to propose his 'Vision for a Digital Garden City Nation'. Infrastructure improvement is a core initiative, starting with a digital superhighway using submarine cables (to be built in roughly three years), a dozen or more regional data centres (five years), and 99.9 per cent coverage by optical fibre (by 2030). Plus 90 per cent 5G coverage by March 2024!

Another focus is human resources with digital skills, which we will look at in Chapter 7. And third, digital services for rural areas will be developed, including smart agriculture, mobility services, logistics, and ICT education, as well as teleworking and export promotion. Most immediately, however, 10,000 'digitalization supporters' were to be mobilized.[27] Just as Kishida's

---

[26] https://www.city.aizuwakamatsu.fukushima.jp/docs/2020102000010/files/supercity_teiansyo.pdf (accessed 23 July 2021).
[27] *Kizuna*, 25 January 2022 ('Vision for a Digital Garden City Nation: Achieving Rural-Urban Digital Integration and Transformation').

'new capitalism' was inspired by elements of the postwar model, including income doubling, so too the digital garden city vision appears to recreate elements of the urban–rural income equalization measures of the high growth period, this time through digital means. However, the above targets are likely to be aspirational rather than realistic, and despite the tailwind provided by the Covid-19 pandemic which produced some outward migration from metropolitan centres, it will be very difficult to achieve them in a context of population decline and ageing, rather than population growth.

A Note on MaaS

A crucial component of any smart city is its transport system. Somewhat surprisingly, only recently has Mobility as a Service (MaaS) featured as such in most smart city projects in Japan. This may have something to do with conceptual and bureaucratic demarcations—a blind spot in joined up thinking—or ironically, Japan's strength in the automobile industry. Finland is widely acknowledged to be a front-runner in MaaS. There both transport and communications were placed in the Ministry of Transport and Communications, lowering obstacles to developing systems which connect the two.[28] Finland also has Nokia, but no car makers. When service providers opened their API codes the Finnish startup MaaS Global launched the Whim app. in 2015. MaaS Global's vision was to allow people to 'move anywhere, at anytime and by any mode of transport without needing to own a vehicle'.[29] Toyota Financial Services and Denso became early investors (as did Mitsui Fudōsan, noted above); MaaS is closely connected with the CASE revolution, so it matters a lot both for Japan's smart cities, and its leading industry automobiles.

Like autonomous driving, MaaS is sometimes depicted in terms of levels, such as:

0 No integration—single, separate services
1 Integration of information—multimodel travel planner, price information
2 Integration of booking and payment—find, book, and pay a single trip
3 Integration of service offer—bundling/subscription, contracts, etc.
4 Integration of societal goals—policies, incentives, etc.

---

[28] Kusuda and Moriguchi, 2020. This section draws extensively on this source.
[29] https://whimapp.com/helsinki/en/finnish-company-maas-global-completes-funding-round-raising-e14-2-million/ (accessed 7 September 2021).

In contrast to many European countries, in which authorities responded to rising congestion and pollution in the 1960s with a revival of public transport, bringing them under unitary authorities and/or issuing unitary passes, in Japan there are typically multiple service providers. Private car ownership *increased* in the late twentieth century. In this decentralized and multiple service provider context, a large number of MaaS-like systems have sprouted, mostly at Level 1 or sometimes Level 2 in the above classification. Companies like Odakyu and Tokyu, which run trains and buses, as well as JR East, and taxi groups, not to mention Toyota, Hitachi, mobile portal companies like DeNa, car share companies, and others are extending or entering into new alliances, out of which multiple configurations are emerging.

Promotional materials almost invariably draw attention to challenges of social participation faced by groups such as the elderly in rural areas, where pressure on public finances has led to bus route closures. On demand, online systems (as in Aizuwakamatsu above) will enable the elderly to visit their doctor. The Universal MaaS consortium, led by ANA, Keikyu Railway, Yokosuka City, Yokohama National University, and others, features in its promotional material a young lady in a wheelchair whose journey requires multiple modes of transport; her app. enables this, and it alerts the train station and bus operators as to when she will be arriving, so they can provide support.[30]

To approach MaaS more strategically and promote interoperability, METI set up a 'New Mobility Service through IoT and AI' research group in 2018, which encompassed autonomous vehicles. MLIT convened New Mobility Services for Cities and Regions, which proposed five types of MaaS—for metropolitan areas; metropolitan suburbs; regional cities; regional city outskirts and outlying areas; and tourist destinations, each with its own design requirements. Together the two ministries launched a Smart Mobility Challenge in which 28 pilot cities were chosen—9 by METI, 15 by MLIT and 4 by both.[31] Lessons from the pilots are to be diffused to other cities. As well, an organization called JCoMaaS brings together private and public sector parties, including universities. MLIT has estimated that the MaaS market in Japan will grow from less than ¥100 billion in 2018 to ¥6.3 trillion in 2030.[32] Intersecting DX, GX, and smart cities, this will undoubtedly be a fertile area in the 2020s for startups and alliances, but it will also pose many technical and organizational challenges.

[30] https://www.youtube.com/watch?v=xOF7l2c1Zv4 (accessed 7 September 2021).
[31] https://www.meti.go.jp/english/press/2019/0618_005.html (accessed 7 September 2021).
[32] *Forbes*, 30 November 2020 ('Japan Is Innovating Mobility as a Service and Creating a $61 billion Market').

Concluding Comments

Smart cities have become a global phenomenon in a remarkably short period of time. They are at the heart of the digital economy, enabling new services, experimentation, and even the allure—or threat, depending on one's viewpoint—of a 'programmable city'. They are also closely linked with green objectives such as relieving congestion and pollution, and improving resource efficiency. But they are also controversial, raising questions about who the cities are smart for, who gets to design the information architecture, and who gets to use what data.

In contrast to the grand Technopolis vision of the 1980s and early 1990s, Japan's current generation of smart city projects is the result of cumulative smaller scale projects, often focused on energy and compacting in the 2000s, as well as resilience, and only in the last few years on IT infrastructure and large-scale digital transformation. Table 4.1 depicted policies implemented by multiple ministries with different objectives, which only recently have become systematically coordinated. Yet as the number of participants in smart city consortia—especially the Smart City PPP Platform—show, there is now a substantial ecosystem oriented towards design and implementation, which will only grow with the Super City projects. This ecosystem forms the basis for Japan's participation in smart city projects overseas.

Citizen participation and data control protocols have also evolved. The concept of 'Data Free Flow with Trust' has been transplanted from strategic diplomacy to smart city principles. Smart cities are supposed to reflect the aspirations and needs of their citizens. But there are two possibilities here. One is for genuine 'bottom up' participation right from early design stages through to ongoing management and monitoring. The other is for a more tokenistic form of participation.

There is a sense that the 'issues' selected and taken up reflect broad national discourse more than genuine bottom-up localized realities. Realities which lie outside that national discourse may be passed over. Overwhelming emphasis in promotional materials is placed on access to services by the elderly by autonomous vehicles or telemedicine. And while the importance of diversity is acknowledged, the majority of people encountered in designing smart city projects are male. Women are typically introduced as users of the services, in need of help. Despite such criticisms, what these Japanese cases have shown is a path towards a digital—and green—socio-economy which navigates, by design, between market domination on the one hand, and central state control on the other.

Chapters 2 and 3 were concerned with policy at the macro level. This chapter considered cities, at a meso level. The following two chapters turn to industries, companies, and entrepreneurs, managers, and investors, focusing first on innovation and DX, and then on investor relations and the incorporation of ESG into corporate governance.

5

Innovation and the Shifting Sands of Industry

There was a time when 'industry maps' of Japan were quite predictable. Placed prominently on bookshop counters annually, the books told of discrete industries dominated by a 'big three' or four majors, and of their key suppliers, all Japanese companies. Other maps would depict major shareholders and capital links between *keiretsu* companies, again quite predictable, reflecting the postwar economy. Fast forward to the 2020s, and the industry maps are hardly recognizable. Tōyō Keizai's *Kaisha shikihō gyōkai chizu 2021* lists as 'industries to watch' 5G, Cashless, Venture/VC, Telework, MaaS, Skillshare, AI, Quantum computing... Turning to older industries, the reader is confronted with complicated maps of capital alliances spanning the globe, new names, and companies which straddle many headings. The publishers bravely try to make sense of these shifting sands, and how the economy is changing.

In Chapters 2 and 3 we looked at how the government is trying to shape the new digital and green economy, while in Chapter 4 we looked at how this is playing out in smart cities. Government policies and incentives matter, but the companies and entrepreneurs, managers and investors who make investment decisions and create the goods and services are the on-site builders. In this chapter we turn to industries, companies, and entrepreneurs which are at the forefront of change, and to the organization–technology dyad. We focus on digital technologies, starting with electronics and IT, the sector that spearheaded the digital revolution. Japan once challenged the US in this sector, but in the past quarter century faded, caught in between Silicon Valley and emerging Asia. Japanese electronics and IT companies have experienced divergent fates; some have disappeared, but others have re-invented themselves, combining elements of the postwar firm-level productionist model with digital technologies. Within this diverse sector we will look at how one giant general electric group—Hitachi—has re-invented itself, and in doing so has become a driving force for Society 5.0, with a distinctively Japanese approach to platforms. We will also look at the rise of specialist manufacturers

Building a New Economy. D. Hugh Whittaker, Oxford University Press. © D. Hugh Whittaker (2024).
DOI: 10.1093/oso/9780198893394.003.0006

through participation in global value chains (GVCs), and briefly at Japan's approach to 5G.

The second and increasingly central pillar of Japan's economy has been the automobile industry. As electronics stumbled, automobiles went from strength to strength, sustaining the economy in difficult times. In the past decade, however, the changes which swept electronics and IT in the 1990s and 2000s have begun to engulf the automobile industry, even more powerfully, as encumbants have become locked in an existential battle with IT companies and new startups. The battle has several fronts, expressed as CASE (connected, autonomous, shared/subscription, and electric), and the outcome will have a profound impact on Japan's economy, and prospects for Society 5.0. Japan's heavyweight champion in this battle is Toyota, which like Hitachi is betting on the continued importance of manufacturing in cyber-physical systems but has so far been slow to embrace electric vehicles (EVs).

Third, finance is an industry and economic enabler. Japanese banks fuelled the country's postwar high growth, and in the late 1980s appeared ready to sweep the world. But they fell heavily in the 1990s and were forced into restructuring. Caught between the past and the future, METI's 'digital cliff' report could have been written about them. Yet digital finance and fintech startups are now gaining a foothold in Japan, forcing megabanks to become more agile. The latter are now taking a more active role in GX, at home and abroad.

Fourth, the flame of entrepreneurship once burned brightly in Japan, in established firms, and in startups. Over time established firms became stewards of past success, while startup rates declined, just as they were rising in other high-income countries in the 1980s and 1990s. *High growth* startups fuelled by venture capital, moreover, became emblematic of the Silicon Valley model; Japan's startups were fewer, smaller, and grew more slowly. In the 2010s, however, a distinctive IT startup ecosystem was established in Tokyo, with its own institutional practices and norms, complementing the mainstream corporate culture. The fourth section assesses this scene, as well as the established SME sector. Small firms are typically lumped together and criticized for being impervious to DX, but the sector is very diverse.

Other sectors might fruitfully be considered, such as the care sector, which plays an increasingly important role in an ageing society (Wright, 2023). While not exhaustive, the above four sectors give an overview of the types and sources of innovation which may bring Japan nearer to Society 5.0. Together they reinforce the observation that DX in Japan is about cyber-*physical* systems, an insistence—which some will interpret as path dependence—that the strengths of the postwar productionist model are still necessary. Relatedly, there is an expectation that finance will play an *enabling* role, and that financialization, especially the *financialization of IT*, should be kept in bounds. Startups are fêted not for heroic individualism and creative destruction, but for their contribution to DX, GX, and solving social issues. And for reinvigorating established firms rather than replacing them.

IT Platforms and Electronics

From the 1990s Japanese electronics and IT businesses came under intense pressure from two mutually reinforcing sources (Chapter 1). The first was the emergence of East Asian competitors who were very quick to master Japanese manufacturing techniques but had significantly lower labour costs. Surveys in the early 2000s showed Japanese companies losing ground to Asian competitors in a wide range of IT product categories, even in ones they had created, like LCD panels (Cole and Whittaker, 2006). Where Japanese quality was higher, it came at a cost, and hence lower profitability, as in DRAM memory chips. Lower profitability put semiconductor makers at a competitive disadvantage when it came to new rounds of capital investment.

The second source emanated from the US, namely the transformation of electronics and IT industries, from vertical integration to vertical specialization, in a series of inter-related technological, design, and managerial developments. Mainframes gave way to desktop and laptop computers, modular product architecture opened the door for new entrants and production was broken up into value chains, leading to outsourcing and offshoring. Ironically competitive pressure from Japanese manufacturers played a part in setting the ball rolling, as did pressure from shareholders. Japanese companies were cautious about going down the same route because, as Fujimoto (2004) noted, they perceived their competitive strength to be in 'integral (product) architecture' which enhances product functions, as well as 'integrated manufacturing'.

The challenges intensified in the 2000s, with the emergence of platforms as an organization form. Platforms build on vertical specialization and horizontal integration but are organized around a few key technologies which integrate the supply and delivery of products and services, potentially on a global scale. They are mainly software-based, and utilize new sources of data, cloud computing, big data analytics, and artificial intelligence (AI). The emergence of platforms posed a direct threat to Japanese manufacturing, as much of the profit generated in platform-mediated activities accrues to the platform owners, which are concentrated in Silicon Valley.

The Giants

Japan's giants especially struggled with these developments, including its general electric companies. Hitachi's profitability declined markedly in the 1990s. Its cash cow of the 1980s—semiconductors—became a loss-making albatross in the second half of the 1990s, and the company made its first-ever postwar loss in 1998, of $3 billion. The *Asahi shinbun* lamented: 'Japan's economic woes have now reached the major electric machine companies which support the nation's very economic foundations. The picture of this giant battleship, Hitachi, losing its way, unable to take effective measures before this massive loss materialized is the very picture of Japan today' (4 September 1998). The company and its group of 1200 companies embarked on wide-ranging reforms, covering divestments and acquisitions, consolidated group management, organization restructuring, corporate governance, and HRM.[1] The managers were tempted to try to emulate GE, which was riding very high under Jack Welch, but opted to plot their own course, with mixed success until the 2010s.

Hitachi began its evolution from a product-based company in a series of steps which laid the foundations for its own platform. Unveiled in 2016, 'Lumada' uses 'business domain knowledge, co-creation and digital technologies to resolve social and management issues'. The platform has a customer-facing level in which problems are defined, or 'co-created', a middle tier which makes available curated data from a data base of existing cases (over 1000 in April 2021, compiled since 2016), and a third tier, which is the actual product or service level. Products and services may come from the Hitachi group itself, or outside it in a network of collaborating 'partner' businesses. It is a cyber-physical system platform, combining operations technology with information technology (OT/IT, or 'OT x IT x product'), rather than an IT-only platform.[2]

Hitachi describes itself as a 'social infrastructure' or 'social innovation' group, and there is a strong resonance with the Society 5.0 vision.[3] It has organized its businesses around IT, energy, industry, mobility, and 'smart life', repositioning—and globalizing—through divestitures and acquisitions. Companies which were still considered important were nonetheless sold. Conversely, acquisitions included JR Automation (2017), ABB's power grid

---

[1] A detailed account of these reforms is given in Inagami and Whittaker, 2005.
[2] In 2020–2021, over 10 per cent of consolidated revenue (¥1.1 trillion) was attributed to Lumada. This segment on Hitachi draws on publicly available information, as well as interviews, 20 April 2021 and 1 June 2021, and 5 April and 1 May 2018.
[3] The former Chairman of Hitachi, and of Keidanren, Nakanishi Hiroaki, was in fact one of the driving forces of Society 5.0.

business (2020), and Thales' railway signalling and train control system division (2021). Significantly, Hitachi purchased the US firm GlobalLogic in 2021. With its 20,000 employees in 14 countries, including 10,000 software engineers, it boosted the group's IT capabilities outside Japan at a stroke, helping to internationalize the Lumada platform.

Much else has changed in Hitachi over the past two decades, including the Board of Directors. From having only token independent directors, all Japanese, by 2021 ten of the 13 directors were independent, and six were non-Japanese. Where there were no non-Japanese executive directors, now there were four. The HRM (human resource management) director described how his work content had changed dramatically: half of his reportees were now non-Japanese, and he spent most of his time working with colleagues in English, in different time zones. He now had smartphone access to a global HRM data base that covered all employees and enabled a shift to job-based HRM. It was, he commented, about visiblizing work, and people, for real-time management. The focus was on the types of employees needed for the Lumada business, through recruiting, internal training and job matching, and acquisitions.

Although Hitachi's managers don't necessarily talk about it in these terms, their technologies and businesses are intimately connected to Society 5.0. To give one example, building on the vehicle-to-home (V2H) and vehicle-to-everything (V2E) trend, the company is designing a system for EVs to be dispatched to localities following a natural disaster. The system selects the most appropriate vehicles and routes to provide battery power to evacuation centres and other facilities when power is down.[4] Hitachi plans to become carbon neutral by 2030, and throughout its supply chains by 2050, through visibilizing and optimizing energy use and emissions, which it links with its internal carbon pricing mechanism.[5]

From being lambasted as a battleship losing its way, Hitachi has managed to recreate itself as a global company, but with a distinctively Japanese approach to DX and GX, in which manufacturing still plays an important role, through cyber-physical systems. Its revival contrasts with fellow general electric business Toshiba, whose problematic purchase of Westinghouse, accounting scandals and corporate governance tensions have brought its very existence into question (Chapter 6). Panasonic is somewhere in between.[6]

---

[4] *Nikkei Asia*, 9 March 2023 ('Hitachi Offers EV Dispatch System to Blackout-Hit Areas').

[5] *Nikkei Asia*, 14 September 2021 ('Hitachi to Eliminate Greenhouse Gases from Supply Chain by 2050').

[6] Panasonic is not a general electric company. In 2022, after years of defensive restructuring—and its centenary in 2018—Panasonic became a holding company with eight main operating companies. Its own

In terms of market capitalization, however, the giants have been eclipsed by focused specialists, which we now turn to. These have ridden the wave of global value chains to become global suppliers.

The Specialists

The electronics and IT sector has become very complex. The mobile phone industry, for example, consists of handsets, network infrastructure and network operators, while the handsets integrate a host of technologies, products, and services, including an operating system, different types of semiconductors, display, camera, battery … in fact several hundred components which must be able to work together, be produced and assembled just-in-time, *and* be constantly upgraded. All of this is done at extremely high volumes—in other words, *complexity at scale and speed*. This cannot be achieved, Thun et al. (2021) argue, through market coordination alone (because of limits to complexity) or through relational coordination (because of limits to scale), but it is achieved through what they call 'massive modular ecosystems' (MMEs).

Japanese specialists have strong market positions in digital cameras, photocopiers, audio equipment, semiconductor materials and equipment, as well as electronic components. Some have grown remarkably quickly through their integration into GVCs and MMEs, such as sensor maker Keyence, miniature electric motor maker Nidec, and capacitor maker Murata Manufacturing.[7] This is reflected in their stock market capitalizations. In 2000 the top rankings were dominated by long-established manufacturing, finance, and electric power companies, with the exception of Murata Manufacturing, ranked 18. By 2020 a number of what were once middle-sized specialized manufacturers had climbed into the top 20, including Keyence, Nidec, Shin-Etsu Chemical, Murata Manufacturing, and Tokyo Electron, indicated in *italics* in Table 5.1.[8] Ranked 16 in 2000, by contrast, giant Hitachi fell to 25th in 2010, and 29th in 2020.

Semiconductor manufacturing is similarly complex, involving chip design and design tools, production equipment, complex materials, assembly, and

'PX' (Panasonic's DX) accelerated in 2021with the acquisition of US software, supply chain management and consulting company Blue Yonder. It also rebooted a stalled GX drive, and HRM is moving in a similar direction to Hitachi: Senior manager interview, 25 November 2021.

[7] All are headquartered outside the Tokyo Metropolitan region; Keyence in Osaka, Nidec and Murata Manufacturing in Kyoto. See Ibata-Arens, 2009, on the 'Kyoto model'.

[8] M3, a highly profitable medical portal founded in 2000, marks the entry of internet-based service businesses.

Table 5.1 Top 20 stocks by market capitalization 2000, 2010, 2020, TSE, 1st section

	2000	2010	2020
1	NTT DoCoMo	Toyota Motor	Toyota Motor
2	Toyota Motor	Mitsubishi UFJ	Softbank Group
3	Sony	NTT DoCoMo	*Keyence*
4	NTT	Honda Motor	Sony
5	Mizuho Holdings	Canon	Fast Retailing
6	Takeda	Sumitomo Mitsui FG	Chugai
7	Matsushita Electric	Mitsubishi Corporation	*Nintendo*
8	Seven-Eleven Japan	Nissan Motor Co.	*Nidec*
9	Bank of Tokyo-Mitsubishi	NTT	Daiichi Sankyo
10	Honda Motor	*Nintendo*	*Shin-Etsu Chemical*
11	Nomura Securities	Mizuho Financial Group	Recruit
12	Tokyo Electric Power	Tokyo Electric Power	KDDI
13	Sumitomo Bank	Takeda	NTT
14	Canon	Softbank	Daikin
15	NEC	*Fanuc*	M3, Inc.
16	Hitachi	Sony	*Murata Manufacturing*
17	Fujitsu	Panasonic	Oriental Land
18	*Murata Manufacturing*	Denso	Mitsubishi UFJ
19	Sakura Bank	Komatsu	Softbank Corp.
20	Oracle Corporation Japan	Mitsui & Co.	*Tokyo Electron*

Source: Tokyo Stock Exchange monthly statistics (databank-*geppō*), figures taken from December.

testing for a wide range of semiconductors, each with their own value chain and integration standards. Although the Japanese semiconductor industry is not what it once was, the country still produces 14 per cent of the global industry's value added (BCG and SIA, 2021: 31). It is particularly strong in back-end processes where companies like Disco, Ibiden, JSR, and Shinko Electric dominate global niches. Even less visibly, little-known Tokyo-based Valqua produces most of the world's super-clean steel containers necessary for storing and transporting chemicals used in chip manufacture.[9] And while Kodak went out of business following the switch to digital cameras, Fujifilm has become a major player in semiconductor photoresists and chemical-mechanical polishing slurries.

With the erosion of Japan's position in the industry, these specialists have set up factories outside Japan where new ecosystems have been formed (Kamakura, 2022). The US–China trade and technology war, Covid-19 and the war in Ukraine, however, have raised hopes for a Japanese renaissance. In 2021 Taiwan's TSMC agreed to build a research facility in Tsukuba, northeast

[9] *The Japan Times*, 20 March 2023 ('TSMC's Container Maker is the Jewel of Japan's Chip Industry').

of Tokyo, and then, with substantial subsidies from the Japanese government, a production plant for 20–28 nanometre (nm) chips next to Sony's image sensing plant in Kumamoto, once a hub of Japan's domestic semiconductor industry. Denso subsequently joined the venture.[10] US giant Micron Technology similarly agreed, with subsidies, to produce advanced memory chips in Hiroshima, while Japanese manufacturer Renesas is re-opening a shuttered factory to make power semiconductors for automobiles. Materials, parts, and equipment suppliers followed suit with new investments.

In 2022 a consortium of eight Japanese companies—Denso, Kioxia, MUFG Bank, NEC, NTT, SoftBank, Sony, and Toyota—created Rapidus (again with significant government subsidies), which has signed a licensing agreement with IBM to produce 2nm chips at the other end of Japan, in Chitose, Hokkaido in an attempt to re-establish Japan as a force in cutting edge semiconductor development and manufacturing. This in turn attracted investments from the US giant Advanced Materials, and Belgium's IMEC, while Samsung announced it would set up a semiconductor development facility in Yokohama, and Taiwan's PSMC chose Miyagi Prefecture.

This is seen as another 'last chance' scenario. METI, which is extending ¥2 trillion in support to the semiconductor industry in 2023–2025—a sizable portion of this to Rapidus—is hoping to triple Japan's semiconductor sales by 2030, but the rapid downturn in 2023 served as a reminder that this is a volatile industry and will not be easily returned to national containers.[11] And there is a question of where the human resources for these ventures will come from (Chapter 8). Be that as it may, whether the future lies in partial reshoring, or 'friendshoring' or something else, Japan's electronics specialists will continue play important roles in the global electronics industry, even if those roles are largely invisible to consumers.

'Beyond 5G'

Tensions between the globalizing forces which have produced MMEs, and decoupling and reshoring/friendshoring, converge with network infrastructure. To date base station hardware and software have been integrated, and dominated by Huawei, Ericsson, and Nokia, but a movement called open

---

[10] *Nikkei Asia*, 16 December 2021 ('Can TSMC Give New Spark to Japan's 'Silicon Island'?') TSMC is said to be planning to build a second plant in Kumamoto to produce 6nm chips: *Nikkei Asia*, 12 October 2023 ('TSMC Plans to Produce 6-nm Chips in 2nd Japan Plant').

[11] Batteries were also designated a strategically critical product in 2022, enabling Sony and GS Yuasa to receive a substantial subsidy for their joint lithium-ion battery factory venture in 2023, as well as Toyota for its joint ventures with Panasonic focusing on next-generation batteries.

RAN (radio access network) would open them to new participants through modularization and standardization. The multinational O-RAN alliance, formed in 2018, has been at the forefront of this effort. On the other hand, technology friction and security concerns have led to efforts to exclude Chinese vendors, and Huawei in particular. Network infrastructure is part of the US–Japan Competitiveness and Resilience (CoRe) Partnership, as well as the US–Japan-initiated Global Digital Connectivity Partnership (GDCP), both launched in 2021. Both trends offer new opportunities for Japanese telecoms companies and suppliers to recover some of the ground they have lost since the 1990s.

Japan's 5G roll-out began in March 2020, almost a year after the US, South Korea, and a number of European countries. Even with the ambitious base station expansion and investment plans announced by Japan's carriers DoCoMo, KDDI, Softbank, and Rakuten Mobile, it will in fact still take several years before the country is fully served by 5G. The question then arises: 5G for what? Like DX, 5G is not simply about making existing business faster and more efficient, but it will enable qualitatively new ways of doing business, and new businesses. 5G will form the infrastructure of the Internet of Things (IoT), AI, intelligent transport systems, autonomous driving, and more.

Yet 5G is still insufficient for the architects of Society 5.0, for whom real-time cyber-physical systems will require an even more advanced infrastructure. In 2020 the Ministry of Internal Affairs and Communication (MIC) brought together a 'Beyond 5G Promotion Strategy Roundtable' to prepare a 'roadmap towards 6G' in 2030, with the 2025 Osaka Expo a milestone along the way.[12] A corresponding Beyond 5G Promotion Consortium was set up, with a $500 million annual budget.[13] The word 'ultra' appears frequently in Beyond 5G deliberations—ultra fast (10x current 5G network access, 100x current core network access), ultra latency (1/10 of current 5G latency, hence ultra-reliable), ultra-numerous connectivity (10x more simultaneous connections than current 5G), ultra low power consumption, and ultra security and resiliency.

The project brings government, business, academia, and international collaborators (US and Finnish initially) together to create a core infrastructure of Society 5.0. The geopolitical winds which will shape how 5G and 'beyond 5G'

---

[12] The Roundtable was chaired by Tokyo University President Gonokami Makoto, one of the formulators of Society 5.0.

[13] https://b5g.jp/en/ and https://b5g.jp/en/randdpromotion.html Softbank, too, plans to spend ¥2.2 trillion over 10 years on 5G/6G https://www.softbank.jp/en/sbnews/entry/20210204_01 (all accessed 26 August 2021).

unfold may yet give Japan's IT and electronics industries new wind in their sails, but it will also require heavy investments in DX and GX, *and people*, to create a new ecosystem.

The Automobile CASE

As Japan stumbled in electronics and ICT, it went from strength to strength in automobiles. Toyota, and the Toyota production system came to symbolize Japanese manufacturing prowess. The year that Hitachi made its first loss, Toyota launched its hybrid Prius, and entered the echelon of top three global car makers, a position it has not relinquished. In fact for much of the 2010s it was the world's top car maker in terms of sales. As shown in table 4.1, it was also Japan's largest company by market capitalization.

Yet the winds of revolutionary change which swept the electronics and ICT industries are now blowing towards the automobile industry, with even more ferocity. The electronics share of value added contained in cars is rising year by year—from around 20 per cent in 2000, it is expected to reach 50 per cent by 2030 according to some estimates. This presents Japan's car makers with complex strategic dilemmas and raises the possibility of a similar fate to that which befell the electronics industry. (On the other hand, it presents an opportunity for Japanese electronics companies to expand their presence in a rapidly growing market.) The challenges are often summarized in the acronym CASE (or ACES), standing for Connected, Autonomous, Shared/Subscription, and Electric. Let us look at them in turn.

Connected

A car connected to the cloud generates a lot of data. This can be very useful to the driver, for example in locating the best route to a destination, or signalling that maintenance is due, connecting the driver to a nearby garage, and sending information back to the dealer or manufacturer to improve future designs. It can be useful to advertisers and service providers—restaurants along the route the car is travelling, for example. Ultimately, what is a connected car—still a car which happens to be connected, or an i-phone on wheels as Foxconn's Terry Gou is fond of saying?[14] Connected cars are a new frontier for IT companies, typically through alliances. But who should control what data? For car makers controlling the central 'gateway' which integrates the different electronic systems of the car is crucial for safety. Car

---

[14] *Nikkei Asia*, 20 August 2021 ('An i-phone With Four Wheels: Inside Foxconn's Bid to Build EVs')

makers also want to control the networks which link cars with their supplier and maintenance networks. But for IT companies, the more data they can access, the greater the value of the wheeled terminal. This 'frontier of control' dilemma has different implications for strong car makers and weaker ones, who might want to cede more control to an IT business to make their cars more attractive.

Autonomous

Again there is a difference in approaches between car makers, who typically wish to take an incremental approach towards autonomous driving, focused on safety and driver experience, and an IT approach, which is more focused on resolving data and sensing challenges for higher levels of automation. Autonomous driving is generally conceived in six levels, shown in Table 5.2. Not only are there technical and commercial challenges in moving from one level to the next, but regulatory and even philosophical challenges as well. In the early 2020s, many cars were equipped with Level 1, 2, or 2+, despite some vendors suggesting they were operating at a higher level. The question is, at what point, and in what road and traffic conditions, is it safe for a driver to turn their attention elsewhere, leaving control of the car to the car's computers? If a driver is expected to take control in an emergency, how quickly can they do it? When does responsibility shift from the driver to the car, and what does 'the car' mean?

Although Japan and Japanese car makers have been cautious over autonomous driving, in 2020 the Japanese government surprised many by

Table 5.2 Levels of autonomous driving

Level	Automation level	Control of tasks
0	No driving automation	Driver performs tasks such as steering, braking, accelerating...
1	Driver assistance	Vehicle performs limited functions like cruise control, adaptive cruise control
2	Partial automation	Advanced driver assistance (ADAS): car can assist with steering, accelerating, decelerating, but driver is in control, and responsible for critical tasks
3	Conditional automation	Car can make informed decisions, but driver must be ready to intervene; at lower speeds no intervention is needed
4	High automation	Cars don't need human intervention in most circumstances
5	Complete automation	Full automation, human attention not needed

recognizing the car as potentially responsible for Level 3, the first country in the world to do so. As noted in Chapter 2, it required many ministries and agencies working together to prepare the legal and regulatory environment. Commented one observer:

> The [Japanese] automobile manufacturers first threw the ball into the government's court, because regulations made it impossible for them to commercialize the technology.… But it was Tokyo which threw back the ball to industry by changing its laws ahead of anyone else in the world. And the player that caught that was Honda.[15]

The ball Honda caught was a Level 3 car. However, its production was limited to 100 expensive vehicles. Tricky questions about conditional automation remain, but regulatory hurdles for Level 4 autonomous driving in designated areas were also cleared by 2023, opening the way for autonomous shuttle services, and beyond that to public transportation in depopulated areas by the late 2020s.[16]

Shared/Subscription

Is the future of mobility personally owned vehicles (PoV), or shared/ subscription vehicles, or MaaS? After all, most cars are idle most of the time, which is an inefficient use of resources. The decline of car sales in Japan— down by roughly a third in 2020 compared with 1990—is not just because of a declining population; younger generations appear less enamoured of owning their own vehicle. The spread of 'ride share' (stretching the meaning of 'share') and 'car share' services raises the question for car makers of who the customer is, and what features cars will need if they are not PoVs (Nakanishi, 2020).

Electric

EVs are powered by a battery, whose current is changed from DC to AC by an inverter. They are very different from internal combustion vehicles, which are powered by thermal energy from petrol or diesel. EVs are currently more

---

[15] Kazuo Shimizu, motor journalist, former racing car driver, and member of a government working group for autonomous driving, cited in *Nikkei Asia*, 24 February 2021 ('Back Seat Driver: How Honda Stole the Lead in Autonomous Cars').

[16] *Nikkei Asia*, 28 October 2022 ('Self-driving Cars: Japan Opens Roads to Level 4 Vehicles in April'). Tesla's 'Autopilot', which prompted a federal investigation in 2021, is considered a Level 2 system. Waymo (owned by Alphabet, Google's parent company) launched a Level 4 self-driving taxi service in Phoenix in 2020, using Arizona's permissive regulatory environment. A limiting factor for Level 4 is three-dimensional maps. Cf. *The Conversation* 14 October 2020 ('Robot Take the Wheel: Waymo Has Launched a Self-Driving Taxi Service').

expensive, but they require 40–50 per cent fewer parts. As such, the shift from internal combustion engines to EVs has far-reaching implications, not just for car makers, but for their networks of suppliers. Many businesses and jobs are at stake, as Toyoda Akio, then President of Toyota, reminded the Japanese government as it contemplated banning the sale of new petrol and diesel cars by 2035.[17] He also reminded them that not all electricity which charges EVs is clean, especially in Japan (Chapter 3).

So how quickly should the shift from internal combustion engines happen? Is there a future for hybrids? What about hydrogen-powered fuel cell vehicles (FCVs)? Who is going to pay for the infrastructure needed for EVs and FCVs? Who will make the batteries, and what kind of batteries? The stakes are very high for Japan's automakers, electronics companies, and for the whole Japanese economy. And the threats come from many directions—front-runner Tesla, nimble European and US car makers, BYD and other Chinese producers vying for dominance in the world's biggest EV market, IT entrants, Foxconn which is trying to entice Japanese suppliers to join its 'open source' platform of software and chassis designs....

Toyota's Response

Toyota's embryonic CASE response came in 2015 with the establishment of the Toyota Research Institute (TRI) in Silicon Valley to develop autonomous driving technology, robotics and 'other human amplification technology'. It took a further step in 2018, when Toyoda Akio announced at the CES (Consumer Electronics Show) in Las Vegas that Toyota was transitioning from car maker to mobility company, and unveiled the e-Palette, a 'mobility services platform' designed to deliver a range of mobility services with partners including Amazon, DiDi, Pizza Hut, Uber, and Mazda.[18] The same year Toyota Research Institute-Advanced Development (TRI-AD) was started to develop software for CASE, as well as an 'open vehicle programming' software platform called Arene on which multiple service providers—partners, startups, etc.—could integrate their services.

TRI-AD was renamed Woven Planet Holdings in 2020, with three operating companies—Woven Core (products of the future), Woven Alpha (innovation) and Woven Capital. The group was headed by Dr James Kuffner, co-founder of Google's robotics division, and part of Google's initial team

---

[17] The automobile industry in Japan was estimated to employ 5.5 million people in 2020, over 8 per cent of the total workforce: Kusuda and Moriguchi, 2020.

[18] https://global.toyota/en/newsroom/corporate/20546438.html (accessed 27 August 2021).

working on autonomous vehicles. In fact, many of the key positions in TRI and Woven Planet are held by non-Japanese, and many have a background in software. These new departures highlight the future relationship between software and hardware. Toyoda himself has used the term 'software first', but usually stresses the equal importance of hardware and software. Toyota, like Hitachi, appears to be adopting an OT/IT cyber-physical strategy, symbolically indicated by Toyota on the one hand, and Woven Planet on the other. This relationship is taking the group in new directions, including Woven City. As Toyoda himself has pointed out, Toyota started out as an automatic weaving loom business—the company still exists—before making cars, and this is the next stage in its evolution.

In re-orienting itself, Toyota has entered into an enormous array of alliances, in addition to its capital ties with Daihatsu (which it fully owns), Subaru, Mazda, and Suzuki. Alliances and joint ventures as of 2021 included:

- Commercial Japan Partnership Technologies: Toyota, Isuzu, and Hino, and later Suzuki and Daihatsu for commercial vehicle autonomous driving, logistics, EV, hydrogen[19]
- Toyota, Suzuki, Subaru, Daihatsu, and Mazda for next generation vehicle communications
- Toyota, Denso, Softbank, Uber ATC for automated ridesharing services
- Toyota-Softbank Monet consortium: 88 companies as of March 2019 for next generation mobility services
- Toyota, GM, Arm, Bosch, Continental, Nvidia, NXP, Denso in Autonomous Vehicle Computing Consortium
- Toyota and Amazon Web Services for mobility services platform
- Toyota and Uber; as well as DiDi, Grab and other ride-share, car-share, and leasing services
- e-Palette alliance with Amazon, DiDi, Pizza Hut, Uber, and Mazda, as mentioned above
- Toyota and BMW for fuel cells and a sports car
- Toyota, Mazda, Honda, Nissan, Subaru, Denso, Panasonic, Mitsubishi Electric, Aisin, and Jatco for model-based development/design
- Toyota and Panasonic for lithium-ion, solid state and other next generation batteries

Some of these alliances may be for 'insurance' purposes, but even Toyota and its group of companies cannot face the CASE upheavals alone. Toyota set the

---

[19] In 2023 Toyota and Daimler Truck together made a holding company to bring together scandal-tainted Hino Motors and Mitsubishi-Fuso respectively.

pace for hybrids, but it is having to play catch-up with EVs. Its EV sales in 2022 were a little over 20,000, compared with Tesla's 1.3 million, and BYD's 810,000, leading some to question whether Toyota can really compete in EVs. To spearhead the company's EV drive, a new president was appointed in 2023, tasked with producing 1.5 million EVs in 2026 and 3.5 million in 2030. Despite Toyoda's avowed concern for suppliers and jobs, competitiveness, and survival were placed in the front seat, with the company announcing it would phase out the traditional conveyor belt in favour of 'gigacasting', in which many separate parts are incorporated into aluminium casts, reducing the number of steps, equipment and space needed. It also announced break-throughs in solid state batteries which it claimed would double the range while reducing charging time to ten minutes. Perhaps Toyota acted just in time.

Japan's other car makers are also in the throes of change. Nissan was the first company to mass produce EVs, but struggled to capitalize on its early start. Its alliance with Renault and Mitsubishi is being revamped to accelerate its transition, while Honda has teamed up with Sony and Qualcomm. Elsewhere Panasonic has partnered with Amazon and Stellantis to produce EV cabin systems. Nidec, Denso, and other Japanese companies are participating in Foxconn's i-phone-like EV consortium. The alliances—and there are many more—are part of a complex game of chess, re-writing the industry maps referred to in the introduction of this chapter, the outcome of which will have a profound impact on the building of Japan's new economy.

DX and Financial Services

Slowly but irresistibly DX is also penetrating the financial services industry in Japan. The pace might be interpreted as resistance to change, or caution until the contours of change and risk are better understood, or both. Since the mid-nineteenth century, nation states have adopted a two-tier structure of central bank and commercial banks to deal with different types of monetary flows and information but sharing a common currency and basis of trust. This structure has allowed for innovations in the commercial banking sector, such as cheques, ATMs, and wire transfers, but digital technologies have the potential to change the structure itself, by generating huge amounts of data on which new sources of trust and currencies can be built (Yamaoka, 2022). They also have the potential to create new forms of systemic risk.

METI's 'digital cliff' DX Report (Chapter 2) might have been referring to Japan's banks, especially to regional banks and trust banks, in its criticism of reliance on legacy systems installed by vendors, IT budgets consumed by maintenance rather than investment, lack of knowledge and involvement of top managers, and lack of IT personnel (BoJ, 2019, 2021). With their rigid decision making, Japan's established banks are anything but agile. A culture of caution is pervasive, shaped by a regulatory system that emphasizes safety and security. Symptomatically, smartphone apps for online banking are seldom user-friendly. To adapt to DX banks need to re-design their IT systems so that they can innovate in user-facing systems while maintaining the integrity of their payment systems (Sonku, 2020).

Facing a structural pinch on profits, many traditional banks are focused on cutting costs and efficiency instead. Low interest rates, reduced borrowing and a declining population have affected both savings and loans business. Whereas banks in many countries have responded to such challenges and the rise of digital finance by closing branches, in Japan branch numbers actually *increased* between 2007 and 2018. They 'have been upgrading their offices' sales functions to offset a decline in net interest income through growth in fee/commission revenue rather than radically revamping their branch networks' (NRI, 2020: 8). They are strong in face-to-face customer interaction, and their customers, who are older—and wealthier—than those of digital-only banks and financial services, tend to shun online banking. However, many traditional banks have announced *plans* to reduce branches, and regional banks are now pinning survival on a joint cloud-based base payment system.

Megabanks meanwhile are taking advantage of a relaxation of ownership restrictions to pursue equity-based startup and turnaround deals. MUFG, for example, announced new funds of ¥30 billion for startups and ¥20 billion for drug discovery in early 2023. Some have teamed up with online banks and financial services businesses which sprang up in the 2000s. MUFG acquired the online brokerage kabu.com (now Kabucom Securities) in 2007; Mizuho Financial Group (through Mizuho Securities) created PayPay Securities with Softbank in 2020 and acquired 20 per cent of Rakuten Securities shares in 2022; and SMBC entered into a capital and business alliance with SBI Holdings in 2022.

Fintech

Banks have also begun to engage with fintech startups. METI's 2017 'Fintech Vision' defines fintech as 'the use of cutting-edge technology, including internet of things (IoT), big data analysis, artificial intelligence (AI) and blockchain, to create innovative financial services provided through mobile terminals and other devices'. In the future, according to this Vision, finance will be reshaped around the needs of users managing and using their own personal data. Application programming interfaces (APIs) will break down data walls, allowing startups to access data held by banks and to offer new services. Electronic data interchange (EDI) will bring commerce and finance together, eliminating paper. Cashless payments and digital finance will become the norm, backed by a secure digital personal identification process.[20] Blockchain ledgers will be widely applied, it predicted.

In 2018 the Banking Act was revised to encourage banks up to pursue new uses of their data, new types of investment, and new services, developed and delivered in collaboration with fintech startups. They responded cautiously. The government's target of at least 80 banks with open APIs by June 2020, was surpassed in 2019, but having an open API and using it are different matters. Many banks did not see much value in working with fintech startups, and set high fees to defray maintenance costs. By September 2019 only 57 of 130 banks had actually signed a one-to-one agreement with a fintech. And just 25 out of 59 eligible fintech businesses had secured an agreement.[21]

Some fintechs, however, have become firmly established in the financial sector, including Money Forward, freee, and Moneytree, all founded in 2012, and active in personal finance management (PFM) and/or cloud-based software tools for SMEs. They received funding from financial institutions—including megabanks and regional banks—and built significant client bases of both individuals and SMEs. Money Forward boasted 5 million PFM users in 2021 and had made customized apps for a number of financial institutions. freee claimed 55 per cent of the cloud-based SME accounting software market in 2019, and 40 per cent of the payroll/HR market. And Moneytree's app. had been installed over 1.5 million times by mid 2021. Its non-Japanese founders launched the Fintech Association of Japan.[22]

Fintech startups have been enabled by a changing regulatory environment, which has simplified licensing and relaxed investment restrictions. The Zengin payment platform is being opened up to non-banks, with a view to create an API Gateway by 2027. In a further shift from a prohibitive to a permissive stance, the government introduced a 'sandbox' system which enables new business models to be tested in a controlled environment, such as Crypto

---

[20] The share of cashless payments to total payments rose sharply, from 20 per cent in 2019 to over a third in 2022, spurred by the Covid-19 pandemic, and redemption of My Number points. New measures, such as allowing wages to be paid directly into digital wallets, are expected to raise this ratio towards that of Western countries.

[21] *The Japan Times*, 27 January 2020 ('Japanese Banks' Fortress Mentality Puts Them on Trailing Edge of Fintech Revolution'). 'Fintech' is almost synonymous with 'fintech startup' in Japan.

[22] https://getmoneytree.com/au/company/profile https://corp.freee.co.jp/en/service/ https://corp.moneyforward.com/en/about_moneyforward.pdf (all accessed 29 August 2021).

Garage's platform for rapid settlement between digital currency exchanges.[23] Fincity.Tokyo estimated the size of the Japanese fintech market at $1.4 billion in 2017, at $3.2 billion in 2019, and with a compound annual growth rate of 51 per cent, expected it to reach $11 billion by 2022.[24]

Digital Currencies and Blockchain Ledgers

Cryptocurrencies were at the forefront of the fintech ferment in the mid 2010s. Their evangelists believed they would re-invent money and radically change the social order. But new technologies are themselves shaped by social relations, and cryptocurrencies and blockchain technology are no different. Cryptocurrency exchanges in Japan have had a chequered history, with two spectacular heists, but rather than banning them, Japanese financial authorities decided to regulate them under the Financial Services Agency in 2016. In 2022 the Japan Virtual and Crypto Assets Exchange Association listed 31 member exchanges, dealing in some 40 cryptocurrencies.[25]

Banks started issuing stablecoins, which are pegged to national currencies, in 2018, initially for intra-group use. MUFG subsequently created Progmat, which quickly evolved into a major stablecoin and tokenization platform supported by other major financial institutions, with the aim of replacing conventional trade finance.[26] At the same time, a Digital Currency Forum, started in 2020 with 83 organizations, including the three mega-banks, industrial and transport corporations, and government observers, founded a holding company (DeCurret Holdings) and an operating company (DeCurret DCP) in 2021 to commercialize their digital currency concept, tentatively called DCJPY. This will be issued by banks, and denominated in yen, building on the current financial infrastructure.[27] Benefits touted are eliminating paperwork and cash handling, improving supply chain efficiency, and enabling smart contracts and other digital innovations in the business process area. Clean energy certificates will facilitate GX.

---

[23] *Forbes*, 26 June 2019 ('Japan's Blockchain Sandbox is Paving the Way for the Fintech Future').
[24] https://fincity.tokyo/wp-content/uploads/2020/11/1604888710-7041ae1e28863fe098eab163e812bf4f. pdf (accessed 12 July 2022). Fincity.Tokyo was set up in 2019 to boost Tokyo as a global financial centre.
[25] *Nikkei Asia*, 22 March 2022 ('Japanese Crypto Exchanges to Speed Up Cryptocurrency Listings') (accessed 12 July 2022). The heists were Mt Gox in 2014, in which 6 per cent of the world's bitcoins disappeared, and Coincheck in 2018, in which over $500 million disappeared.
[26] *Nikkei Asia*, 5 September, 2023 ('Japan's Megabank Mizuho Joins MUFJ's Stablecoin Platform') (accessed 5 September, 2023).
[27] The system has two parts—a 'business process area' in which goods and services flow between companies, and a 'common area' in which the associated financial information flows and settlement occurs simultaneously. The two are linked by an interoperable interface and built on a blockchain platform: https://www.decurret-dcp.com/.assets/forum_20211124wp_en.pdf (accessed 15 July 2022). See also Yamaoka, 2022.

Finally, the BoJ has been studying what form a central bank digital currency (CBDC) might take—cautiously, given the possibility that it could collapse the overall two-tiered monetary structure and facilitate state surveillance. From proof of concept tests in 2021, through a pilot programme in 2023, the BoJ foresees launching a CBDC later in the decade. In sum, cryptocurrencies and blockchain have not overturned the existing social order, but they are contributing to the changing face of financial services in Japan. Changing financial services, in turn, will contribute to DX and GX elsewhere in the economy, including manufacturing.

Entrepreneurship, Startups, and SMEs

The final section of this chapter will look at both startups and established SMEs, their changing relations with large firms, and their role in building Japan's new economy. Fintech highlights the role of startups in Japan's economic transformation. The Kishida administration set a goal of increasing the annual number of startups and investment in them tenfold (10,000 to 100,000, ¥1 trillion to ¥10 trillion) between 2022 and 2027. It is not clear where these figures come from, but this is a tall order, and probably not achievable. It does, however, signal strong government support for boosting Japan's startup ecosystem, including tax incentives for large companies to invest in startups.[28] Entrepreneurs are now fêted in national award ceremonies, almost like national treasures, in much the same way that medal winners were at the 'Skill Olympics' (*ginō gorin*) at the *monozukuri* peak in the 1960s. 'I've never had a situation like this ... where everybody—government officials, startups or major firms—talks about how ecosystem building is (crucial)', commented the president of a major startup hub in Tokyo.[29] The fervour for startups focuses on high-growth startups backed by venture capital. At the apex of this fervour are 'unicorns'—high growth VC-backed startups valued at $1 billion or more—which have been elusive in Japan. This represents a significant cultural shift from the postwar decades, when large firms were seen as drivers of change, and startups as perpetuating a dual structure.

The ground for a startup boom in Japan is rather fertile. In the late 1990s a series of policies were implemented to promote startups, entrepreneurship,

---

[28] The 'open innovation tax relief' scheme (2020) allows companies to deduct 25 per cent of their investment from taxable income in priority sectors, under certain conditions. Supposed to be temporary, the scheme was extended in 2022.

[29] *The Japan Times*, 18 January 2023 ('At Long Last, Japan's Startup Scene May Finally Be Ready to Take Big Leap Forward').

clusters, technology transfer, and spinouts from universities, but with limited impact. Japan's prevailing corporate culture, both in large firms and SMEs, was seen as inimical to the venture model of large financial bets placed on early stage firms, which required rapid growth and an 'exit' pathway for investors after 3–5 years. Gradually, however, the venture (capital) model began to take root, at least in Tokyo, with a sufficient depth of entrepreneurs and investors familiar with it, and a pool of managerial talent willing to work in startups. Kotosaka and Sako (2016: 7) describe two co-existing logics in the Tokyo ICT startup ecosystem in the 2010s, one a 'corporate logic' and the other a 'venture logic':

> Under Corporate Logic, actors prioritize sustainability, and do not necessary drive for rapid growth as the basis of their strategy. Successful entrepreneurs under Corporate Logic generally demonstrate stable growth, even the most successful ones, due primary to their reliance on the entrepreneurs' personal savings for seed funding and on cash flow and loans for growth…. They take extra care to retain existing business contacts, and are often hesitant to move beyond the area where they have confidence.
>
> The actors under Venture Logic, in contrast, have a strong appetite for growth. Entrepreneurs obtain funding from venture capitalists to realize promising business ideas, constantly seek additional capital and labour, and sacrifice positive cash flow and stability for the sake of growth…. They actively recruit talented executives and junior staff, with incentive packages that are linked to corporate growth.

Entrepreneurs in the latter ecosystem in Tokyo saw themselves as brave, plucky change agents inhabiting a 'village' surrounded by a terrain of corporate conservatism, or 'old Japan' (Frenkenberger, 2021). After the fall from grace of flamboyant financial entrepreneur Horie Takafumi in 2006, they were careful to present themselves as working for the future of Japanese society rather than their own enrichment. And gradually with the growth of servicing and intermediating institutions in that ecosystem, and the flow of financial and human resources from the corporate sector, interaction between the two worlds increased. The notion that Venture Logic would supplant Corporate Logic gave way to a more nuanced picture of interaction, as with banks and fintechs.

The number of startups estimated to be receiving venture capital, corporate venture capital or similar funding more than doubled between 2011 and 2018, from 1067 to 2428 per year, before dipping during the Covid-19 pandemic, while funding more than quadrupled over the same time, from

$1.06 billion to $4.16 billion in 2018. Thus average funding increased as well (INITIAL, 2021).[30] By sector, the most funding in 2020 went to AI, software-as-a-service (SaaS), Fintech, Clean Tech, and the 'Sharing' Economy. Not surprisingly amidst the pandemic, drug discovery and manufacture also made it into the top ten (ibid.). The funding and funders are concentrated in Tokyo, where information networks and events are densest, and IT and software engineers, and managers with international experience, are most plentiful. There are startup ecosystems in other parts of Japan, such as in Kansai and Fukuoka, but on a much smaller scale (Kapturkiewicz, 2021); by and large the Corporate Logic prevails elsewhere.

SMEs and Digital Transformation

In contrast to venture-capital-backed startups, existing SMEs have been shunned once again. In recent years they have been decried as zombies, and as a drag on DX and GX. Of course the sector is varied, and there are many entrepreneurial small businesses. However, a common characteristic of these is a cautious approach to growth, a gradual accumulation of technological capabilities, and a 'lifework' orientation of the founders (Whittaker et al., 2009). Resilience over effervescence. This was necessary in an environment of conservative finance, conservative transacting, pressure from large firms, and social expectations. Firms like Nidec, which grew rapidly through M&A, were the exception.

Surveys show that SMEs invest less in software than large companies, that DX is a high priority only for a minority, and that many see no clear link between IT investment and increased labour productivity, which may be down to the fact that the investment is not coupled with changes in organization or company culture. SMEs themselves cite as obstacles to DX an 'analogue company culture', lack of clear purpose, lack of IT literacy, and not wishing to disturb client relations. Over half lack sufficient IT staff. Few have prepared for a cyber attack, despite one-fifth experiencing one. And while US counterparts invest in IT to analyse and respond to market and customer trends, for Japanese SMEs it is more about reducing costs, work reform to address difficulties in recruiting staff, and reducing long working hours (Chūshō kigyōchō, 2021). There is some justification, then, in seeing SMEs as a drag on DX.

---

[30] The figure for 2020 was $4.32 billion. The average deal was $1.39 million in 2011 and $3.07 in 2020, and the median rose from $0.15 million to $0.94 million. The top corporate investors (by amount) were NTT DoCoMo, Itochu, Sompo Holdings, Softbank, and Link and Motivation (INITIAL, 2021).

On the other hand, many small businesses survive *because* they do work which cannot be easily automated. Ota Ward in Tokyo is home to a vast concentration of SMEs, even though their numbers have halved since the mid 1990s. Commented one industry promotion veteran: 'Ota supply chains are complex, and many of the small factories have 200+ customers. They do small batches and are not in *keiretsu*. They have many different kinds of transactions. For some of them, analogue is rational.' Promoting DX, he said, has to align with their reality. When it comes to GX, too: 'Some see the future in green certification and green business, but for others it just means more paperwork loaded onto them— Restrictions on Hazardous Substances, and all that. They feel they get dragged around by customers and the government changing what they want.'[31]

DX and GX look different from the 'bottom' looking up. Small factory owners complain that savings from investments in new technology are appropriated by large company customers. And that the quality of the technical drawings they get from the latter is declining. When they offer ideas for improvement, far from being compensated, in the digital age their ideas are easily stolen. Such a situation led to the creation of I-OTA, a consortium of 30+ small businesses which aim to transform themselves from subcontracting to one-stop manufacturing consulting, while promoting DX for work and information flows to cut out waste, and to deliver on QCD (quality, cost, delivery).[32] Digital Ota is another network of small businesses in Ota Ward using the Tailor Works platform to create an online community, one of the aims of which is to promote peer-based digital awareness and DX.

A similar philosophy and approach can be seen in the Industrial Value Chain Initiative (IVI), whose membership encompasses both large and small firms, with many working groups. IVI's founder characterized the approach as follows:

Smart manufacturing, as the term is used in Europe and North America, refers to top-down reforms that seek to establish a new type of manufacturing. On the other hand, it is bottom-up reforms that are better suited to the manufacturing industry in Japan.... IVI working groups start by defining an 'as is' model of how the issue being addressed currently manifests, and a 'to be' model that could be

---

[31] Interviews, 31 March 2021 and 28 October 2021. On the role of Ota's small factories in Japanese manufacturing, see Whittaker, 1997.

[32] Tsujimura, 2022. I-OTA is a word play on Innovation-Ota, and IoT.

done using the IoT and other technologies, and then determines things like where digitalization is needed to address the issue and the requirements for system implementation.

(Nishioka, 2020: 27)

IVI seeks to create 'gradual' de facto standards through the interactions of its members, combining IT with hardware and manufacturing—mirroring in some respects the approach of Hitachi and Toyota. One outcome has been a system for trading manufacturing data between companies using a 'connected industries open framework'.[33]

After the outbreak of Covid-19, IT investment did become a greater priority for many SMEs, so that meetings could be held online and employees could work from home, and for sales and consultations. But while the pandemic provided a boost for DX, outside the metropolitan centres many SMEs lacked the necessary skills.[34] Thus there may be a two-speed engagement with DX, geographically and otherwise, while the meaning of DX and the way it unfolds in the SME sector is likely to be quite different from the large firm sector.

Concluding Comments

The industries on which Japan built its postwar economy are in a state of flux. Boundaries are being redrawn by technological innovation, changes in production systems and changes in business models. Many electronics and IT incumbents have struggled to navigate these changes—even Hitachi is forced to constantly change, divest, and acquire to maintain profitability, without revenue growth. Specialists have fared better through GVC engagement, but are now caught in the turbulence of US-China friction and decoupling.

Schaede (2020) makes a strong case for the business re-invention of Japan. Japanese companies, she argues, have strategically repositioned, claimed strategic niches in advanced equipment and materials, and undergone organization renewal. To be sure, there are many examples of this, but there are many casualties, strugglers, and stragglers as well.

The divergent ability of companies to respond to their challenges can be seen in Table 5.1. Banks, which topped the TSE table in market capitalization

---

[33] Cf. *The Japan Times*, 25 April 2016 ('Internet of Things in Japan: Quietly, Systematically Plowing Ahead').

[34] Cf. Chapter 8. Some rural SMEs turned to part time IT freelancers in the metropolitan centres, who were also working from home: *Nikkei Asia*, 31 August 2021 ('COVID Pushes Japan's Non-Metropolitan Companies to Digitize').

in the early 1990s had dropped off it by 2020, even in their mega-merged forms. The financial system which powered the postwar economy became both a victim and a contributor to the 'lost decade' travails. Clear demarcations within the sector and with other sectors are now breaking down, or rather are being eroded by fintech startups.

The biggest current upheaval, however, is in the automobile and associated industries which are central to the Japanese economy, with simultaneous revolutions described as CASE. The question here is whether the apex companies—assemblers—and their suppliers will fare better than their electronics and IT counterparts when they face competition from many different directions at once. The future of Toyota is particularly consequential. Although it still sold more cars than any other maker worldwide in 2022, it made a slow start in the shift to EVs, in part by betting on the durability of its hybrid technologies.

Spokespersons for the company defended its stance in terms of the need for different solutions in different markets, and in terms of social responsibility—with multiple tiers of domestic suppliers and employees, a precipitous shift from internal combustion would risk mass redundancies and social chaos, they said. But Toyota has had to yield to the pressures of change by introducing 'gigacasting' and racing to develop new batteries. The dilemma for Toyota echoes other distributional issues, which we will return to later in the book. Similarly, startups are now seen as important drivers of change, but despite official rhetoric about disruptive innovation, there are expectations that they will benefit from working with large established firms, and vice versa. Overall, the preference is for a more organic form of metabolic renewal than surgical Schumpeterian 'creative destruction'.

6
Corporate Governance, ESG, and 'New Capitalism'

The stock market reacted negatively to Mr Kishida's 'new capitalism' when he was elected leader of the LDP and hence Prime Minister. Investors fretted about backsliding on structural reforms, a return to the 'bad old days' of industrial policy, and most of all, that he would fund 'distribution' by raising taxes on investment income:

> The Japanese stock market has suffered an eight-day losing streak unbroken by the election of a new prime minister, an event that typically produces a rally, in what some have dubbed the 'Kishida shock'. The Nikkei Stock Average has retreated 6.8% since Fumio Kishida won the race to lead the ruling Liberal Democratic Party on Sept. 29. About 80% of the benchmark index's gains since August have been wiped out.... Fuelling this anxiety is Kishida's declared goal of a 'virtuous cycle of growth and distribution'.[1]

In the face of such criticism, Kishida appeared to backtrack, and emphasize the 'growth' part of the virtuous cycle. His 'income doubling' plan became '*investment* income doubling', intended to mobilize ¥1 quadrillion of household savings held in banks and cash. When his draft economic agenda was released in late May 2022, many wondered whether there was anything new in 'new capitalism'.[2]

Kishida was under pressure not to deviate from Abenomics as well. However, Abenomics was unable to deliver a new growth model for Japan. It boosted corporate profits, as well as returns to investors, but it exacerbated inequality and the pinch in household incomes. Corporate investment flowed overseas rather than into the domestic economy. The materials put before Kishida's Council of New Form of Capitalism were sobering (Table 6.1). Between 2000 and 2020 labour costs of large firms (capitalized at ¥1 billion

---

[1] *Nikkei Asia*, 7 October 2021 ('"Kishida Shock" to Stocks Shows Fear Japan will Slide on Reforms').
[2] *The Japan Times*, 2 June 2022 ('Kishida's "New Capitalism" Not so New, Economists Say, But on the Right Track').

Building a New Economy. D. Hugh Whittaker, Oxford University Press. © D. Hugh Whittaker (2024).
DOI: 10.1093/oso/9780198893394.003.0007

Table 6.1 Key corporate statistics, 2000, 2020 (¥ trillion)

	2000	2020
Labour costs	51.8	51.6
Capital investment	21.8	20.7
Operating profits	19.4	37.1
Cash and deposits	48.8	90.4
Internal reserves	88.0	242.1
Dividends	3.5	20.2

Source: 'New Form of Capitalism' office (November 2021), Cabinet Office 'Chingin, jinteki shihon ni kansuru dētashū' (Data on Wages and Human Capital).
Note: Figures for large firms capitalized at ¥1 billion or more.

or more) *declined* (¥51.8 to ¥51.6 trillion), as did (domestic) capital investment (¥21.8 to ¥20.7 trillion). On the other hand, operating profits almost *doubled* (¥19.4 to ¥37.1 trillion), as did cash and deposits (¥48.8 to ¥90.4 trillion). Internal reserves almost *trebled* (¥88.0 to ¥242.1 trillion), and dividends rose *sixfold* (¥3.5 to ¥20.2 trillion), almost equalling capital investment. Investment in employee education and training, already low by international comparisons, declined further.[3]

How did this happen? This cannot be answered by just looking at DX, GX and Society 5.0, which have been the focus of the book so far. To answer this question we must consider not only processes of value creation, or 'growth', but questions of 'distribution' as well. Kishida was right that together these can create a virtuous cycle, and his critics were correct in sensing this had implications for them. The two come together at the company level in corporate governance, which is the main focus of this chapter. Corporate governance has an increasingly crowded agenda, which has come to include ESG (environment, social, governance). As we shall see, investor relations have become the core institutional nexus, replacing employment relations, and as such, also a nexus of tension.

As well, we will begin to look at Keidanren's 'sustainable capitalism' and Kishida's 'new capitalism', which seek to create a macro-framework for a 'virtuous cycle of growth and distribution'. As we transition from a focus on DX, GX, and Society 5.0 to new capitalism, moreover, we need to clarify how the many terms come together (or not). As a simplification, if DX and GX are

---

[3] Naikaku kanbō atarashii shihonshugi jitsugen honbu jimukyoku (November 2021) 'Chingin, jinteki shihon ni kansuru dētashū' (Data on Wages and Human Capital), p. 2.

wheels of a cart, and Society 5.0 is the destination, capitalism is the cart itself. But who is in the cart, and are they all travelling in the same class?

The first section traces the corporate governance reform movement, from the leadup to the Stewardship and Corporate Governance Codes, to the requirements for listing on the Prime section of the re-organized Tokyo Stock Exchange in 2022. While pushing managers to be more responsive to investor concerns, these developments do not mandate shareholder interest maximization per se. Instead, they urge managers and shareholders to work together for 'sustainable corporate growth and increased corporate value over the mid-long term'.

A towering presence in investor relations is the Government Pension Investment Fund (GPIF), which in 2015 was mandated to raise the share of domestic stocks in its portfolio from 12 per cent to 25 per cent. Its stance would help determine the success or otherwise of the Stewardship Code. As well, however, in 2015 GPIF signed up to the UN's Principles for Responsible Investment (PRI), and it thus became a driving force for the spread of ESG. This is taken up in the second section.

The third section is a reflection on tensions in corporate governance and investor relations, from the ongoing drama at Toshiba. Despite 'unitary' expectations of managers and investors to work together to create corporate value, their interests are actually plural. It is possible to see in Toshiba's investor relations a new 'frontier of control', in much the same way as employment relations were a century ago. Tensions can be a force for transformation, and perhaps Japan can resolve them as skilfully as it did with labour conflict, which paved the way for its postwar manufacturing-centred growth model.

This sets the scene for considering sustainable and new capitalism. First we consider how GPIF, Keidanren and others have tried to conceptually integrate the veritable flurry of economic and business reforms. We then look at Keidanren's 'sustainable capitalism', and Kishida's 'new capitalism'. Their claim to be 'people-centred' will be taken up in the next chapter. In market terms, whereas Chapter 4 focused on competition and product markets, this chapter is indirectly concerned with financial markets, and Chapter 7 is concerned with labour markets.

Shareholder Voice and Corporate Governance

In the 1980s investors in the US and UK began to pressure managers to prioritize profits and shareholder returns, marking the end of 'managerial capitalism' and the rise of 'shareholder capitalism', with a corresponding shift in corporate governance practices. In the 1990s, as corporate profits in Japan slumped, and financial institutions started to unwind reciprocally held shares and foreign investors purchased them, the tide of corporate governance reform began to wash Japan's shores. This coincided with the US economic resurgence and technology boom and Japan's prolonged downturn. The postwar Japanese model was discredited, but what followed was not a simple re-enactment of what had played out in the US and UK.

As pressure mounted on Japanese companies to restructure, the government passed a large number of facilitating laws. The postwar ban on holding companies was lifted, transfers of undertaking were simplified, stock swaps and share buy-backs were allowed, and labour markets were partially deregulated, unpicking some of the interwoven legal threads of the postwar model. The Commercial Code revision in 2002 introduced a US- and UK-inspired 'company with committees' system of corporate governance that separated boards and management, and placed a majority of external directors on nomination, remuneration, and audit committees. In the wake of the dotcom bubble burst and with opposition from Keidanren, the new system was made optional, and only a minority of (mainly internationally exposed) companies adopted it.

A second area of contestation was the 'market for corporate control'. Previously Japanese law and practice had supported management defences against hostile takeovers, but this began to be tested in the early 2000s with the arrival of activist shareholders, who scored early wins in forcing medium-sized companies to disgorge some of their cash reserves to shareholders, but did not succeed in establishing shareholder sovereignty. Effectively activists were bought off (Buchanan et al., 2012). The Livedoor, Bulldog Sauce and J-Power cases, followed by the Global Financial Crisis, brought an end to aggressive shareholder activism in the 2000s. It did not end the corporate governance question, however, and activists shifted to a quieter, more measured form of engagement.

At stake was what structures and processes could best ensure companies were delivering 'value', and for whom. A METI-sponsored Corporate Value Report, issued at the height of Livedoor's attempted takeover of Nippon Broadcasting System in 2005, insisted that 'corporate value' was not the same as 'shareholder value'. The issue resurfaced under the second Abe administration, which sought to entice more foreign investors to Japan by promising an investment-friendly environment. Another METI-sponsored report—the Ito Review—held that continued low profitability had pulled Japanese managers towards 'short termism', a curious claim given that the accusation is more often directed towards shareholders, but in the context of prolonged recession, perhaps as plausible as the depiction of Japanese managers as wisely investing corporate profits for future growth. The source of future growth, the review opined, was an inflow of long-term capital—again a curious claim as Japanese companies were amassing retained earnings.[4]

Be that as it may, when the review argued that (short-termist) managers needed to engage with (long termist) investors, it was not with a view to *maximizing* shareholder returns. Returns needed to be raised to a level where they at least covered the cost of capital, but the rationale for investor relations was to deliver 'sustainable growth', which meant increasing 'corporate value' over the medium to long term. Thus on the one hand it urged managers to pay more attention to shareholder returns, but on the other it created an image—and normative expectations—of investors as interested in investee companies in the long term. Shareholder activists who pushed managers to maximize profits in the short term, or who engaged in corporate raids and asset stripping, were not fulfilling *their* role.[5]

In 2014 a new stock index—JPX-Nikkei Index 400—was launched for companies with 'high appeal for investors, which meet requirements of global investment standards, such as efficient use of capital and investor-focused management perspectives.'[6] Inclusion criteria emphasized return on equity (ROE) and operating profit, which Japanese companies were constantly berated for performing badly on. An ROE figure frequently cited in the media was the Topix 2004–2013 average of 6 per cent (with a mode of 3–4 per cent) versus the MSCI World Index average of 12.6 per cent. Now the absolute floor for respectability became 5 per cent, and the 'global standard' 'at least 10 per cent'. The initiative had an effect; some companies were said to be shamed by being left off the new Index and many began to allocate substantially more of their profits to dividends.

The Stewardship Code and the Corporate Governance Code

In 2014, a Financial Services Agency (FSA) council of experts published the 'Principles for Responsible Investors (Japan's Stewardship Code): To promote sustainable growth of companies through investment and dialogue'.

---

[4] The full name of the report was the 'Ito Review of Competitiveness and Incentives for Sustainable Growth: Building Favourable Relationships between Companies and Investors' (Ito et.al., 2014).

[5] A second Ito Review exhorted both managers and investors to work together in 'collaborative creation' focused on intangible assets (Ito et.al., 2017). Some saw these reports as an attempt by METI to retain its influence over corporate governance reform, which was being steered by the Financial Services Agency (FSA) and Tokyo Stock Exchange (TSE) .

[6] 'The new index will promote the appeal of Japanese corporations domestically and abroad, while encouraging continued improvement of corporate value, thereby aiming to revitalize the Japanese stock market.' https://www.jpx.co.jp/english/markets/indices/jpx-nikkei400/ (accessed 4 September 2021).

As fund stewards, institutional investors were duty-bound to 'enhance the medium- to long-term investment return for their clients and beneficiaries by improving and fostering the investee companies' corporate value and sustainable growth through constructive engagement, or purposeful dialogue, based on in-depth knowledge of the companies and their business environment'.[7] Key words were engagement, corporate value, sustainable growth and in-depth knowledge. No longer could institutional investors remain disengaged; henceforth they were expected to exercise voice, not shrilly, or for short-term returns, but constructively, for the medium to long term. By the end of August 2014, 160 institutional investors had signed up to the Stewardship Code.

The following year, shortly after the OECD's Principles of Corporate Governance, another FSA/TSE council of experts introduced the 'Corporate Governance Code', which was designed to complement the Stewardship Code—as 'two wheels of a cart'. Similarly subtitled 'seeking sustainable corporate growth and increased corporate value over the mid- to long-term', it defined corporate governance as 'a structure for transparent, fair, timely and decisive decision-making by companies, with due attention to the needs and perspectives of shareholders and also customers, employees and local communities'. The 'timely and decisive' phrase reflected the view that without a clear direction from the board, managers were afraid of taking risks. They needed to be 'free from such restrictions and establish an environment where healthy entrepreneurship can flourish and where the management's capabilities can be given full force'.

The Corporate Governance Code exhorted boards to engage constructively with investors. It set out principles rather than rules, with 'comply or explain' requirements. Whereas the Companies Law (2015) required companies to explain if they had no independent external directors, the Corporate Governance Code specified at least two, strengthening the requirement for meaningful external voice. The code was revised in 2018, with new requirements for board diversity, reductions in relational shareholding and active stewardship of corporate pension funds. It was accompanied by 'Guidelines for Investor and Company Engagement', which covered amongst other things CEO appointment/dismissal and responsibilities of the board. Both were further revised in 2021, setting higher disclosure standards, a requirement for at least one-third of prospective TSE Prime market company directors to be external and independent, and targets for women, mid-career, and non-Japanese hires. The Stewardship Code was also revised in 2020, emphasizing

---

[7] https://www.fsa.go.jp/en/refer/councils/stewardship/20,140,407/01.pdf (accessed 4 September 2021), p. 2.

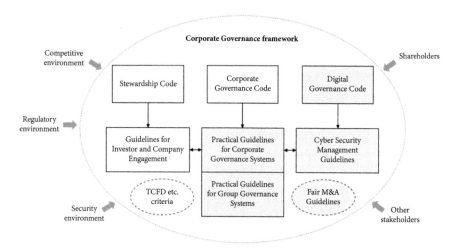

Figure 6.1 Evolving and expanding corporate governance framework

Source: Adapted and modified from METI and IPA, 2023: 9, https://www.meti.go.jp/policy/
netsecurity/downloadfiles/CSM_Guideline_v3.0_en.pdf (accessed 21 June 2023).
Note: Shaded code and guidelines from METI, unshaded from FSA.

medium to long-term sustainability of investee companies, and ESG 'consistent with investment strategies'. The evolving—and expanding—corporate governance framework is shown in Figure 6.1.

Reorganization of the Tokyo Stock Exchange, 2022

From 2014 there has been a ratcheting up of corporate governance and investor relations engagement expectations, justified by the expectation that this will be beneficial not just for shareholders, but for medium- to long-term growth of 'corporate value'. The ratchet was tightened yet again in 2022 with a reorganization of the TSE into Prime, Standard, and Growth sections, with the intention of making the Prime section more attractive to international investors. Historically many companies treated listing on the first section of the TSE as a badge of honour, which once gained could be enjoyed almost indefinitely with little chance of demotion. All were included in the TOPIX index.

The new Prime section, by contrast, would be limited to companies with a market capitalization of more than ¥10 billion that continued to meet performance and disclosure requirements. Market capitalization would be calculated on the basis of *traded* shares, excluding relational or reciprocally owned shares which were a pillar of the postwar system. Prime section companies would need a minimum of one-third external directors, and qualifications for director appointments would have to be published. Procedures for appointing CEOs and board chairs, and holding of annual general meetings, have been gradually tightened, shrinking the scope for management discretion.

For some investors the reorganization did not go far enough, but like the codes, this is an evolving process which nudges companies in a direction of compliance. But will it ultimately deliver 'corporate value' and sustainable capitalism, or simply a more investor friendly environment? To consider this, we first need to consider some related developments.

GPIF, ESG, and Integrated Reporting

We at Government Pension Investment Fund (GPIF) are responsible for providing stable income to multiple generations of retirees, and thus our investment horizon spans several decades. Within such a long timeframe, the latent risks associated with negative externalities generated by individual companies—that is, environmental, social, and governance (ESG) issues—will very likely materialize. This has the potential to significantly impair the value of the assets we invest in. Similarly, since our portfolio includes virtually all investable assets, the sustainability and stable expansion of the market as a whole is critical in protecting and growing the pension reserves entrusted to us by beneficiaries. We work to limit these externalities and promote the holistic growth of the market through ESG investment.[8]

There was a further reason for the government to want companies to improve their ROE. Japan has a 'pay as you go' pension system, meaning that current contributions are used to pay the pensions of retirees. When the population was young, a surplus was built up, which was entrusted to what became the Government Pension Investment Fund (GPIF), sometimes called a 'whale' because of the size of its assets, and for being the largest investor in Japanese stocks (until early 2021, when it was overtaken by the Bank of Japan).[9] The better the returns that could be generated from GPIF's investments, the healthier its reserves, which matters a lot for a rapidly ageing population.

---

[8] https://www.gpif.go.jp/en/investment/esg/gpif_publishes_the_fy2019_esg_report.html (accessed 5 September 2021).

[9] It had ¥197 trillion worth of assets invested in March 2021, including ¥50 trillion in domestic equities. https://www.gpif.go.jp/en/annual_report_summary_2021_en.pdf (accessed 20 July 2022).

Table 6.2 GPIF's changing asset allocation framework

	2001–2015	2015–2020	2020–
Domestic bonds	60	35	25
Foreign bonds	11	15	25
Domestic shares	12	25	25
Foreign shares	12	25	25
Other (short term assets)	5		

Source: GPI, https://www.gpif.go.jp/en/performance/pdf/adoption_of_new_
policy_asset_mix.pdf, https://www.gpif.go.jp/en/topics/
Adoption%20of%20New%20Policy%20Portfolio_En.pdf (both accessed 20 July 2022).
Note: Figures are targets, with +/- ranges, which are not shown here. GPIF was allowed to invest in startups from 2022.

GPIF's asset portfolio framework was changed in 2015, when the domestic bond ratio was reduced to 35 per cent, and the proportion of domestic shares was doubled, to 25 per cent (Table 6.2). This was controversial, as Japanese stock markets were not performing well at the time, and there was an increased element of risk as well. For the sake of Japan's future pensions, increased ROE and long-term growth—increased 'corporate value'—were crucial, as the above quote suggests. GPIF entrusts most of its equity funds to fund managers rather than managing them directly, but as it was increasing its exposure to the domestic stock market performance, it had every reason to be keenly interested in how those managers were fulfilling their stewardship responsibilities. The introduction of the Stewardship Code in 2014 gave it both a mandate and a responsibility to do so.

GPIF and ESG

Coincidentally, GPIF sent shock waves through Japan's investor and management communities in 2015 when it signed up to the UN's Principles for Responsible Investment (PRI). The Stewardship Code *and* ESG signalled a new set of issues to take on board. By way of background, UN Secretary-General Kofi Annan initiated the Global Compact in 2000 in an attempt to align business behaviour with UN principles and objectives. Its ten principles spanned human rights, labour, environment, and anti-corruption. In 2004 Annan wrote to the CEOs of some of the world's leading financial institutions and invited them to take part in this initiative. This resulted in two reports—'Who Cares Wins' and 'Innovative Financing for Sustainability'—which were the origin of 'ESG'.[10] ESG figured prominently in the PRI, launched in 2006.

GPIF established its own Stewardship Principles in 2017. As 90 per cent of its portfolio was held in passive investment accounts, it called for applications for 'engagement-intensive passive managers', and selected two to establish appropriate key performance indicators (KPIs) and milestones. It also called for proposals for ESG indexes and selected three: the FTSE Blossom Japan Index, the MSCI Japan ESG Select Leaders Index, and the MSCI Japan Empowering Women Index. In 2018 it added two S&P Dow Jones Indexes which focused on corporate greenhouse gas emissions (GPIF, 2020). And it began to extend its ESG criteria to fixed income assets, establishing partnerships with the World Bank, other multilateral development banks and government financing agencies to provide opportunities for its asset managers to invest in green, social, and sustainability bonds.

GPIF joined the (US) Thirty Percent Coalition and (UK) Thirty Percent Club—aiming for 30 per cent share of female board members—as an observer in 2016, and the Thirty Percent Japan Investor Group when it was formed in 2019. It joined Climate Action 100+ and aligned with the Task Force on Climate-Related Financial Disclosures (TCFD) in 2018 and the International Corporate Governance Network in 2019. Thus GPIF actively sought to establish a climate for ESG in investment and corporate governance.

GPIF presented this as a win–win scenario for investors. It argued that ESG and returns on investment are positively correlated, and: 'Skeptics that continue to question the growing role of sustainability within the global investment community should realize that they are quickly becoming the minority. With a large majority of research in a meta-analysis of over 2200 studies [Friede et al., 2015] showing a positive relationship between ESG investment and returns—and around 90% showing at least a non-negative effect—they should also be aware that the evidence is not on their side.'[11]

---

[10] The full titles were 'Who Cares Wins: Connecting Financial Markets to a Changing World', and 'Innovative Financing for Sustainability: A Legal Framework for the Integration of Environmental, Social and Governance Issues into Institutional Investment'.
[11] https://www.gpif.go.jp/en/investment/Our_Partnership_for_Sustainable_Capital_Markets.pdf (accessed 5 September 2021).

GPIF Survey

GPIF carries out an annual survey of listed companies. In 2020 one-third of respondents said that investors were now coming to meetings better prepared, almost double the figure of two years previously.[12] Almost half had been approached by activists or engagement funds. Most had responded, with discussions focusing on financial results, management, and business strategies. A majority responded that this was worthwhile.

In terms of ESG, their priorities were:

- Corporate governance, 71 per cent
- Climate change, 54 per cent
- Diversity, 44 per cent
- Human rights and community, 35 per cent.

Almost all of the companies had knowledge of the (UN) Sustainable Development Goals (SDGs) and had taken action or were considering taking action related to them. Three-quarters voluntarily disclosed ESG and other non-financial information, using a variety of guidelines and benchmarks which included Global Standards for Sustainability Reporting (GRI), International Integrated Reporting Framework (IIRC), Guidance for Collaborative Value Creation (METI), and Environmental Reporting Guidelines (Ministry of Environment). Unsurprisingly most said they had reviewed their ESG evaluation methods against the GPIF-supported indexes, and over a third had had dialogue with FTSE, MSCI, and/or S&P over ESG. A fifth said they endorsed the TCFD and 9 per cent disclosed information consistent with it. It appears from surveys such as this that ESG is taking root in the board rooms and management structures of large firms, and also that Japanese managers—and investors—are participating in a global alignment of corporate governance indicators.

Integrated Reports

In fact, Japanese companies appear to have embraced integrated reporting with some enthusiasm; 565 companies produced one in 2020.[13] Investors

---

[12] Respondents were weighted towards large firms, representing two-thirds of total market capitalization (GPIF, 2020b).

[13] An integrated report is 'a concise communication about how an organization's strategy, governance, performance and prospects, in the context of its external environment, lead to the creation of value in the short, medium and long term' (IIRC, 2013: 7).

were not convinced, however, seeing the reports as long, and long on sto-
ries but short on 'materiality'.[14] They complained that the link with company
value, risk, and corporate strategy is missing, and that many reports are so
vague that is difficult to know what company they come from (WBCSD,
2019). Similarly, Eccles et al.'s (2019: 41) comparative analysis of integrated
reports concluded that: 'While the growth in Japan has been rapid and the
number of integrated reports is high, the overall quality is low.'

Reporting aligned with the TCFD is similarly patchy, although it is becoming a requirement for Prime listing (as are diversity targets for women,
mid-career and non-Japanese hires). TCFD was established in 2015 at the
request of the G20, and published guidelines for voluntary disclosure in 2017.
A Japanese TCFD Consortium was formed, and an annual TCFD summit
has been held since 2019. Japan reported the highest number of companies
supporting the TFCD in 2020 (334), rising to 527 in 2022, but KPMG found
that when it came to reporting 'the most urgently needed information is often
the most lacking'.[15] Preferring exhortation over punishment, GPIF launched
Excellent Integrated Reports and Excellent TCFD Disclosure awards.[16]

In sum, companies are being pressed by investors for more concrete information. Larger companies have more resources to allocate to this process,
and are further along the learning curve, but some companies are yet to be
convinced of the benefits of dialogue with investors. As dialogue develops,
they are expected to open sensitive information to people who may not be
entirely on their side. A good example is how company presidents are chosen,
which tends to score very low in the disclosure and investor satisfaction ratings. Should they really let investors take part in this process, which disclosure
implies?

A Reflection on Toshiba

Schaede (2020) argues that Japan maintains 'balanced capitalism' in the face
of substantial change because of its 'tight culture', strong norms as to what
is right behaviour, and ostracism for those who flout those norms. Soft law
fits well with this tight culture, enabling modification through nudging and

---

[14] Information is material 'if omitting, misstating or obscuring it could reasonably be expected to influence the decisions that the primary users of general purpose financial statements make on the basis of
those financial statements.... The materiality of narrative information should be judged based on whether
or not it is material to investors' decisions' (JPX/TSE, 2020: 3).

[15] https://www.ftserussell.com/blogs/incentivizing-japans-net-zero-vanguard-enterprises   (accessed
20 July 2022). KPMG 2022: 37.

[16] Seventy-seven companies received the former, and 27 domestic companies and 34 non-Japanese
companies were awarded the latter in 2022: GPIF, 2022.

shaming. Instead of changing Japanese capitalism, she charts how private equity (PE) funds themselves have changed in order to successfully operate in Japan.[17] In the 2000s Japanese CEOs viewed them as 'predatory vultures and a noxious outgrowth of Wall Street greed' (p. 139). By the 2010s, however, the funds had changed, and CEOs came to see some of them at least as partners for restructuring.

> The takeaway is that Japan has developed its own culture and norms of appropriate behaviour for these market transactions, and through a variety of mechanisms, including exclusion, is nudging participants into assuming more long-term, value-creating strategies. Selling highly valuable assets means parting with businesses that are near and dear ... trust is a precondition, to assure that their business units end up well. Through this insistence, slowly but surely, Japanese companies have developed a new set of rules, and even hard-core Wall Street players are abiding by them.
>
> **(Schaede, 2020: 140)**

Schaede cites the battle to buy Toshiba's NAND flash memory business in 2017. Western Digital believed it had the inside track by virtue of its existing joint venture with Toshiba but its CEO 'alienated Toshiba executives by repeatedly violating all of Japan's business norms' (p. 149). Bain Capital entered the fray with a group of foreign investors, and a deal was struck in which Toshiba and Hoya together kept a majority of the voting stock in the new company Toshiba Memory Corporation. The deal was about price, but also etiquette, long-term value creation, and dignity.

Share buybacks might also work differently in Japan. De-regulated in the early 1980s, they have been widely used in the US to drive up stock prices, and to boost executive compensation.[18] They were legalized in Japan in 1994, and in 2022 the amount spent on them was ¥8.5 trillion—almost half as much as dividends.[19] Together with the statistics in the introduction of this chapter, this suggests a significant tilt towards shareholder primacy, which is why, for example, Hara (2017) calls for restrictions to be placed on them. However, Miyajima and Ogawa (2022) argue that share buybacks

---

[17] Altura et al. (2021), too, showed how Airbnb and Uber had to change their practices substantially to establish themselves in Japan.

[18] Lazonick (2014: 4) provides a startling statistic: the 449 companies in the (US) S&P500 Index which were publicly listed from 2003 to 2012 spent 54 per cent of their earnings on share buybacks, and a further 37 per cent on dividends. More recent figures put the combined ratio at almost 100 per cent! *Nikkei Asia*, 8 June 2023 ('Japan Inc. Annual Dividends at Record Levels Again').

[19] Sumitomo Mitsui DS Asset Management Market Daily figures 5 July 2022 (in Japanese). https://www.smd-am.co.jp/market/daily/marketreport/2022/07/news220705jp/ accessed 19 July 2022.

in Japan have often been triggered by restructuring companies, especially banks, wishing to sell relational shares. Companies which issued those shares have acquired them off the open market and retained 60 per cent as treasury stocks, using some to raise new funds later, some to forge alliances or for M&A, and some to allocate to third parties, including managers and employee shareholding associations. Share buybacks in Japan, they insist, have not been contrary to the aims of 'new capitalism', but broadly in line with them.

This is debatable. The continued surge of both dividends and buybacks in 2023—expected to continue in 2024—appears to be driven more by the TSE's new requirement that listed companies with a price-to-book (P/B) ratio of less than 1 disclose and implement measures to raise it. Following ROE 8 per cent, P/B ratio >1 has become the new FSA/TSE rallying call, which for many companies means opening up their internal reserves.[20]

This points to another reality, which subsequent drama at Toshiba illustrates. When an accounting scandal and its Westinghouse debacle forced Toshiba to sell off some of its crown jewels and to raise fresh capital in 2017, the door was opened to shareholders who were hostile to the incumbent management team, and willing to act on it. Toshiba was one of the first companies to adopt the company with committees system in 2003, which was supposed to loosen insider control and improve corporate governance. Now the independent directors not only opposed incumbent management, but in 2020 commissioned an investigation into collusion between them and METI over reappointment of Toshiba's officers. Toshiba's management sought respite by entering into discussions with PE group CVC Capital Partners to take the company private, which was ill-considered given that its new CEO had once headed CVC's Japanese operations. The subsequent plan to break the company up was also voted down, and in December 2023 the company was due to be delisted following a successful tender offer from a consortium led by Japan Industrial Partners.

As in the mid 2000s, activist investors appeared to be pitted against Japan Inc. Drawing substantial funds from outside Japan, Singapore-based Effissimo Capital Management and 3D Investment Partners had become Toshiba's first and second shareholders respectively. Effissimo was started by two former Murakami Fund managers in 2006. In an effort to distance themselves from Murakami, Kousaka and Imai had adopted a low profile, insisting that their investments were made with a 5–10 year horizon, although

---

[20] *Nikkei Asia*, 8 June 2023 ('Japan Inc. Annual Dividends at Record Levels Again').

Effissimo had led a vote against the appointment of Kawasaki Kisen's CEO in 2017, a major shipping company in which it had built a 37 per cent stake. The Toshiba case has been dramatic but is not isolated. Shareholder proposals have risen, to 292 in 2022 and 314 at the end of May in 2023, and institutional investors are increasingly willing to back them.[21]

Frontier of Control, or Necessary Tension?

A century ago, Goodrich (1920) documented the contested and shifting frontiers of control between workers and managers in British mines and factory shop floors. The study was set against a background of a growing labour movement, which was growing increasingly radical. *The Frontier of Control* inspired many workplace studies of industrial relations, creating a 'pluralist' tradition which held that worker and manager interests are in essence different. At the same time in Japan—1919—Japan's Home Ministry and business leaders including Shibusawa Eiichi established the Kyōchōkai (Industrial Harmony Association) which insisted on a 'unitary' stance of shared capital and labour interests to ward off the growing labour movement, but also to force both capital and labour to serve the higher goals of the nation (Kinzley, 1991). A century later, the 'frontier of control' has shifted to investor relations against a background of rising shareholder capitalism. The Stewardship Code and Corporate Governance Code, and the GPIF, seemingly adopt a unitary position, but Toshiba calls this into question, testing as it does unitary assumptions.

Will shareholder returns empty the internal reserves that companies have built up? We saw in Chapter 3 that companies are also increasing capital spending, and many also intend to increase their spending on human resources, in the form of both wages and training (Chapter 7). Just how this three-way tug will be apportioned over the medium term remains to be seen, but it does appear that the trend towards building up internal reserves at least may be going into reverse, and the P/B requirement is a factor in this. If so, and critically, can investor relations provide the spark for sustained private sector capital expenditure in DX and GX needed to usher in Japan's new economy, as asserted by the Corporate Governance and Stewardship Codes? With the postwar tension gone from industrial relations, and the main bank system eviscerated (many companies switched to loan-free management in the early

---

[21] *Nikkei Asia*, 3 June 2023 ('Record Number of Japanese Companies Face Shareholder Proposals'). The proposals in 2023 were directed at 82 companies.

2000s, and reciprocally held shares were sold off),[22] will investors force managers to react more proactively to the challenges they face, and to fulfil the multiplying roles expected of them? How will this now crucial institutional nexus evolve?

Worryingly, there is little convincing evidence that shareholder-favouring policies and shareholder primacy bring about greater investment in innovation (O'Sullivan, 2000; Belloc, 2013). Leading Japanese companies like Toyota and Canon have also questioned the link (Jacoby, 2005). Given the need for innovation directed towards solving social and sustainability issues envisaged by Japanese STI policy and Society 5.0 in particular, tilting the balance of corporate governance towards investor relations is a big bet on Japanese exceptionalism and the countervailing strength of Japan's stakeholder and communitarian norms. METI seems to be making the same bet in releasing Fair M&A Guidelines in 2023 to sit alongside the Cybersecurity, DX, and other guidelines (Figure 6.1), placing the onus on boards to consider 'equitably' proposals brought by engagement (and presumably activist) funds.

Society 5.0 and 'New Capitalism'

Society 5.0, DX, GX, ESG, SDGs, new capitalism ... point towards the possibility of a new institutional configuration, albeit one submerged under a proliferation of change initiatives which risks confusion. In this section we will first try to bring some order to this proliferation, as participants themselves see it. We will then outline Keidanren's 'sustainable capitalism' and Kishida's 'new capitalism', and why they have been added to the new economy agenda.

First, some conceptual organization. Keidanren and GPIF, with the Institute of Future Initiatives at Tokyo University, produced a report in 2020 titled 'The Evolution of ESG Investment, Realization of Society 5.0 and Achievement of SDGs'. Given their shared UN origin, it is not surprising to find ESG and SDGs placed together, with ESG at the company level and SDGs at the societal level. But a Keidanren survey found that this lacked a transformative spark, and that 'ESG investment contributing to Society 5.0 for SDGs' resonated more with investors and managers, and would encourage them to focus on the future, and future economic opportunities (Figure 6.2).

---

[22] Note, however, that Japanese companies still relied on loans from financial institutions for 25.8 per cent of their finance in 2020 versus 6.8 per cent in the US: Kurosawa, 2020: 6.

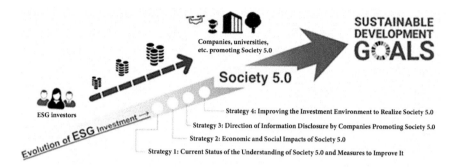

Figure 6.2 Linking ESG, Society 5.0, and SDGs
Source: Keidanren, University of Tokyo and GPIF, 2020: 3.

The economic case for this alignment, which informed the strategies listed in Figure 6.2, came from a related report commissioned by Keidanren called 'Society 5.0 for SDGs: An Economic Analysis of Future Created', which quantitatively assessed two scenarios for 2030 against a 2015 benchmark; business as usual, and the individual and combined impacts of investing in 57 emerging technologies critical for Society 5.0 (Nomura, 2020). In the business as usual case, Japan's nominal GDP would grow from ¥531 trillion to ¥650 trillion, but in the case of Society 5.0 it would grow to ¥900 trillion, with nominal and real GDP growth rates of 3.5 and 2.6 per cent respectively. For this to happen, a cumulative investment of at least ¥844 trillion would be needed—much more than the GX Plan envisaged—but incomes would expand, and household consumption would increase by 2.2 per cent per year rather than 0.7 per cent. Government share of final demand would fall from 20 per cent to 14 per cent, the productivity gap with the US would be substantially reduced, and the GDP share of advanced sectors of the economy like research would increase (Nomura, 2020).

Growth sectors identified by the report included next generation healthcare (¥36 trillion contribution), digitalization of manufacturing (¥29 trillion), smart mobility (¥21 trillion), smart living (domestic robots, teleworking, etc. ¥19 trillion), and next generation energy (¥19 trillion), as well as cross-sectoral technologies and services such as AI (¥153 trillion), IoT (¥86 trillion), and 5G (¥87 trillion). In sum, the joint report declared: 'If ESG investment and Society 5.0, which have common features, are combined, the problem-solving innovation ecosystem will evolve autonomously, Society 5.0 will be realized, and SDGs will be truly achieved' (p. 14). Very clearly, then, these initiatives were conceived as part of a growth model, which should be promoted abroad as well, the report added.

Sustainable Capitalism

At the same time, in the context of growing criticism of the excesses of financialized, shareholder capitalism abroad, and fresh concerns in Japan, Keidanren issued a statement on the future of Japanese capitalism.[23] This proclaimed that it would re-invent Japanese capitalism through its 'New Growth Strategy' (2020) and 'Future Vision for 2030' which would 'bring together the wisdom of diverse stakeholders and establish sustainable capitalism with Society 5.0, which creates diverse value through DX'.

> Declaring a basic philosophy of 'sustainable capitalism' as a new form of capitalism, Keidanren proposes a growth strategy that the business community should pursue.... (W)e are resigned to the fact that the extension of our current path of gradual reform offers no future for capitalism, and we intend to take bold steps to embark on this new strategy.[24]

Given disillusionment with shareholder capitalism, Keidanren argued:

> Japan's business community must redefine and reaffirm the traditional business principle of *sanpō-yoshi* (that business should benefit buyer, seller, and society).... We are convinced that the updating of Japanese capitalism and the realization of growth that is sustainable and resilient against various types of risk would make Japan a pioneer in establishing a new vision for capitalism around the world.[25]

In other words, Japan's new growth model should be based on sustainability and a re-assertion of stakeholder principles. Although Japan had a stakeholder model in the postwar period, which was partially emasculated, there was an important nuance in Keidanren's line-up of stakeholders. Corporate 'value co-creation' will be achieved, it claimed, with consumers, employees, local communities, environment, and 'the global community'. Investors are not mentioned, presumably not because they are absentee landlords, as in the postwar model (Clark, 1979), but because they are assumed to be part of the central investor–manager axis. Conversely, employees become simply

---

[23] Criticism from abroad included BlackRock's CEO, who called on companies to have a social purpose, and not just a financial one; the (US) Business Roundtable which called for the recognition of stakeholder interests beyond shareholders; the World Economic Forum which called for stakeholder capitalism as the institutional vehicle for the fourth industrial revolution.... Cf. also Mayer, 2018. Keidanren may also have felt pressure from domestic groups arguing it had not been decisive enough on either DX or GX, such as the Japan Association for the New Economy (JANE) and the Japan Climate Initiative: cf. Katz, 2021b, c.

[24] https://en.kkc.or.jp/international-platform/20,210,618.html (accessed 26 September 2021); https://www.keidanren.or.jp/en/policy/2020/108_proposal.html (accessed 3 September 2021).

[25] Ibid.

one stakeholder among several, on the receiving end of strategic decisions made in board rooms, but not participating in the making or monitoring of them.

'New Capitalism'

Kishida's 'new form of capitalism' resonates strongly with Keidanren's 'sustainable capitalism'. Shortly before becoming Prime Minister, Kishida published a 'vision' book which emphasized growth through S&T-based innovation, a 'digital garden city nation', carbon neutral and economic security. It also emphasized distribution with wage growth, rebuilding the middle class, and better wages and conditions for daycare and nursery workers (Kishida, 2021). Kishida went on to propose 'new capitalism', which implicitly drew upon elements of the postwar model in its original income doubling aspiration (which quickly became *investment* income doubling) harking back to the 1960s policies of then Prime Minister (and head of Kishida's LDP faction) Ikeda Hayato. Departing from supply side orthodoxy and structural reform, he possibly had in mind an updated version of the spring wage offensive (*Shuntō*) which powerfully linked productivity gains, wage increases, and consumption in the 1960s, but which had become largely moribund by the late 1990s.[26]

Another source of influence was said to be Hara Joji (George), Japanese national, Silicon Valley entrepreneur and venture capitalist, and advisor to the Japanese government in various capacities. Hara published a book called *Atarashii shihonshugi* (New Capitalism, 2009) in the aftermath of the Global Financial Crisis, which was highly critical of US financialized capitalism and urged Japan to build on its strengths, provide tax incentives for innovation, and rediscover social purpose. His 'public interest capitalism' advocates concrete measures including restrictions on share buybacks and on decision-making rights of short-term shareholders, class shares (like Toyota's AA shares), and abolishing quarterly reporting requirements.[27]

In a speech in London, Kishida outlined four priorities for his 'new capitalism': people; science, technology, and innovation (STI); startups; and DX and GX; with a particular emphasis on the first—people—in terms of 'flow', or wages and working conditions, and 'stock', or investment in human capital

---

[26] So weak had *Shuntō* become that the Abe government took to cajoling and offering tax incentives to employers to increase wages, a policy which the Kishida administration maintained.

[27] Hara 2009, 2017. Also https://diamond.jp/articles/-/286,154 (accessed 12 June 2022). Toyota has historically been sceptical about corporate governance reform, and Toyoda Akio has commented favourably on public interest capitalism.

formation through vocational education and training (VET) and lifelong learning. This, too, arguably echoed the postwar model, of schools producing providing highly literate and numerate leavers, companies raising their human capital further through on-job training (OJT) and sometimes off-job training and suppressing status and wage differences between blue-collar and white-collar workers. After three decades of neglect: 'The reality is that investment in education and training in the corporate sector in Japan is much lower than in other countries. My government has already introduced a three-year, 400 billion yen package' to support VET and recurrent education, Kishida declared.[28]

We will shortly turn to people, skills, and employment, as well as STI, in Chapter 7. The other emphases—startups, DX, and GX—are an extension of the new economy building efforts we have described in previous chapters. The distinctiveness of 'new capitalism' is less that it is 'new', but first that it appears to recognize the importance of consistent institutional linkages between the micro- and macro-levels of the economy to create a 'virtuous cycle of growth and distribution', and second that like Keidanren's *sanpō-yoshi* (business should benefit buyer, seller, and society), it seeks to return Japanese capitalism to traditional notions of a moral economy; closer also to Shibusawa Eiichi's *gapponshugi*, or bringing capital, labour and management together to serve the public interest. Just over 150 years since he founded the First National Bank, Shibusawa is set to become the new face of the Japanese ¥10,000 note, reminding users of the roots of Japanese capitalism.

Concluding Comments

Pursued over two decades, corporate governance reform has brought important changes to capitalism in Japan, although to those who take shareholder sovereignty for granted—such as the lawyer commissioned by Effissimo who gave a four-minute speech on why shareholder rights must not be infringed at an extraordinary general meeting of Toshiba shareholders in 2020—they have not gone nearly far enough. The Stewardship Code and Corporate Governance Code were the twin drivers of reform in the 2010s, intended to make managers more attentive to investors. Although they did not stipulate shareholder primacy per se—the codes stressed that managers and shareholders should work together to build 'sustainable corporate value' in the mid- to

---

[28] Guildhall speech, London, 5 May 2022.

long-term—they did bring about a very significant rise in shareholder returns (Table 6.1).

Into this context ESG was introduced, forcefully by GPIF, raising new questions, but also consolidating the centrality of corporate governance at the company level (Figure 6.1). *Corporate governance and investor relations have become the central institutional nexus of Japanese capitalism at the company level,* and employment and industrial relations have been correspondingly downgraded. This nexus is a nexus of tension, despite efforts by GPIF and others to present it in unitary terms. The tension appears within the Japanese government itself, with the FSA pursuing an investor-centric logic, and METI an industry-centric one.

Without disturbing this axis (so far), both Keidanren and the Kishida administration have joined the backlash against shareholder sovereignty and financialized capitalism and re-asserted a stakeholder vision for Japan's new economy. This is necessary, they argue, to create a virtuous cycle of growth and distribution, without which growth itself will break down. They have good reasons for doing so, which are rooted in the sustainability of Japanese society itself, as we shall shortly see.

Ultimately Japanese companies and the Japanese government may be successful at harnessing the tensions around corporate governance and stake-holder capitalism to create a new form of public interest capitalism, much like they resolved the postwar tensions in employment relations to produce a potent form of producer stakeholder capitalism. Perhaps ESG can help them to do so, becoming an aid to transformation rather than a reporting chore. ESG does raise a number of difficult questions. (Just how aggressively should companies pursue each of E, S, and G? How should companies respond when one set of shareholders demands prioritization of shareholder returns, and another more forceful pursuit of GX? Toyota has been a notable target of the latter.)[29] But as the Keidanren-GPIF-U-Tokyo report suggests, it might also accelerate the transformation of Japan's economy, towards the SDGs.

ESG and green funds and investment are rising rapidly in Japan. Tokyo is modifying its pitch and is now seeking to become a global *green* financial centre. Between 2017 and 2020 private sector ESG funds in Japan increased six-fold to ¥30 trillion, or 10 per cent of the global total (FSA, 2021: 11). Green bonds issued by Japanese companies increased four and

---

[29] Some CEOs who have pursued sustainability too enthusiastically—like Emmanuel Faber of the French giant Danone—have been forced out by investors who believe they should be focusing on delivering returns to shareholders. BlackRock's own former head of sustainable investment created a stir in 2021 when he declared ESG investment a 'dangerous placebo'.

a half times, and almost doubled in 2021 alone, to ¥1.9 trillion, while sustainability bonds increased five and a half times, and topped ¥1 trillion in 2021. Sustainability-linked loans, too, increased fivefold from 2020 to 2021, reaching ¥357 billion.[30] Hardly a day goes by without a new major green investment being announced in the business press. This does not appear to be a case of business as usual masquerading as green; when it comes to investment in general, and especially ESG and green investment, Japanese companies appear to be responding positively. How much of this may be attributed to investor stewardship and the 'G' of ESG is impossible to say, however.

---

[30] Ministry of Environment: http://greenfinanceportal.env.go.jp/en/bond/issuance_data/market_status.html
http://greenfinanceportal.env.go.jp/en/loan/sll_issuance_data/sll_market_status.html (both accessed 19 July 2022).

7

People, Skills, and Employment

'People' are at the heart of the new economy, and increasingly at the heart of deliberations about how to build it. Consider the following:

> Investment in human capital is at the heart of the growth strategy of the Kishida Administration. In the new era, intangible assets such as human capital, intellectual property and innovation will become more important than tangible goods.... We must produce maximum value with a shrinking pool of workers. We need to expand investment in people.[1]

A 'broad middle class' (*buatsui chūkansō*) will support the realization of 'sustainable capitalism' and play a central role in the economy and society. The formation of a broad middle class will help solve the problem of inequality and will create more demand and stimulate economic activity. In other words, the 'virtuous cycle of growth and distribution' can also be described as a 'virtuous cycle of sustained economic growth and the formation of a broad middle class'.[2]

> We have moved from an era in which 'careers are given by the company' to one in which 'each individual chooses his or her own career'. We must shift to a system that allows workers to re-skill and choose their jobs by clarifying the skills required for each job. This will open the door to hiring experienced workers from outside the company, seamlessly link the internal and external labour markets, and allow workers to move of their own choice, helping Japanese companies and the Japanese economy to grow more rapidly.[3]

The Prime Minister's speech acknowledged that the Japanese government had underinvested in human resources in recent decades, and that the

---

[1] PM Kishida, London Guildhall speech, 5 May 2022.

[2] Keidanren (2023), 'Sasuteinaburu shihonshugi ni muketa kōjunkan no jitsugen: Buatsui chūkansō no keisei ni muketa kentō kaigi hōkoku' (Achieving a Virtuous Cycle Towards Sustainable Capitalism: Report of the Deliberation Group on Building a Broad Middle Class), Tokyo.

[3] Atarashii shihonshugi jitsugen kaigi ed. (2023) 'Dai 18kai: Sanmiittai rōdō shijō kaikaku no ronten'an' (New Form of Capitalism Realization Council, Meeting No.16: Draft of Issues in Trinity Labour Market Reforms), Tokyo.

Building a New Economy. D. Hugh Whittaker, Oxford University Press. © D. Hugh Whittaker (2024).
DOI: 10.1093/oso/9780198893394.003.0008

declining labour share of GDP had acted as a drag on the economy. Further-more, signalling that he has not given up on 'distribution', at a special meeting of the government's Council on Economic and Fiscal Policy in May 2023, he asserted: 'We will distribute corporate profits to workers in order to restore a large middle class', and suggested that the government and Bank of Japan should work together to raise wages and expunge the threat of deflation. Kei-danren concurred. Its 'Rebuilding the middle class' report opened with the reflection that 'excessive focus on shareholder capitalism and market funda-mentalism had created various social problems, such as environmental and ecosystem destruction, and the expansion and reproduction of inequality'. Building Japan's new economy means rebuilding the threatened middle class, it continued. Both Kishida and Keidanren agreed that this goes far beyond above-inflation wage increases—which they both support—and requires a fundamental reshaping of labour and associated policies.

Two weeks earlier, the New Form of Capitalism Realization Council had complied a package of policy proposals dubbed the 'new trinity labour mar-ket reforms'.[4] The underlying assessment was that wage and productivity growth in Japan have been hampered by a lack of job mobility, causing peo-ple to be stuck in the wrong jobs, or out of jobs, and the problem was likely to get worse with DX and GX. People were unlikely to change jobs if their wages fell, which typically happens with wage systems which reward length of service (or 'membership-based employment') rather than skills. And they would also be unlikely to take the plunge without a safety net, and oppor-tunities to gain the skills which might be rewarded in growing areas of the economy? Hence the inter-connected 'trinity' of labour mobility, job-based employment, and reskilling.

The trinity touch on many other institutions, such as pensions, employ-ment protection, employment adjustment subsidies, unemployment benefits, vocational education, and training—in other words, the whole edifice of the postwar employment system which was premised on employment security and welfare delivered through companies (Miura, 2012). Modifying these also presents a serious challenge to enterprise unions. If implemented then, the new trinity reforms would constitute a fundamental break with post-war 'Japanese-style employment'. Conceptually they would take Japan in the direction of European flexicurity, and the 'social investment state', which would require higher levels of taxation. But is such a break plausible, and if it is only partial, what might the eventual outcome be? It is too early to

---

[4] The original 'trinity' reforms, as noted in Chapter 4, were Koizumi's neoliberal decentralization measures of the early 2000s.

answer this last question, but we can at least assess recent developments, and whether the would-be reforms are likely to gain traction, which will require buy-in from a wide range of social actors.

The first section of this chapter addresses the changing supply and demand for labour, including attempts to increase the labour supply through women, elderly, and foreign workers, each presenting challenges to existing employment practices. It also assesses the growing role of employment and dispatching agencies, which have begun to play a role in re-shaping labour markets, increasing fluidity and, it is hoped, improving human resource allocation. The second section looks at attempts to chip away at the rigidities of postwar 'Japanese-style employment', first through Abe's work-style reform package, then the more fundamental attack of the 'new trinity' labour market reforms under the slogan 'from membership-based to job-based employment'. This is deemed necessary to secure human resources and improve productivity, as well as to address the challenges of diversity, changing values and social sustainability. Changing employment practices, then, are part of a wider debate about the social division of labour, and by implication, the nature of Society 5.0.

The third section briefly considers the boost to teleworking from the Covid-19 pandemic, as well as the limitations to such work which the pandemic exposed, giving impetus to work-style reform and job-based employment. The final section concerns the re-discovery of 'investment in people' which stagnated from the 1990s, and 'rebuilding the middle class'. Investing in people is necessary for rebuilding the middle class, but it comes with a bill, as does revamping the social security system. After considering Keidanren's report, we will look at government investments in reskilling, and in upgrading Japan's education system for Society 5.0, returning the discussion to DX, GX, and innovation.

Supply and Demand for Workers in a Changing Landscape of Work

Japan's greatest asset—its people—has turned into its greatest challenge. The youthful and inexpensive labour of the high growth era, equipped with solid literacy and numeracy skills and receptive to further in-house training, was a potent force for high productivity growth. Now Japan's labour force is ageing, there are not enough people to fill the jobs available, there is a skills mismatch, and human resources are wasted. Challenges, however, can bring forth innovation, and this may be the case when it comes to human resources.

The ups and downs in the supply and demand of labour can be seen in the ratio of job openings to job seekers (Figure 7.1). From the highs of 1.43 jobs for every job seeker in the 'bubble' years, it fell to two seekers for every job in the 'recruitment ice age' of the late 1990s, rose again in the 2000s, plunged after the Global Financial Crisis, and then began a relentless climb. Even the Covid-19-induced layoffs did not bring the ratio back below 1.0. There is thus an obvious numerical shortfall, which with an ageing and shrinking population is destined to intensify, and three possible (human) sources of relief—females, the elderly, and especially foreigners. Each brings a substantial set of challenges to the postwar employment system, and to social relations, which we consider in the first part of this section.

While these supply challenges have captured headlines, the trinity reform formula highlights the *allocation* of human resources, especially of middle-aged workers who have skills that are not optimally deployed or who are in need of reskilling. The second part of this section looks at the growth of intermediary agencies which have been laying the foundations for increasing labour market fluidity, and have the potential to shrink the skills gap and mismatch. It is difficult to imagine a shift from 'membership-based' (lifetime) employment to 'job-based' employment without them.

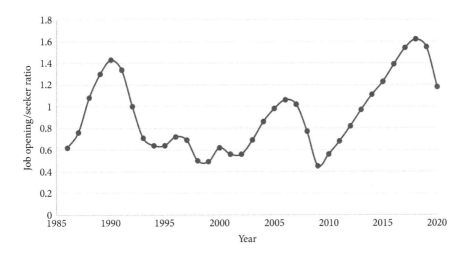

Figure 7.1 Ratio of job openings to job seekers, 1986–2020

Source: Adapted from Ten-navi.com; originally MHLW, https://ten-navi.com/hacks/article-280-25,516 (accessed 7 May 2022).

Foreigners, Females, and Elderly Workers

Who Will Supply Japan's Labour Force: Foreigners, or AI/Robots? asked Terada et al. (2017). The concern about AI in Japan is less to do with labour displacement than its augmentation. Can Japan address its labour shortage in areas like healthcare through robots, the book asked, or will it need to rely on care workers from Southeast Asia? While officially maintaining an anti-immigration stance, the Japanese government has been forced to open the country wider to foreign workers, whose numbers quadrupled between 2007 and 2017 to 1.3 million, and rose further to 1.7 million in late 2021.[5] Some 350,000 were enrolled in government-approved (on-job) trainee programmes, and another 330,000 were part timers, mainly foreign students. The majority had come from China, Vietnam, and the Philippines.

Yet this is just a drop in the bucket for Japan's needs. A Japan International Cooperation Agency (JICA) report in 2022 estimated that Japan would have to quadruple the number of foreign workers by 2040 to 6.7 million, but may have trouble recruiting them from Southeast Asian countries, whose own populations would be beginning to age and decline, forcing Japan to look as far afield as Africa, with its still youthful population.[6] The hole in Japan's labour force is not limited to lower-skilled workers moreover. Increasingly companies have looked abroad for engineers and other professionals, as well as entrepreneurs. In doing so, they are meeting competition from their counterparts in other countries who are less reticent to offer attractive packages for the right skills. New measures in 2023 to simplify the visa application process for 'highly skilled professionals' and to extend the stay of graduates of elite (mainly Western) universities, and opening the 'specified skilled worker' category to longer stays and to family members in 2024, were widely seen as inadequate and ineffective.

The intensifying competition for 'highly skilled professionals' is one factor in forcing Japanese companies to reconsider their remuneration and employment packages, and work environment, which we will consider in the second section. Such workers have difficulty accepting the relatively meagre wages, exacerbated by the declining value of the yen in 2022, and often menial tasks assigned to new recruits. At the other end of the skill spectrum, many trainees abandon their designated employer in search of better conditions. In fact the current trainee programme will be scrapped. Attracting foreign workers long-term has implications for housing, education of children, pensions,

---

[5] Keizai Koho Centre, 2018: 40–41; *Nikkei Asia*, 3 February 2022 ('Japan to Require Four Times More Foreign Workers, Study Says').
[6] https://www.jica.go.jp/jica-ri/news/topics/20220203_02.html (accessed 22 June 2023).

voting rights … which civil society organizations say need reform if Japan is to become truly welcoming of non-Japanese workers. The social implications are far-reaching.

They are far-reaching when it comes to women as well. Women make up over half of the population, but have been subject institutionally and attitudinally to a highly gendered social division of labour. This persisted and mutated after the passage of the Equal Employment Opportunity Law in 1986. As Emmott (2020) points out in *Japan's Far More Female Future*, in 1985 just over 10 per cent of women were enrolled in four-year university courses; by the late 2010s the figure had risen to over 50 per cent. Almost half of those enrolled in universities are women, although women are considerably under-represented in STEM (science, technology, engineering, mathematics) subjects, especially engineering. The labour force participation rate for women aged 15–64 has risen continuously as well; in the 2010s it rose from roughly 60 per cent to over 71 per cent, which is above the OECD average. In 1975 only 43 per cent of women aged 25–29 were part of the labour force; by 2021 this had reached almost 80 per cent. The proportion of dual-income households has risen to double that of single-income households.[7]

Women may not be a vast untapped resource in quantitative terms, but qualitatively they are. Much of the recent rise in womens' labour market participation has been in part-time and other 'non-regular' work. Up until the mid 1980s the vast majority of women were 'regular' employees, but by 2002 the figure had dropped to 51 per cent, and by 2012, to 43 per cent, before rising slightly to 46 per cent in 2020.[8] (The corresponding figures for men were 93, 85, 78, and 79 per cent.) Even those in regular employment are often put on a separate, clerical track, with limited prospects for advancement. As Macnaughton (2015: 14–15) put it: 'Since the late 1980s, the more Japanese policy seems to strive toward gender equality, the more employers' implementation of policy has served to differentiate the management of male and female employees, even widening the gap between the sexes.'

As a result, the gender wage gap is large by any measure. It is reinforced by the tax system, which is still premised on a male breadwinner model, by imbalances in household duties, and by the caring responsibilities of women

---

[7] JILPT, 2017; https://www.gender.go.jp/about_danjo/whitepaper/r04/zentai/html/zuhyo/zuhyo02-02.html (accessed 13 May 2023).

[8] https://www.gender.go.jp/about_danjo/whitepaper/r03/zentai/html/honpen/b1_s02_01.html (accessed 22 June 2023). From 1986 to 1996, 93 per cent of the growth in women's employment was in part time jobs (Dalton, 2017: 99).

which have come to include elderly parents. The birthrate has declined more or less continuously since 1973, to 1.26 in 2022. Without changes to working practices, it might decline even further, especially if more women stay in the labour force on a full-time basis. Needless to say, this has serious implications for social sustainability. So to the extent that he was serious when he announced in 2013 that Japan must create a 'society in which all women shine', then PM Abe was proposing far-reaching change. His 'womenomics' included a package of work-style reform measures, which we will look at in the second section, while Kishida has grasped the baton with the launch of a Children and Families Agency, and a range of childbirth and childrearing support measures (many of them financial), in 2023. In sum, there remains a yawning gap between what women currently contribute (excluding unpaid labour) and what they *could* contribute to building Japan's new economy and closing that gap itself requires social transformation.

Despite a declining working age population, Japan's labour force continued to expand, at least until 2020. This was not just due to an increase of foreign workers and women, but of older workers as well. In 2021 29.1 per cent of the population was aged 65 or over, the highest proportion of any country. Instead of retiring, an increasing proportion has continued working; between 2011 and 2021 the proportion of 60–64 year olds (both men and women) who were working rose from 57 per cent to 72 per cent, and 65–69 year olds from 36 per cent to 50 per cent.[9] The government is raising the basic pensionable age towards 65, and has pushed employers to provide employment until age 65, but longevity with health, meagre pensions, and economic hardship, as well as labour shortages on the part of companies, have contributed to the trend. Companies generally responded by keeping their mandatory retirement age at 60 and re-hiring employees reaching that age on new contracts with less pay. In fact, most over-60s are employed on a part time basis. Skills accumulated over their careers are often poorly used (Jones and Seitani, 2019). As with non-Japanese and female workers, there is much scope for improvement, not least in skills matching, which we will now consider.

Matching People and Jobs

The term 'labour market' is something of a misnomer when it comes to Japan, at least for core, regular workers. Hired straight out of school or university, their careers have been 'given by the company' (in the words of the

---

[9] https://www.stat.go.jp/data/topics/topi1322.html (accessed 22 June 2023).

quote at the beginning of this chapter) through internal allocation. Indeed, school-to-work transition in the postwar period was also managed through extra-market placement, such as school recommendations to employers. The system began to break down in the 1990s but was not replaced by the invisible hand of the market.

There is a visible hand, which has grown larger since the 1990s, namely employment agencies, whose flag bearer is Recruit. Founded in 1960, the company's first product was a job-hunting magazine for university students. Recruit did not just grow *with* the market for placements, but it helped to *create* the market through its magazines and subsequently online media. With the admonition to 'follow your heart' it also became famous for in-house start-ups and spin-outs. And it became a global company through acquisitions such as Indeed Inc. (2012) and Glassdoor (2018). As Table 5.1 shows, it was ranked 11th in TSE market capitalization in 2020.

Recruit and other large employment agencies have accumulated a wealth of labour market data, and are able to offer increasingly sophisticated services in addition to two-sided placement platforms. They have expanded into personnel and HRM consulting, including matters which would formerly have been considered part of the internal labour market, such as remuneration. This has led to some blurring of the divide between external and internal labour markets (Zou, 2023). Agencies reported a doubling of placements for those aged 40+ between 2015 and 2020, with one agency specializing in the placement of older workers reporting a 2.7-fold increase in registrations between 2019 and 2021 alone.[10]

Specialized employment and dispatching agencies have played an important role in the mobility of professionals, such as TechnoPro for IT engineers. Studies by Nakata and colleagues (2011, 2018) highlighted a growing trend for engineers, especially IT engineers, to change jobs as a result of dissatisfaction with long working hours, poor pay, and other conditions. Comprehensive and specialized employment agencies together helped to prepare the ground for the trinity labour market reforms, and the movement towards 'job-based' employment.

Dismantling Japanese-style Employment

The need to secure an adequate supply of labour has opened a Pandora's box of social issues. Conversely, the social and demographic issues cannot be addressed without changes to employment and employment policy. What

---

[10] *Nikkei Asia*, 24 April 2022 ('Middle-aged Job-Hopping Booms in Japan').

started as an attempt to make 'Japanese-style' employment more flexible, and suited to a new era, has in rhetoric at least turned into an attempt to dismantle it.

Work-style Reform

From promoting labour market flexibilization and corporate restructuring, labour market, and employment policy began to change after 2006, and more forcefully after 2012 under the second Abe administration. Vogel captures the changes succinctly:

> [Policy] was more interested in improving working conditions than in helping firms to cut costs, because this would help increase the workforce and raise productivity. It was more interested in raising the status of women and nonregular workers than in giving employers more flexibility in hiring nonregular workers, because this would make it easier for women to combine work and childrearing. And it was more interested in raising wages than in suppressing them, because this could lift consumer demand.
>
> **(Vogel, 2018: 262–263)**

Vogel also notes the growing involvement of the Cabinet Office. Abe's 'dynamic society of 100 million people' in which 'all women can shine' envisaged changes to work practices and work-life balance, including improved childcare, uptake of parental leave (and regular holiday entitlement), and tackling the yawning gap in wages and conditions between regular and nonregular workers, which persisted despite a tightening labour market. The Council for the Realization of Work Style Reform which considered these matters submitted its report in 2017, and legislation was passed in the 2018 'Work Style Reform Diet'.

This had three main parts, all of them contentious. The first was overtime, which was restricted in principle to 45 hours per month, but allowed up to 100 hours a month in exceptional circumstances and 720 hours per year. The second addressed equal pay for equal work for regular and nonregular workers, banning inequality except where differences can be justified as 'reasonable'. The third concerned overtime exemption for 'high-level' professionals earning over 10.75 million yen (then just under US$100,000) per year, but at the same time stipulating four days' holiday every four weeks and at least 104 days' annual leave.

Optimists argued the legislation would force employers to restrict over-time and improve conditions for women, while simultaneously improving productivity. Others insisted that it would perversely increase unreported overtime, and encourage employers to dilute conditions for regular workers, as Japan Post Holdings had done in 2018. The 'reasonable' clause for equal-pay-for-equal-work was a let-off for employers, enabling them to avoid making fundamental changes to remuneration systems, and would not shrink pay differentials. Exemptions would open a new front for exploitation rather than productivity enhancement. All in all, any changes were going to be incremental, driven by the modification of norms rather than the immediate effects of legislation, and unlikely to bring about a radical shift to Society 5.0.

Job-Based Employment

At around the same time, Keidanren began to promote the idea of 'job-based' employment for Society 5.0, in contradistinction to 'membership-based' postwar 'Japanese-style employment'.[11] Keidanren's chairman was an enthusiastic advocate, and his vision was probably an extension of the transformation of employment relations which he had seen, and overseen, at Hitachi.[12] Globalization, increasing diversity, a shift from products to solutions business, and rapid technological change had pushed the company towards 'job-based' employment, in which all work was classified into roughly 70 'jobs' at 6–7 levels. Workers are recruited externally or internally to these, and compensation is based on duties and job scope. The transition took two decades.

It may sound trite, but there is a chasm between job-based and membership-based employment in Japan, at least conceptually. (In practice, the careers of employees under membership-based employment are already 'job-based' in a broad sense: Nakata, 2023.) In terms of compensation, this echoes an old distinction, which took the form of whether to base the pay system on ability (*shokunō*) or job duties (*shokumu*) in the 1960s, with Nikkeiren (later merged with Keidanren) coming down on the side of

---

[11] Cf Nakamura, 2020. The terms 'job-based' and 'membership-based' employment came from Ham-aguchi, 2009.

[12] Chapter 4; Inagami and Whittaker, 2005. Hitachi's definition of job-based employment is 'a system that assigns personnel to tasks upon defining the duties and job scope and determines the compensation according to the details of the work and status of execution' as opposed to a membership-based system that 'allocates tasks to personnel without defining the scope of duties and determines compensation according to the ability based on the expected contributions as a member of the organization' (in-company presentation material).

shokunō, setting the direction for Japan's postwar 'membership-based' system. In 2019 Keidanren decided that without reversing this system, Japan would remain stuck in Society 4.0. It set about trying to convince members to abandon the annual hiring processes and induction rituals through which 'members' have been collectively recruited and inducted. It was helped by the disruptions caused by the Covid-19 pandemic, when the term 'job-based' employment spread, but the pandemic also showed the distance many companies have to travel for such a transformation, as we shall see.

The 'New Trinity' Labour Market Reforms

The work-style reforms affected the conduct of 'Japanese-style' (membership-based) employment but did not touch its foundations. The campaign for job-based employment began to tinker with them. The New Form of Capitalism Realization Council opened a direct assault at its 16th meeting in April 2023 with a document called Proposal for Trinity Labour Market Reform Issues, which went well beyond labour market institutions, and included supporting institutions which would simultaneously need to be changed. Salient issues included:

1. Reskilling
   Re-design the system in which most of the subsidies for reskilling are paid to companies to one in which the majority is paid to individuals; i.e., direct support. As well, expand the subsidy limit, expand the range of courses recognized for subsidy, allow individuals to receive support even when they don't change jobs, strengthen public and private sector vocational education and training (VET), and increase the number of students studying 'overseas' (including online courses).

2. Job-based wages
   Produce model cases of job-based wages which companies can refer to and adapt according to their own circumstances, while recognizing the importance of performance as well. Encourage companies to visibilize their employment and wage systems. Reform the human capital reporting in company and integrated reports. Work towards shrinking wages for the same job between Japanese and foreign companies.

3. Encourage labour mobility to growth sectors
   Reduce the time needed to obtain unemployment benefit when quitting a job for personal reasons. Increase the tax exemption on lump sum retirement or severance payments. Reconsider whether companies

should reduce severance payment when employees quit for personal reasons. Strengthen public and private sector career consulting and information sharing, noting Denmark's detailed locality and job-type data, which is part of its flexicurity system.

The 'trinity' idea is that all are necessary, and that if one is missing, the other reforms will fail, but the underlying assessment was that wage and productivity growth in Japan have been hampered by a lack of job mobility, and incentives for job mobility, causing people to be stuck in the wrong jobs, or not in jobs. And with DX in particular, there is a drastic shortage of people with the right skills which needs to be addressed quickly.

The labour union confederation Rengo (JTUC) responded that reskilling should be about enhancing the security of workers in jobs, not about promoting mobility. If reskilling is positioned as a means to promote labour mobility, why would employers, who will have to provide much of the training, engage in it? The measures risk becoming a cloak for restructuring, moreover. 'In order for workers to work with peace of mind and fully demonstrate their abilities, it is essential for companies to take responsibility for human resource development and skill development; support for companies as well as individual workers should be maintained and expanded.' These issues should be taken up at the Labour Policy Council and other forums with management and union participation...'[13] The proposals certainly did raise questions, not least because two of the trinity elements—job mobility and job-based wages—are associated with marketization, and this in turn (usually) with neoliberalism, which 'new capitalism' is supposed to be diverging from, as well as from the postwar model.

Diversity and Disparity

In fact there was a fourth element in the 'trinity' proposals, namely 'Respect for diversity and addressing disparity'. This was about raising the minimum wage to the elusive (yet very modest by international standards) ¥1000 target nationwide—¥1500 by the mid 2030s—making sure large companies don't raise wages at the expense of SMEs, stricter implementation of equal pay for equal work (closing the ¥600+/hour gap between regular and non-regular workers), and boosting career education. The underlying idea was that there

---

[13] Yoshino Tomoko, Rengo Chairperson to the New Form of Capitalism Realization Council, of which she is a member, Meeting No. 18, May 2023. Yoshino also repeatedly questioned what the reforms mean for SMEs.

should be diverse ways of working, but this should not increase disparities in earnings and opportunities, unlike the 'portfolio' practices which heightened disparities from the 1990s.

Diverse ways of work include telework, side jobs, and multiple jobs, which have been increasing in recent years. 'Spot' work, in which people use apps to find work for as little as a single shift, has mushroomed. According to the Japan Spot Work Association the number of people registered with four leading agencies more than doubled between December 2020 and May 2023 to reach 10.7 million.[14] Investigating 'quasi-employment', a Ministry of Health, Labour and Welfare (MHLW) interim report in 2019 estimated that there were 2.3 million persons who were 'entrusted with work by a client, provide services, and receive remuneration while operating primarily as individuals'—1.7 million as their main job, and 600,000 as a side job.[15] How to regulate the growing number of gig and similar jobs has been a subject of debate in many countries, namely whether it is best to expand the category of employee or worker; to add an extra, intermediary category between the employed–self-employed binary; or to deal with issues under current regulation on a case-by-case basis. To date, Japan has opted for the third option, deeming current laws as applicable to most situations. Not only that, but the growth of such jobs has been actively encouraged. Yet surveys of such work show a (gendered) bifurcation. Nishimura (2021: 39), for example, writes of the two types of crowdwork (CW):

> One can be categorized as 'household income-supplementing CWs'. Many of them are women, and they are engaged in tasks that can be done with general capabilities. The amount of compensation tends to be low, and they tend to be somewhat dissatisfied with their work styles. The other can be categorized as 'independent CWs'. This group consists mostly of men, and is engaged in work that requires specialized skills. Some of them earn relatively high compensation among [independent contractors] in general. They tend to be satisfied with the CW work style, and to be satisfied with their incomes to a certain extent.[16]

Rather than taking Japan towards Society 5.0, then, such work extends the trajectory established from the 1990s, of growing polarization and inequality accompanying flexibilization. In fact it may do more than that; Lucács (2020)

---

[14] The number is inflated by multiple registrations *Nikkei Asia*, 22 June 2023 ('Japan Sees Explosion in "Spot Workers" in Hotels, Bars, Stores').

[15] 'MHLW's Interim Report on Points of Controversy Regarding Employment-like Work Styles', *Japan Labour Issues*, 3(19): 2.

[16] Crowdworkers were defined as 'people who receive orders for self-employed work only through crowdsourcing companies'.

depicts how, lured by the prospect of avoiding discrimination in traditional employment and building an online entrepreneurial career, many young women in Japan have inadvertently ended up providing unpaid labour to platform owners. Frenkenberger's (2021) study of employment in startups in Tokyo, too, found many of the same narratives and motivations, namely a celebration of freedom from the constraints of the 'old (corporate) Japan', in which individuals can pursue their dreams, but an everyday reality in which dreams are betrayed or shattered.[17]

This is a far cry from Keidanren's optimistic vision of sustainable capitalism and Society 5.0 in which workers will 'command digital technologies with rich imagination and creativity and will create value through flexible work styles that are not confined by time or space'. The 'disparity' part of 'respect for diversity and addressing disparity' needs more attention, which Keidanren itself recognizes.

Covid-19 and Teleworking

The Covid-19 pandemic could have provided a big boost to work-style reform, and to mobility, as companies were urged by the government to let their employees work from home to lower the risk of virus transmission on crowded commuter trains and in offices. If anything was going to shift working patterns, this was it. Teleworking was not new; an MLIT survey in 2002 estimated that as many as 6 per cent of the workforce were teleworking (Sakamoto et al., 2003). That proportion appears to have doubled to 13 per cent by early 2020 according to an employee survey carried out by the employment agency Persol. A month later, after a state of emergency had been declared in key prefectures, the number had doubled again to 28 per cent.[18] Over 30 per cent of companies had implemented teleworking by that time according to company surveys by the Japan Productivity Centre (JPC). But would this translate into long-term change?

The evidence is mixed. From the high point in April–May 2020, the number of teleworkers began to drop, then they climbed again, to 29 per cent in February 2022 in the Persol employee survey. In the JPC surveys the percentage of companies implementing telework hovered around 30 per cent in the Tokyo metropolitan area, but was under 20 per cent in many other parts of the country. Just over half had telework on 0–2 days per week, while only 4

---

[17] Cf. Neff's (2012) study of dotcom workers in New York's Silicon Alley in the 1990s.
[18] https://www.persol-group.co.jp/en/ir/upload_file/m005-m005_06/integrated-report_2020_en.pdf (accessed 28 April 2022).

per cent were using telework full time, again with a gap between the wider Tokyo area and the rest of the country.[19] And from the initial optimism about changing work styles and productivity gains, doubts began to emerge, as did a gulf between many employers and their employees.

Companies were not prepared for long-term teleworking. They had concerns about setting up employees for teleworking, physical environment at home, internet and VPN access, and data security. There were issues with communication, personal seals, contact with clients, mixing work and home duties, and employment concerns about fair evaluations in diverse working environments, as well as isolation, morale, and productivity.[20] Some surveys reported a drop in productivity for certain types of work (creative, group work), types of HRM (seniority-based), level in the company (management), and overall.[21] Company investment in employee education and training, already comparatively low, declined further between 2019 and 2021. A Recruit survey found the proportion of both regular and non-regular workers who said they had no opportunity to acquire new knowledge or skills increased, and attributed this to the sudden take-up of telework without sufficient company preparation.[22]

Workers were much more positive than managers. A large majority wanted to continue working from home at least two days a week—every day for younger employees according to one survey, while older workers preferred a balance.[23] The gulf between employers and employees surfaced when employees were asked to go back to work. Commuting distances which had been tolerated in the past were now a toil. Some workers decided to seek a new employer who would allow teleworking; others decided to change their lifestyles. In an indirect way, then, the pandemic may have given a push towards the diversification of work styles. However, while some large companies are not only using teleworking but moving towards a four-day work week, confident that productivity will not decline, many others, especially provincial companies and SMEs, prefer face-to-face working as the basis of cohesion and efficient working. Covid-19, it seems, produced, or at least

---

[19] https://www.nippon.com/en/japan-data/h01004/ (accessed 28 April 2022). For the first time in many years the population of Tokyo dipped as companies and employees moved out of the capital in search of premises and apartments more suited to teleworking.

[20] Ibid.

[21] Cf. Morikawa, 2021; Ovsiannikov et al., 2022.

[22] *Nikkei shinbun*, 7 August 2022 ('Hito e no tōshi: Daikaikaku no kakugo wa' ['Investment in People: Are We Prepared for Major Reform?']).

[23] The survey of 4494 workers—predominantly engineers—in the greater Tokyo region was carried out by *fabcross for Engineers* magazine in August and September 2021: https://soranews24.com/2021/12/01/survey-reveals-most-japanese-workers-want-to-work-from-home-at-least-twice-per-week/ (accessed 28 April 2022).

brought into the open, a two-speed Japan in terms of work-style reform. This most probably maps onto the shift to 'job-based' employment as well.

Investing in People, Rebuilding the Middle Class

In 2023 Keidanren released a report which called for the rebuilding of Japan's middle class, necessary because 'an excessive focus on shareholder capitalism and market fundamentalism' had depleted it.[24] Summarized in Figure 7.2, the proposal incorporated the trinity labour market reforms. The government and Keidanren appear to be moving in step, although Keidanren goes further in its advice to the government about reforming the social security system and creating a safety net, while the government wants companies to do more to reform their employment system.

This combination is significant. First, rebuilding the middle class is seen not just as a matter of trimming the excesses of shareholder capitalism; the employment system and the social security system also need to be reformed. Second, however, that inevitably means adjustments to the respective roles of the state and companies (the 'market'). The first part of this section will

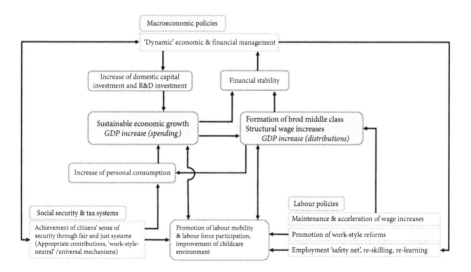

Figure 7.2 'A virtuous cycle' of growth and distribution towards the formation of a broad middle class

Source: Keidanren, 2023.

---

[24] The report was titled (in Japanese) 'Achieving a Virtuous Circle toward Sustainable Capitalism: Report of the Deliberation Group on the Formation of a Thick [*buatsui*] Middle Class'.

explore this prospect. The second part builds on this by looking briefly at government initiatives to boost VET and upgrade Japan's education system for Society 5.0, returning the discussion to DX, GX, and innovation. Whereas previous sections focused on mobility and employment reform—two of the trinity targets—overall this section focuses on reskilling.

Figure 7.2, which summarizes Keidanren's report, is an attempt to create conceptual coherence in the sustainable/new capitalism reforms, and especially between the micro- and macro-levels of the economy. Lurking within the figure, however, is the question of who will pay for 'investment in people'. Keidanren's answer is given in Table 7.1. Companies have to increase their capital expenditure and investment in R&D, commit to wage increases, and invest more in training and education. This would mean a significant shift for many employers. Japan often prides itself on on-job-training (OJT), which is difficult to measure, but as Miyagawa (2018) argues, this typically prepares employees for existing work rather than for new departures. Its contribution to intangible asset growth is therefore limited. Moreover, surveys have shown that Japanese companies spend much less on off-JT than their counterparts elsewhere, and that what they do spend has diminished significantly over time.[25]

In an interesting twist, a survey by the Life Insurance Association of Japan found that investors are more strongly interested in investing in people than managers are. Asked to give three top mid-to-long-term investment and financial priorities from a list of nine, the former rated IT investment, R&D investment and just behind at 58 per cent, investment in people. Company executives ranked investment in people fifth at 31 per cent, well behind capital investment, IT investment, R&D investment, and investor returns![26] Investor interest has grown as part of the 'social' in ESG, and because it appears to differentiate company performance, both in terms of sales growth and returns on investment.[27] Some managers, it seems, need to re-learn that lesson, but as Table 7.1 suggests, they have the means to do it in the form of 'excessive corporate savings'. While they dipped into these for capital expenditure and pay rises in 2023, they continued to increase dividends and share buy-backs even more.

---

[25] For example a survey cited in the 2018 White Paper on Labour showed off-JT expenditure of at least 1 per cent of GDP in the US, France, Germany, Italy, and UK, while in Japan it had declined from 0.4 per cent in 1995–1999 to just 0.1 per cent in 2010–2014: Kōsei rōdōshō, 2018: 89. The same White Paper reported fewer Japanese companies providing OJT than the OECD average (p. 87).

[26] Nikkei shinbun, 7 August 2022 ('Hito e no tōshi: Kigyō kachi o sayū, sukoa jōi no kabuka 7 waridaka' [Investing in People: Affecting Corporate Value, Share Price of High Scorers 70 Percent Higher]).

[27] Ibid.

Table 7.1 Government and company roles for rebuilding the middle class

	Roles of government	Roles of companies
Macroeconomic policies	• Improving corporate investment environment through regulatory reforms, long-term government investment (which increase predictability for corporate investment), etc. • Ensuring 'wise spending' and concentrated financing in priority fields (solving social issues, improving productivity, promoting innovation and new business, etc.)	• Increasing domestic capital investment and R&D investment (and as a result, resolving excess corporate saving) • Establishing a distribution structure appropriate for multi-stakeholders (in particular, structural wage increases which include SMEs)
Social security and taxation systems	• Realizing fair, just, and appropriate contributions and distribution (changing current structures that place too heavy a burden on the working generation) • Realizing a universal system (which is 'neutral' with regard to work styles) • Thoroughly utilizing 'My Number' and promoting DX in social security fields	• Promoting 'investment in people' • Maintaining and accelerating wage increases • Supporting smooth labour mobility • Promoting 'work-style reforms' and developing work–life balance support • Instilling DE&I (diversity, equity, and inclusion)
Labour policies	• Shifting employment 'safety net' from an 'employment maintenance' mode to a 'labour mobility facilitation' mode	

Source: Keidanren, 2023.

As for the government, not surprisingly Keidanren wants clarity, less waste, and public investment to induce private investment. It also calls for a universal social security system which is 'neutral' with regard to work styles, and reduces the burden on the working age population (hence companies), and shifts the social safety net from employment maintenance to one that enables labour mobility.

In other words, it wants 'active labour market policy'. In fact, it seems to have in mind something akin to the 'social investment state' (preferably without the bill). Seen as a successor to the postwar welfare state and its redistribution policies in Europe, or alternatively to neoliberalism which undermined the welfare state and treated social expenditure as a cost, this situates social policy and expenditure as an investment. Policy emphasis is on labour market activation, skills and training, flexibility with security, policies to support women's employment, active ageing, higher education and lifelong education, and skill upgrading (Morel et al., 2011). Leoni (2016: 196) observes:

> Focusing on human capital and the labour market as anchors for individual well-being, SI acknowledges that the capacity to acquire and update skills is of central importance to secure employment opportunities, and that employment is in turn the best prevention against social risks, which have become more difficult to insure against.

Arguably Japan's postwar 'developmental state' did this as well, but it did it through companies, 'membership-type' employment and legislative measures to ensure employment stability (Sugeno, 1996). The state's current interventions seek to expand the labour force and provide the skills for the digital economy. 'Social investment' has been criticized on a number of counts, including the economic instrumentalization of the social, neglect of poverty, and focus on activation at the expense of job quality. Some of these criticisms would apply to Japan, which is a long way from achieving 'a secure society based on work', as Rengo puts it. 'Decent work', or a combination of meaningful work and social protection (Kamimura, 2021), appears to be a particular lacuna, which 'respect for diversity and addressing disparity' does not touch.[28] In other words, workers who 'command digital technologies with rich imagination and creativity' appears to be more wishful thinking or aspiration than a concrete goal.

Digital Skills and Education for the Future

The government insists it is doing its part, at least when it comes to reskilling. Soon after he became Prime Minister, Kishida announced a ¥400 billion package for VET and lifelong learning. But when it comes to skills, the role of the government is much more extensive, encompassing the whole education

---

[28] Kamimura cites Odaka's (1941) formulation, which combines labour (wages), vocation (meaning) and occupation (social integration/contribution). Those who enjoy all three are few and fortunate. SDG No. 8 stipulates 'inclusive and sustainable economic growth, employment and decent work for all'.

sector. We conclude this section with a brief look at reforms in the education sector, returning us to innovation, DX, GX, and Society 5.0.

One of the many debates about education in Japan has concerned digital skills. A professor of the National Institute of Informatics caused a stir in 2018 with her book *AI vs Children Who Can't Read Textbooks*. Her project had shown that a 'robot' (AI) could not (yet) pass Tokyo University's entrance exam, although it could almost certainly pass many others. But her survey had also found that one third of middle school and high school pupils and company employees could not properly decode even relatively simple sentences. A generation raised on SNS texts were beginning to lose the ability to understand written matter that might make their jobs secure from AI. (They also lacked the stamina necessary for manual jobs like construction, which would also be safe from AI, she opined.) Her prescription was to get people reading again.[29]

A group meeting for the Ministry of Education, Culture, Sports, Science and Technology (MEXT) on the types of human resources and learning necessary for Society 5.0 was in partial agreement, proposing amongst other things literacy, numeracy, and information skills for all, and transcending the science–arts divide (STEM to STEAM).[30] Individually optimized learning, however, would be achieved through online learning portfolios and study logs using ed-tech. The Global and Innovation Gateway for All (GIGA) School Programme (2018) was to provide one device for each pupil, as well as ensuring high speed internet access. Although most pupils already used electronic devices for texting and games, they were much less adept at using them for finding, organizing, and presenting information. GIGA would help them to engage in investigative learning, improve their production and presentation skills, learn with distant partners—universities and overseas schools—and learn about ethics and fake information. 'Computers in schools' was by no means new.[31] A push in the early 2000s stalled through budget cuts and other factors. By 2018 many schools faced the same problems that were identified by METI's 'DX Report'—ageing hardware and software in computer rooms, and a lack of people with the right skills to maintain and upgrade them. Already overworked teachers would struggle to acquire the necessary skills themselves. The programme acquired a new urgency and momentum, however, with the onset of the Covid pandemic.

---

[29] Arai, 2018; Arai and Sato, 2021.

[30] 'Ministers Meeting on Human Resource Development for Society 5.0' (2018). STEAM adds 'arts' to science, technology, engineering, and mathematics.

[31] The idea that Japanese education crushes individuality was old hat as well. Reforms intended to produce 'learner-centred' learning have consistently failed, and have instead loaded extra work onto already overworked teachers. Cf. Kariya and Rappleye, 2020.

Universities as Powerhouses of the Digital Economy

Although only 20 per cent of four-year university students were enrolled in STEM subjects in 2020, higher education institutions are expected to shoulder much of the task of reskilling production of digital human resources. A succession of programmes has been introduced to raise digital literacy, some of them shown in Table 7.2.[32] These in turn have provided an incentive for tertiary institutions to create data science departments and programmes, but supply side constraints—especially qualified faculty—are severe.

On the demand side, the 18-year-old population has been in decline since 1993. This was counterbalanced by a rising proportion of school leavers going

Table 7.2 Tertiary education programmes promoting digital skills and digitalization

Advanced IT Specialist Education Promotion (2016)

Targeting Masters students—6 education 'bases' with 28 participating universities and 76 companies selected in 2016, a further 2 with 8 universities and 15 companies in 2017;[*] project-based learning with 216 graduates in 2018, 198 in 2019 from the first batch, 320 graduates goal by 2020 for the second batch.

Maths, Data Science and AI Smart Higher Education (MDASH)-Literacy Level (2021)

With the goal of all higher education students (or 500,000 per year) mastering introductory-level mathematics, data science, and AI, a certification programme promoted by MEXT, METI, and the Cabinet Office. 11 universities selected in the first round, 67 in the second. An Advanced Literacy level aiming to certify 250,000 students per year to be added.

Digital Tertiary Education Upgrading Plan (2021)

Two sub-themes of 'realizing learner-centred education' and 'improving the quality of learning' with digital technologies and innovation, like virtual reality, digital contents, etc. 44 universities selected for the first theme, 10 for the second (9 overlapping with the first theme).

Student-centred Higher Education through Digitalization (Scheem-D) (2021)

Aiming to promote digitalization of universities, with a focus on combining cyber and physical systems. Activities include ed-tech pitches and promotion.

Digital x Specialist Area (2021)

¥46 billion allocated from 2021 Supplementary Budget to promote digital skills in applied areas like agriculture, manufacturing and construction. 39 universities chosen in 2021.

Source: Compiled from various MEXT sources.
[*] Also open to junior college and technical college students.

---

[32] Others include enPIT (education network for Practical Information Technology, from 2012), Data Science for Super Smart Society (2018), and Smart DX Specialist Education (2022).

on to university, reaching 53 per cent in 2017, when the absolute number of university students began to decline.[33] The Central Council for Education's (2018) 'Grand Design for Higher Education Toward 2040' anticipated an increasingly diverse student population, consisting of more non-Japanese, and older people returning for recurrent education courses.[34] To accommodate them, universities would need to modify their offerings and specialize—some striving to become top-tier global universities and others serving local economies and communities.

Universities are often seen as the powerhouses of innovative postindustrial economies, an expectation which Japan has shared but not obtained. As companies closed their central research labs or curtailed R&D in the 1990s, universities were expected to pick up the slack. Emulating the US, Japan passed a succession of laws from 1998 to 2002 to encourage university-originating technology transfer and commercialization through technology licensing offices, university spinouts, and university–industry collaboration. And emulating the UK, public-sector research institutes, hospitals, and universities were turned into independent administrative institutions.

Arguably Japan ended up without its erstwhile corporate-based innovation system, or a new one. Academic papers published by researchers in leading companies declined sharply from around 1997. The number of academic papers published by all researchers also flattened out and began to decline markedly in areas like physics, material science, biochemistry, and molecular biology.[35] And whereas the number of PhD graduates increased in many countries, in Japan they declined as job prospects in both academia and industry dimmed. From a peak of 11,637 in 2003, the number had halved to 5963 by 2020.[36] Japanese universities slipped down global rankings. To counteract the slide the government announced in 2021 a massive ¥10 trillion university endowment fund, with the expectation that grantee universities will tap other sources of funding as well. Areas like AI, quantum technology, and biotechnology are especially targeted. It remains to be seen whether this will be a game changer for Japanese universities, both in terms of STI, as well as human resources; there is much to be done.

---

[33] A further 5 per cent went to two-year junior colleges, and 22 per cent to specialist or professional institutions, making an overall advancement rate of 80 per cent: MEXT, 2018.

[34] The number of foreign students—mostly from emerging Asia—doubled between 2006 and 2019, to roughly 230,000, before plummeting during the Covi-19 pandemic, as Japan shut its borders.

[35] Yamaguchi, 2019, citing Iijima and Yamaguchi, 2015. In Yamaguchi's view there were several reasons for the 'crisis' in Japan's innovation system, a crucial one being that Japan imitated the US Small Business Innovation Research (SBIR) programme in form only.

[36] *Japan Today*, 13 October 2020 ('The Number of Doctoral Students in Japan Is Now Almost Half What It Was 17 Years Ago').

Concluding Comments

'People' are at the heart of the new economy, and increasingly at the heart of deliberations about how to build it. There is a good reason for this—Japan's greatest asset has become its greatest challenge, most obviously because of population decline and ageing. Of all the 'last chance' scenarios we have encountered so far, the declining birthrate is perhaps the most severe. According to Prime Minister Kishida in January 2023, 'Japan is on the verge of whether we can continue to function as a society.... It is now or never when it comes to policies regarding births and child-rearing. It is an issue that simply cannot wait.'

To date the workforce has not declined, due largely to increased participation by non-Japanese, women, and the elderly. Each of these brings a set of challenges which require modification to 'Japanese-style employment', which served Japan so well in the postwar decades in terms of economic recovery and growth. Abe attempted to address these challenges through work-style reform, with limited effect. Work-style reform did not touch the foundations of 'Japanese-style' employment. Keidanren, meanwhile, began to advocate a shift from 'membership-based employment', which it associated with Society 4.0, to 'job-based employment', which it associated with Society 5.0. Job-based employment, it opined, is necessary to address pent-up social and economic problems, such as work–life balance (hence birth rate), diversity (both in terms of diversity of work types and DE&I), allocative efficiency, and productivity.

The New Form of Capitalism Realization Council took this up in its April 2023 Proposal for Trinity Labour Market Reform Issues, namely reskilling, job-based wages and employment, and labour mobility. In the proposal it signalled its readiness to tackle the pro-employment-stability institutional supports of the postwar model, and promised concrete measures and a timeline to follow. Two weeks later Keidanren issued its rebuilding the middle-class report. By this time the language of the government and Keidanren had become virtually interchangeable, but underneath, there are highly consequential issues about the design of the new employment and social security system, and how the costs and responsibilities will be apportioned.

Also significant, as Vogel (2018) noted, is the fact that the Prime Minister and the OPMC have become the drivers of change. This means that institutional design and interest adjustment can be carried out more quickly, and policy coordination—in this case the coordination of social and economic policy—should become easier. It would have been difficult to imagine these proposals coming from the MHLW. The same, it would seem, is beginning to happen with education, tying the education system into reskilling, as well as the other new capitalism priorities of DX, GX, and STI. The challenges of such coordination, of trying to balance state and market responsibilities, and building new social foundations for the new economy by 2030 are formidable. There are inconsistencies, and it is unclear where these reform attempts will take Japan. One possibility is the 'social investment state'—with Japanese characteristics (Chapter 10).

8

Beyond Capitalism

It is often said that capitalism requires non-capitalist ethics and institutions for its survival.[1] Moreover, in a variation of Polanyi's double movement argument: 'Capitalism as we know it has benefited greatly from the rise of counter-movements against the rule of profit and of the market. Socialism and trade unionism, by putting a brake on commodification, prevented capitalism from destroying its own non-capitalist foundations—trust, good faith, altruism, solidarity within families and communities, and the like' (Streeck, 2016: 60). The problem with the triumph of neoliberal financialized capitalism over its ideological opponents in 1989, Streeck writes, is that it lost its 'loyal opposition', and as a result, eroded its own foundations. It was a Pyrrhic victory, and capitalism may have become its own worst enemy.

Financialized capitalism never fully conquered Japan, and the processes of financialization remain partial. We have not properly explored what has impeded its progress, however, except for reference to social norms, and the legacy of the postwar stakeholder model. In fact there is more to it than that, and the institutions and norms which acted as a restraint have seldom been fully acknowledged in depictions of the Japanese economy. This chapter may seem like a digression to those interested solely in changes to mainstream Japanese capitalism, but it is useful to ask whether these institutions and norms are continuing to play a role in shaping Japan's capitalism, and in building its new economy, or conversely, whether they are decaying to the point of irrelevance. We will do so from three perspectives.

The first is from the perspective of the 'social and solidarity economy' (SSE), which encompasses 'activities and organizations of associative, cooperative, and mutual nature created to respond to the need for jobs and the well-being of people, as well as those citizen movements geared toward democratizing and transforming the economy'.[2] In recent years the SSE has been promoted by the United Nations, ILO, and even the OECD. In fact

---

[1] E.g. Hirsch, 1976; Etzioni, 1988; Streeck, 1997; Hodgson, 2001.
[2] http://www.ripess.org/wp-content/uploads/2017/08/RIPESS_charter_EN.pdf; https://www.ilo.org/empent/areas/WCMS_546299/lang—en/index.htm (accessed 27 July 2021); Utting, 2015.

Building a New Economy. D. Hugh Whittaker, Oxford University Press. © D. Hugh Whittaker (2024).
DOI: 10.1093/oso/9780198893394.003.0009

Japan has always had a large social economy, and if the SSE is about putting people and communities first, there should be some overlap with 'new capitalism' and Society 5.0, which claim to be people-centred. Could Japan in fact be reverting to its historical moral economy base, which was temporarily submerged in the rush of 'catch-up' industrialization, as suggested by Keidanren's references to *sanpō-yoshi* in Chapter 6? Or at least re-inventing it?

Second, critics of Japan's efforts at GX sometimes point to the absence of a strong, confrontational environmental movement in Japan. The weakness of oppositional politics in Japan in general and the virtual hegemony of the conservative LDP, moreover, may be seen as impediments to meaningful institutional change. There is, to be sure, a long history of environmental protest and citizens' movements in Japan,[3] but as Avenell (2009) notes, many movements from the 1970s attempted to engage with state and corporate elites rather than denouncing them, and as a result, state, corporate, and civic actors 'fashioned a domesticated and largely apolitical sphere of social activism' (p. 247). The second section looks at NPOs in this light, and in particular two which have focused on environmental activities and awareness raising, engaging rather than denouncing their opponents. It also looks at new networks which sprang up in the wake of the 2011 triple disaster and the attempts of some to democratize DX.

Third, the divide between SSE, civil society, and capitalist enterprise is questioned, in two respects. First, on a spectrum *within* capitalism from profit-oriented, shareholder maximizing corporations on the one hand, to corporations oriented towards public purpose on the other, there is no shortage of Japanese companies that are closer to the latter pole. In other words, public interest capitalism is not entirely new, even if it proposes institutional reforms. And relatedly, there is a spectrum of views of how capitalism should be reformed within Japan, from capitalism harnessed to serve local interests through to creating a more cosmopolitan form of capitalism capable of attracting foreign talent and money.

In brief, although they are typically not seen as part of a mainstream 'Japanese model'—past, present, or future—the organizations described in this chapter may be an important albeit largely invisible part of Society 5.0 and 'new capitalism'. This chapter, looking at possible influences on building a new economy from within, will be complemented by Chapter 9, which looks at influences from outside Japan.

---

[3] E.g. Huddle et al., 1975; McKean, 1981; Sorensen and Funck eds, 2009.

The 'Social and Solidarity Economy'

The 'social economy', sometimes called the 'third sector', encompasses cooperatives, mutual benefit societies, and associations, which are typically assigned a special legal status. Neither controlled by the state, nor run for (maximization of) profits, such organizations prioritize services to members and community. Although the origins of modern cooperatives date back at least to the 1840s,[4] the 1990s saw the rise of new movements, especially in Latin America and Europe, which did not fit the conventional categories of the social economy but shared a common ethos, including emphasis on social and community objectives, as well as pushing back against environmental destruction caused by the activities of global corporations. The commonality was recognized in the more inclusive term 'social and solidarity economy'. The ILO and the United Nations have actively promoted the SSE; the latter setting up an Inter-Agency Task Force on Social and Solidarity Economy (UNTFSSE) in 2013, to which many UN and other international intergovernmental and civil society organizations affiliated. The OECD chimed in in 2020, with its Global Action 'Promoting Social and Solidarity Economy Ecosystems'.

There has always been a caution in Japan about separating the economic from the social and the moral. Indeed, the modern word for economy—*keizai*—is abbreviated from the expression *keikoku (or keisei) saimin*, or 'administering the nation and relieving the suffering of the poor' (Morris-Suzuki, 1989). Edo period (1603–1867) writing was replete with themes stressing the moral economy. Osaka merchants were told at the opening of the Kaitokudō academy in 1727 that 'economic competition must be accurate and fair and be based on a respect for others' humanity and not a selfish desire for aggrandizement' (Najita, 2009: 3).

Mutual aid societies and cooperative organizations such as *mujin kō* and *tanomoshi kō* revolving credit associations flourished, including the Hōtoku self-help movement which helped villages to cope with famine, depopulation, and rising taxes in the nineteenth century. Such organizations persisted into the Meiji period and beyond, often unregistered, and imbued with a 'theme of resistance' to the central government.[5]

---

[4] The International Co-operative Alliance's seven principles derive from the Rochdale Community, set out in 1844: open and voluntary membership; democratic member control; members' economic participation; autonomy and independence; education, training and information; cooperation among cooperatives; and concern for community.

[5] Najita, 2009. The Hōtoku movement resisted attempts at cooption by the Meiji government seeking to use it to spread capitalism and profit-oriented rationality into the countryside. Legendary founder Ninomiya Sontoku *was* coopted, as statues of him as a youth reading a book with firewood on his back were placed outside primary schools throughout Japan to inspire diligent study and hard work.

Debates about the relations between cooperatives and capitalism in Europe were keenly studied by Japanese students sent abroad during the Meiji period, who returned to work in government, especially the Ministry of Agriculture. Ideas flowed from Japan as well, with a particularly rich exchange between Japan and Russia around 'cooperatist anarchism' (Konishi, 2013). Kagawa Toyohiko, a Christian and early organizer of the labour movement who became a leading figure in the interwar and early postwar cooperative movement in Japan, was highly influential in the US and Europe—his 'third way' (neither capitalism nor communism) *Brotherly Economics* (1936) was translated into 17 languages.

Tanaka Shōzō, a Freedom and Popular Rights movement leader, elected to the first national Diet in 1890, became an early environmental activist. Unable to obtain redress through the Diet to the devastating pollution from the giant Ashio copper mine, he went to live with local villagers, espousing a vision of working with nature rather than against it, and personifying protest through his daily life.[6] In brief, both the social economy and the solidarity economy have venerable roots in Japan (Morris-Suzuki, 2020).

Cooperatives

The *World Cooperative Monitor* estimates that there are about 3 million cooperatives worldwide, providing work for 10 per cent of the world's working population, and that the largest 300 cooperatives generate some $2.15 trillion in annual turnover.[7] There is nothing new or marginal about the social economy. Measured by turnover and turnover to per capita GDP, three of the world's top ten cooperative and mutual association organizations are Japanese: Zenkyōren (National Mutual Insurance Federation of Agricultural Cooperatives), Zen-noh (National Federation of Agricultural Cooperative Associations) and Nippon Life Insurance Company.[8] In 2018 the Japan Cooperative Alliance counted over 40,000 cooperatives in Japan, with a total membership of over 100 million.[9] While agriculture cooperatives and consumer cooperatives are more famous, the majority are SME cooperative associations, whose scale is mostly small, often with ten members or less.

---

[6] Stolz, 2014, cited in Morris-Suzuki, 2020.

[7] https://www.ica.coop/en/cooperatives/facts-and-figures (accessed 28 July 2021). The International Cooperative Alliance, which produces the Monitor together with the European Research Institute on Cooperative and Social Enterprises, was itself founded in 1895.

[8] https://monitor.coop/en/media/library/research-and-reviews/world-cooperative-monitor-2020 (accessed 28 July 2021).

[9] JCA, 2021. The number includes multiple memberships; other estimates put the figure at closer to 65 million members: JCA, 2018.

Cooperatives flourished in the postwar years. In agriculture, they were seen as the best hope for effectively growing and distributing food to prevent starvation and clamping down on the black market, not to mention acting as a restraint on rural socialism. Thus the government had an interest in both promoting and regulating cooperatives. It did this to fit its own ministerial structures, meaning different types of cooperative were supervised by different ministries, and regulated under different laws.[10] The number of agricultural cooperatives peaked in the 1950s at around 35,000, of which 13,000 were multi-purpose, meaning they engaged in activities other than joint purchasing and sales, including banking and finance, insurance, retail... In fact they were an all-encompassing part of village life, and served as vehicles for redistribution as Japan underwent rapid (re-)industrialization and urbanization.[11] In return, they provided a powerful rural support base for the Liberal Democratic Party. The entrenchment of these structures, however, meant that they often became obstacles to change, even as the rural population aged, the number of full-time farmers dwindled, and abandoned land proliferated. After mobilizing to oppose Japan's entry into the Trans-Pacific Partnership in the early 2010s, they were targeted for reform under Abe's third arrow. Some, however, have successfully reinvented themselves.[12]

Urban cooperatives followed a different trajectory. An initial postwar flourish of buying clubs seeking to secure scarce food was followed by the establishment of labour union-sponsored cooperatives in the 1950s, and of consumer cooperatives in the 1960s, which grew to become easily the largest category in terms of membership; roughly half of Japanese households are said to belong to one. Members were mostly housewives, who found their way around restrictions and campaigns aimed at protecting small retailers by organizing home deliveries, often on the basis of *han* groups. They became concerned about pollution, tainted food and abuses of corporate power, which they opposed through collective purchasing, and organizing or taking part in citizens' movements. Although faced with growing concentration in the retail sector and declining household incomes, they are still a powerful force, and a vehicle for social participation by women (Kurimoto, 2020).

Small business cooperatives, conversely, were encouraged by the government as a means of overcoming disadvantages related to size and to

---

[10] For example, the Agricultural Cooperatives Act (1947), Consumer Cooperatives Act (1948), SME Cooperatives Act (1949), and Cooperative Banking Act (1949).

[11] They were all-encompassing in terms of membership as well—it was effectively obligatory, despite the first cooperative principle, mentioned above.

[12] On agricultural cooperative reform and attempts to revitalize Japanese agriculture, see Jentsch, 2021; Lollini, 2021; Maclachlan and Shimizu, 2022. In 2022 there were less than 1600 agricultural cooperatives, of which 585 were multi-purpose.

promoting scale and efficiency. As with agricultural cooperatives, many were organized in a tiered structure, with a peak organization which lobbies on behalf of members.[13] Structural change, deindustrialization, and the closure of factories from the 1990s sapped the vitality of many associations, although some have successfully rejuvenated themselves to become vehicles of digital and green transformation in the 2010s (Morishita, 2023).

In line with the global re-evaluation of the SSE in recent years, and seeking institutional renewal, in 2018 the Japan Joint Committee of Cooperatives (JJC) was restructured to become the Japan Cooperative Alliance (JCA). Adopting the motto 'better living and work through sustainable local communities', the JCA is building horizontal links between cooperatives, and extending cooperation to other local organizations. In 2020, after years of campaigning, a new law was passed unanimously in the Diet officially recognizing worker cooperatives—a hopeful sign for the future of Japan's SSE, according to the newly formed Association for the Promotion of SSE in Japan.[14]

Labour Organizations

Labour unions were important for the construction and maintenance of the postwar Japanese economic model, especially the wage–labour nexus (Chapter 1). Membership surged after they were legalized, to a high of 56 per cent of the workforce in 1949. Unions campaigned for job security, living wages, and the abolition of status differences between blue and white collar workers. Even after managers regained the 'right to manage' after some landmark strikes, those gains were largely preserved. They also organized the spring wage offensive (*Shuntō*), which spread the benefits of productivity gains and raised living standards. Fast forward to the 1990s, and amidst a stagnating economy and falling unionization rate, unions became increasingly defensive, protecting their members at the expense of a growing proportion of non-regular, non-unionized workers.

There is more to this story, however, than the rise and fall of organized labour, nor is the story just about enterprise unions. Pempel and Tsunekawa (1979) depicted Japan as a country of 'corporatism without labour'. However, union federations and national centres came together in 1989 to form Rengo (JTUC), explicitly to influence policy. Rengo could not stop the deregulation

---

[13] Others aligned themselves with left-wing organizations such as Minshō (Peoples' Chamber of Commerce and Industry).

[14] https://www.ssejapan.org/yobikakebun (accessed 29 July 2021).

of labour markets in the 1990s and 2000s, nor could it stem the declining unionization rate, which hovered around 17 per cent in the 2010s. With the demise of the left and centre left opposition parties, Rengo edged closer to the LDP, working with Abe on the package of work-style reforms and in urging employers to improve their wage offers, a stance which Kishida has maintained. Labour in this sense has been incorporated into the corporatist polity.[15]

There is another important qualification, however. In the postwar turbulence, a number of labour organizations were formed jointly with cooperatives, including labour banks (*Rōkin*), which were set up in 1950 to provide an alternative to loan sharks for poorer workers, and whose customer base spanned unions, cooperatives and their members (Kurimoto and Koseki, 2019). *Rōkin* helped NPOs get off the ground in the early 2000s and campaigned for legislation against usurious interest rates charged by consumer credit companies in 2006. In 2018 *Rōkin* held ¥20 trillion in deposits, making them (collectively) the 11th largest bank in Japan. *Rōsai* (workers mutual aid accident and disaster funds, 1951) had over 30 million life, fire, natural disaster, car, and other accounts in 2019.[16] As noted, such organizations have a tiered structure, and peak organizations have close links with their respective ministries.

Conversely, local level activities have also become more important. Perhaps the least well known of the postwar labour institutions, but which played an important role in creating many of them, are *Rōfukukyō* (workers welfare associations, 1949).[17] At the local level, they sponsor 'life support centres', support food banks, and run classes in schools on work and financial literacy. Rengo, too, began to put more heft into local organizations, establishing or strengthening 260 local councils (*chiiki kyōgikai*), as well as prefectural organizations (*chihō rengōkai*) between 2010 and 2016. Horizontal links between union organizations, cooperatives and NPOs have strengthened, and they can exert significant influence at the local and prefectural level.[18] Support from organizations such as the Japan Confederation of Retired Persons

---

[15] Addressing Rengo's biennial convention in October 2023, Kishida stressed common objectives of pay increases, workforce expansion and raising the minimum wage. Behind the scenes the government was reportedly attempting to draw the Rengo-backed Democratic Party of the People into its ruling coalition: *The Japan Times*, 5 October 2023 (Kishida's Attendance at Union Event Offers Hint at Electoral Strategy').

[16] *Rōsai* was re-branded in 2019 to emphasize mutuality, becoming Kokumin Kyōsai Co-op (National Federation of Workers and Consumers Kyōsai Cooperatives): https://www.zenrosai.coop/english/english.html (accessed 30 July 2021). Also *Annual Report*, 2020.

[17] Cf. https://www.rofuku.net; Nakamura, 2019.

[18] Nakamura, 2021. Nakamura is a professor of the Institute for Solidarity-based Society, set up in 2015 by Rengō, the Labour Culture Foundation and its host institution Hosei University to run postgraduate courses on and for labour unions, cooperatives, and NPOs.

(*Nihon taishokusha rengō*, membership 800,000), moreover, can be crucial at election time in some localities. In sum, although they face the challenge of renewal, the organizations of Japan's SSE are far from moribund, even as Japan ages. In fact, they form a base on which new social movements can be built.[19]

NPOs and Social Enterprise

New forms of social enterprise, social innovation, and non-profit organizations (NPOs) are emerging in Japan. The Hanshin-Awaji earthquake of 1995 saw a large number of volunteers converge on Kobe—more than a million, it is said—to the extent that already struggling local government bodies were overwhelmed. Many of the volunteers' organizations were not recognized in official government categories, posing difficulties of incorporating them into the recovery effort. A public debate resulted in the Law to Promote Specified Non-profit Activities (NPO Law) in 1998, and a wave of NPO registrations followed in which existing organizations sought legal status, and new ones were set up.

Pekkanen (2000) argues that the NPO Law marked a significant shift in state-civil society relations in Japan, lifting the heavy bureaucratic hand that had stifled civil society, and giving legitimacy to a new kind of social group and social innovation. The government itself then began to see the sector, and social innovation, as a means of tackling Japan's emerging problems, a view that was reinforced after the March 2011 triple disaster, when many NPOs were the first responders on the ground. METI became a strong supporter, and encouraged a network for cross-fertilization of ideas, mentoring, and philanthropy matching. Revisions to the NPO Law in 2012 made local governments responsible for certification, made tax deductions for donations easier, and made it easier to raise funds through access to loan guarantees from Japan Federation of Credit Guarantee Corporations members.

NPOs encompass a wide range of social visions and energies. Given their variety, any attempt to portray a 'typical' social enterprise or NPO would be futile. The remainder of this section echoes Tanaka Shōzō's attempts to prevent environmental damage, first by the Asaza Project, and then by the NPO *Mori wa Umi no Koibito* (The Sea is Longing for the Forest). These are not overtly oppositional environmental projects, but rather aim for change through education grounded in participation.

---

[19] Shinoda Toru, personal communication, 4 May 2022.

The Asaza Project: Ripples on a Lake...

The Asaza Project is based around Lake Kasumigaura, Japan's second biggest lake by area, with a catchment area ten times bigger again. Once a magnet for fishers and swimmers, and an important source of livelihoods for local communities, it became heavily polluted and smelly during Japan's rapid industrialization. Its wildlife was further impacted by public works schemes in the late 1960s which turned natural banks into concrete barriers, emblematic of Japan's 'construction state' (McCormack, 1996). The situation deeply disturbed Ijima Hiroshi, who had lived locally during his high school years, and returned later to find local residents avoiding the lake. He knew that protest would not bring resolution; like his classes at school, which carved knowledge up into discrete disciplines, seeking redress from siloed ministries could even make the situation worse. He adopted a radically different approach, of using the healing power of nature to repair itself, starting with *asaza*—fringed water lilies, or 'floating hearts'.[20]

Once common on the lake, *asaza* helped to absorb the impact of waves, protecting the shoreline reeds, in turn creating a biotope for various species of plant, fish, and insect. Bringing back *asaza* could be the beginning of a restoration process. The Asaza Foundation was set up in 1995. Passionate about holistic education, Ijima approached local primary schools and together they launched 'adopt an *asaza*', a project in which children—eventually from more than 100 schools—created a mini biotope at home to grow the plant. When transplanted back into the lake, however, many asaza were washed away by waves rebounding from the concrete banks.

Ijima consulted a local fishing cooperative, whose head reminded him of the traditional method of making breakwaters from forest brushwood. This solution required the (now) NPO to think about the wider catchment area, and the depleted forests around the lake, and to approach the local office of the construction ministry, whose permission would be needed to construct the brushwood breakwaters. The ministry backed the project, and the Kasumigaura Brushwood Fascine Association was born, creating a new local industry of forest restoration and brushwood fascine production. Meanwhile, researchers from Tokyo University had found that water level controls also affected the survival of *asaza*, and the ministry agreed not only to cease the controls, but to cooperate with the NPO in a major natural restoration project.

---

[20] This segment draws on the Foundation's account, http://www.asaza.jp/en/outline/about/ (accessed 30 July 2021) and Nonaka et al., 2013. Whereas the latter focuses on the journey of the founder, Ijima Hiroshi, the project's website mentions no names, for reasons which will become clear.

Although the network of collaborators was expanding, school children remained central to the project. Ijima recognized that the school catchment areas, about 5km in radius, coincided with the habitats of wildlife. However, few could remember exactly what wildlife had originally lived in them. Children asked their grandparents to recall their childhood days, and in this way local knowledge was re-created, and grandparents became involved. Electronics corporation NEC provided sensors for habitat monitoring and employee volunteers for joint NPO and school projects. In collaboration with fishing and agricultural cooperatives, exotic fish which competed with indigenous species were caught and processed into fertilizer, creating a new source of income. Ultimately, the health of the lake is inseparable from the rivers and catchment areas which feed it. To address depopulation and the increasing abandonment of farmland in the headwater hills and mountains a new project was started with NEC, other NPOs, and local governments to gradually restore this farmland, growing rice for *sake* brewing and soya beans for *miso*.

The 'Asaza Project: Lake Kasumigaura Revival Project Through Uniting Lakes, Forests and People' describes itself as a 'citizen-initiated public works project'. It is conceived as having no centre, and no management hierarchy, with projects loosely coordinated in networks of people sharing common values. School children have been central. The '100 year project' aims to progressively bring back the wildlife, culminating, it is hoped, with the return of the crested ibis, once a symbol of Japan, thus reversing the environmental and social damage done in the previous 100 years. In the words of Ijima:

We are aiming for a society in which everyone's qualities can find a place and develop themselves, without needing a great person or strong organization at the centre.... You don't have centres in nature, but each part is incomplete without the others. It leads you to think that society needs changing, from a pyramid to a horizontal network. Making it possible to create new developments means building a circular society which co-exists with nature. The society we are trying to build is a dynamic network with no centre, which has the potential for unexpected things to happen, continuously, through encounters. It doesn't mean breaking down the existing social system, but 'liquifying' it, dissolving compartmentalizing walls, having membranes that allow inside and outside to abundantly mix.[21]

This is why the NPO's website does not mention Ijima at all. This statement is reminiscent of the worldviews of the 'cooperative anarchists' who

---

[21] Quoted (in Japanese) in Nonaka et al., 2014: 85–86.

opposed the path of modernization adopted by the Meiji oligarchs, and the ensuing pollution, over a century ago (Konishi, 2013). The project created ripples, from the idea of bringing back *asaza*, widening out geographically, biologically, socially, and even economically, bringing together thousands of participants and turning some whose interests were potentially threatened into collaborators. The ripples spread to other parts of Japan, where similar restoration projects have been started.

Mori wa Umi no Koibito (The Sea is Longing for the Forest)

The second NPO is located at Moune, a district of Kesennuma which, like Higashi Matsushima, was devastated by the triple disaster of 2011.[22] As well as bringing rich nutrients from nearby mountains to the coastal oyster farms, during Japan's high growth period the Okawa River carried pollutants, creating 'red tide' algae blooms which threatened the oyster farmers' livelihoods. The villages in the area had been tied together for centuries by a festival held every four years, in which two teams raced from Mount Murone to the sea carrying a portable shrine. Each village had specific tasks, and Moune's was to provide salt for purification. Instead of confronting the upstream Murone villagers, oyster farmer Hatakeyama Shigeatsu appealed to their common history and interests, and they formed an association called *Mori wa Umi no Koibito*, which in 1989 started a tree planting and environmental education programme that mobilized school children and their families.

The association became an NPO in 2009. Two years later Hatakeyama's oyster beds were destroyed by the earthquake and tsunami, which caused the land to subside, flooding coastal areas. The government planned to reclaim the land, but Hatakeyama's son Makoto purchased a 1200 m² tract, intending to leave it as a tidal flat. Clams and small fish started to appear, which attracted birds, which attracted people. The rewilding project was threatened first by adjacent river bank works, and then by the massive new coastal seawall—10 metres high on average—being built to keep out future *tsunami*. As with the *asaza* project, the construction ministry was persuaded to break down the concrete river embankment rather than rebuild it, and the residents united to oppose the seawall, becoming one of only two communities to successfully do so.[23]

---

[22] https://mori-umi.org/eng/ Information based on interviews, 6 January 2022, and published sources.
[23] Cf. https://www.youtube.com/watch?v=xWx-U9q1WYQ (accessed 3 August 2022). On the other side of Kesennuma the seawall makes a short detour; the result of a compromise by (majority) anti-wall residents and (minority) pro-wall residents who both wanted to keep their beach, and years of negotiation with different ministries.

Overlooking the restored oyster beds today is the Moune Institute for Forest-Sato-Sea Studies, with seminar, accommodation, and lab facilities, to which students from a dozen universities, and disciplines ranging from marine biology to social anthropology, come to carry out research. It also organizes a 'Mori-Umi' (Forest-Sea) summer school and other environmental education activities for children. Commented Hatakeyama Makoto, now vice chairman of the NPO: 'It takes a long time to restore the environment by planting trees; cultivating people is a much quicker way.'

Digital SSE

Hatakeyama, who studied biology, made another observation: '3.11 was traumatic. I lost my grandmother, and the boat I was on was overturned. Luckily I was able to swim to shore.... We lost our oyster farms. But after natural disasters, new life appears, with new species, and new ecosystems, like on the tidal flat. I think it's like that with human beings. After the disaster I made a lot of new connections which I would never have made before, with people from other communities around Kesennuma, ministries, companies, NPOs.... Those connections and the trust you build up have been very important for rebuilding and doing new things.'

Similar views were expressed by others in Tohoku. Many reported being initially frustrated at the slow, top-down response from central ministries in Tokyo, and particularly with the Democratic Party of Japan, which was in power at the time. In normal times small regional cities like Higashi Matsushima and Kesennuma would not have dealt directly with central ministries, going instead through prefectural offices. But such was the scale of the destruction, and pressing needs, that things changed. People recruited into the Reconstruction Agency from other ministries and the private sector were generally young, and open to direct, two-way and bottom-up communication. Personal networks encompassing the public and private sectors and NPOs were used to leverage resources. People moved in and out of different reconstruction roles, enhancing those networks. Commented one who had worked for two NPOs and the City Office in Kesennuma before joining DMO Inoutbound (Chapter 4):

> The reconstruction areas were like a massive experiment. Nothing on this scale had been done before. The Reconstruction Agency set up a hackathon, and allowed experimentation, or challenge, which wouldn't have been allowed before. And it came with a budget. Before 3.11 the public and private spheres were quite

separate. But with 3.11 everything was broken, and there was a need to rely on the private sector. People came together who would not have interacted before, and they built a solid trust through working together. If I were to put a word to it, I would call it social capital-ism.[24]

Citing 1977 Nobel Prize winner Ilya Prigogine's work on dissipative structures, and using the example of *miso* soup, the Chief Digitalization Officer of Nishi Aizu town outside Aizuwakamatsu expressed it evocatively:

The government was caught up in the same old pattern of defeat with the Reconstruction budget. Most of it ended up in Tokyo without much impact. It's because they expect that money will change structures, but that's not the way things work. With *miso* soup a difference in temperature creates a current, and that makes the structure of *miso*. You have to start by bringing people together to share ideas—that will create a movement, and structure will emerge, not the other way round.[25]

As a visiting professor of Aizu University, Fujii Yasushi had started 'Code for Aizu', which is part of a national network called 'Code for Japan'. Started in 2013, the network has roughly 100 'brigades' (named after fire brigades) that address local matters, often but not exclusively with a digital technology element.[26] Brigades do hackathons, organize projects and accelerators, and promote participation in smart cities, using software like Decidim. 'Anyone can join, and anyone can leave', he commented in language reminiscent of cooperatives.

Aizu University developed a digital coin using blockchain technology, *byakko*, for campus use, and a digital wallet was part of Aizuwakamatsu's Super City bid. A network of researchers and practitioners nationwide is actively researching the use of digital currencies and blockchain technologies as tools for promoting interaction among local residents, and for local community building and revitalization (e.g. Takagi et al., 2017). They hope that this will reduce the money and information siphoned off by tech giants and governments, and that the technologies can be used to strengthen local economies and communities by retaining more of both. In other words, they share a vision for local, participative digital democracy.

Founders of such networks are now invited onto government advisory councils, given central ministry and Cabinet Office affiliations, and titles such as 'policy advisor', 'digital transformation fellow', 'regional DX advisor',

---

[24] Interview, 6 January 2022.
[25] Interview, 16 November 2021.
[26] https://www.code4japan.org (accessed 2 August 2022).

and 'open data evangelist'. This may account for the increasing emphasis on participation (and experimentation) in smart city guidelines discussed in Chapter 4. The range of networks, study groups, 'salons', and the like which transverse public and private sector, academic, and civil society boundaries, many with a strong ethical undertone, is quite remarkable. They serve as a reminder that the impetus for Japan's DX and GX comes from 'below' as well as from 'above'.

Corporations as Social Enterprise

We return to capitalism itself in the last section of this chapter. Not only have there been historical calls for Japan to practise a different kind of capitalism—*sanpō yoshi* and Shibusawa's *gapponshugi* for example—but many writers have asserted that Japanese capitalism *is* different, and in fact not really capitalist, whether because of ownership (Nishiyama, 1984), culture (Matsumoto, 1991), emphasis on people (Itami, 1987) or some other reason. The claims typically presuppose a hegemonic form of capitalism in which profits are the sole objective and shareholder interests are maximized, and consequently Japan is the exception. More recently Gotoh (2020) has argued that Japan's true capitalists were eliminated after World War II, that its elite politicians, bureaucrats, and even corporate heads have been essentially anti-capitalist, and that this coalition rebuffed attempts by neoliberal reformers to convert Japan in the mid 2000s.

The debate is not our focus here. Instead, we take up the example of a listed corporation which makes explicit its social objectives and has created a structure to achieve them. Whereas the previous section introduced two NPOs working towards environmental and social regeneration through the healing power of nature, this corporation is working towards similar goals through the power of art, architecture, and culture. No claim is made as to its representativeness, but it does illustrate that 'new capitalism' or 'public interest capitalism' is not so exceptional. Second, we will also consider other, alternative calls for the reform of Japanese capitalism, and their normative appeals for a moral economy.

Benesse Corporation and the Art of Island Rejuvenation

In 1986, following the sudden death of his father, Fukutake Soichiro returned to Okayama from Tokyo to become the president of Fukutake Shōten, an education correspondence and publishing company which had grown rapidly during Japan's high growth period.[27] He also took on his father's commitment to the mayor of Naoshima, one of the many islands of the Seto Inland Sea, to develop healthy tourism and a camp where children could come to learn, relax, and exchange ideas. Visiting the island, and talking with its residents, he felt they were happier than people in Tokyo; they had less materially, but they were less stressed. Fukutake decided that Maslow's five stages of self actualization were incomplete, and that there was a sixth stage, of happiness obtained through a happy community.

Over the next few years he re-oriented the company, acquiring Berlitz language schools and starting a new nursing care business, and changing the company name to Benesse (bene + esse), or good living. Contrary to the capitalism of Tokyo which he characterized as 'destroy and create', he began to espouse 'use what exists to create something new'.[28] He was moved by the paintings of Okayama-born Kuniyoshi Yasuo in his father's collection, which expressed the artist's resistance to Japanese militarism, and used the power of modern art for social ends.[29]

The problem, though, was that although the islands of the Seto Inland Sea were themselves beautiful, 'what exists' was also landscapes of environmental degradation from abandoned copper smelting factories, quarries, illegally dumped rubbish, and slopes denuded of vegetation, not to mention ageing communities and abandoned houses. Fukutake enlisted the help of the famous architect Ando Tadao, who supervised the construction of the Naoshima International Camp in 1989. The collaboration expanded, and three years later Benesse House was opened, comprised of a stunning contemporary art museum and hotel. Before long artists were coming to Naoshima to create new art, always with a view to working with the beauty of the island. In 1998 artists and architects began to work with abandoned houses, incorporating the island's culture and traditions. Sceptical islanders were won over and began to participate themselves.

The natural-light-lit subterranean Chichu Art Museum, opened in 2004, houses striking art from contemporary artists around the world, as well as five

---

[27] This account draws on Nonaka et al. (2014), Müller and Miki eds (2011), a presentation by Fukutake, Ando, and Kitagawa at the Foreign Correspondents' Club of Japan in May 2013 (https://www.youtube.com/watch?v=TizGPlAEg1c (accessed 2 August 2021)), as well as discussions between Fukutake Soichiro and the author.

[28] 'The more I thought about the contrast between the current urban situation and the lifestyle of people in the Seto Inland Sea area, the more sceptical I became about living in a "civilization of destruction and creation," where modernization is based on the unnatural process of destroying one thing so that another may be created. I began to feel the need for a "civilization of maintenance and development," one that "uses what exists to create what is to be." Unless we make this transition, the development of our culture will be arrested, and everything that we have created so far is certain to disappear in the future' (S. Fukutake, in Müller and Miki eds, 2011: 25).

[29] Kuniyoshi (1889–1953) moved to the US aged 17, refusing to enrol for military service in Japan.

of Monet's water lily paintings. The project spread to other islands—Inujima in 2008, where an old copper smelting complex became the Seirensho Art Museum, and a shell-shaped museum on Teshima in 2010, the same year the first Setouchi International Art Triennale was held, drawing almost a million visitors. This was a collaboration with Kitagawa Fram, who combined art and community development anchored in 'place'. Kitagawa and Fukutake had worked together to create the Echigo Tsumari Art Triennale, in conjunction with local woodland restoration, terraced paddy field restoration and village regeneration.

'Culture is my economics', declares Fukutake, an integral part of his version of 'public interest capitalism', rather than philanthropy. The Fukutake Foundation uses the dividends from Benesse shares for cultural works.[30]

Spectrum of Capitalism and Beyond

Japan has no shortage of 'post-capitalist' theorists, some inspired by Marx, such as Karatani Kojin (2021), whose view of history feeds into a 'new associationist movement', and Saito Kohei (2020), who argues that Marx was becoming increasingly concerned with the natural world, non-hierarchical organization and sharing, and proposes to take this forward in a 'Capital in the Anthropocene'. From a different theoretical perspective, Uzawa Hirofumi's post-Keynesian critique remains influential. An economy, Uzawa argued, consists of both private capital and 'social capital' (natural, social, and institutional), and as private capital is accumulated, so must social capital be. The postwar balance broke down, however, giving rise to many contemporary socio-economic problems (cf. Morris-Suzuki, 1989).

At a popular, vernacular level, there are 'shades' of capitalism, in addition to the 'sustainable capitalism' and 'new capitalism' we considered in Chapter 5. '*Satoyama* capitalism', for example, shares the Benesse theme of locality-based social and environmental embeddedness and advocates grass-roots international exchange rather than cosmopolitanism. *Satoyama* conjures up images of wooded hills and mountains behind a hometown village, shrouded in nostalgia but also in need of communal care, and nowadays restoration; 'encultured nature' as Knight (2010) calls it. From the early 2000s the newly created Ministry of the Environment began to promote *satoyama* as a model of human cohabitation with nature, bringing it into the 2010 Aichi

---

[30] Benesse sold Berlitz in 2022, and in November 2023 announced plans to delist from the TSE, to restructure its distance learning business, hit by Japan's falling child population.

COP10 summit, and creating the 'Satoyama Initiative' jointly with the United Nations University.[31]

In 2013 former DBJ employee Motani Kosuke and NHK Hiroshima Reporting Team published a book called *Satoyama shihonshugi* (*Satoyama capitalism*), as an antithesis to 'macho' twentieth-century, US-style 'money capitalism'. While the starting point for Benesse's project was the offshore islands of Okayama prefecture, here the starting point was inland Okayama's Maniwa City, whose lumber industry was decimated by cheap imports. With a boldness born of desperation, a struggling sawmill owner installed a power generator that could use his waste chips and shavings, lowering both his power and waste bills, and generating a power surplus he could sell to the local grid. A biomass pallet industry developed. The idea spread to other businesses and industries in the town, giving birth to a quasi-circular economy, flexible, and resilient but not introverted.

A consortium to promote *Satoyama* capitalism was formed, and a sequel was published by Motani and the consortium in 2020 with new examples, arguing for the movement to spread to Japan's cities.[32] The original publication declared that rural towns and cities need to work together to create a new economy, and saw the smart city movement, with its energy management systems as a promising vehicle. Such examples have a hint of nostalgia for what was lost in Japan's rush for modernization and industrialization, but mostly they are forward-looking. They are sceptical of metropolitan capitalism, but not opposed to technology. Although most are not overtly anti-government, they see change coming primarily from grass roots, self-help movements.

Concluding Comments

If capitalism requires non-capitalist ethics and institutions for its survival, then there is a future for capitalism in Japan, provided it meets its contemporary challenges. This chapter has shown that the historical reluctance to separate morals and the economy persists in contemporary Japan and will play a role in shaping Japan's future economy. The NHK drama 'Reach Beyond the Blue Sky', which depicted the life if Shibusawa Eiichi over 41 weekly episodes in 2021, was not just nostalgia for a bygone age, but an appeal to the continued relevance of *gapponshugi*, or bringing capital, labour, and management together to serve the public interest.

---

[31] See also Watanabe et al., 2012. *Satoumi* conjures up similar images of the sea, for those from coastal hometowns.

[32] https://www.japantimes.co.jp/satoyama-consortium/ (accessed 2 August 2021).

It is not just a matter of morals, or ethics, moreover. Nakane Chie (1970), famously depicted Japan as a 'vertical society', in which Japanese people develop strong ties and loyalty to their groups within organizations, vertically, but weak links horizontally. This view coloured the perceptions of many scholars, but this chapter has shown it to be a very partial view. Japan has, and has always had, a vigorous, horizontal social and solidarity economy, not necessarily based on class solidarity, but embodied in institutions such as cooperatives, and more recently in NPOs and myriads of formal and informal networks. As a generalization, earlier expressions of the SSE were bound up in formal organizations, with formal membership, subscriptions, and rules, whereas recent expressions have a tendency towards less formal, less rigid organization, and looser networks which people can participate in flexibly.

Norms and institutions both within Japanese capitalism and on its fringes may remain vital enough to put a brake on the shift towards shareholder prioritizing, financialized capitalism, as observers sometimes claim. As yet unanswered questions from this chapter include how the institutions of the postwar SSE will be re-invented and contribute to building the new economy—many have only recently embarked on that journey—and the terms in which the new networks and NPOs will gain entry to the corridors of bureaucratic and political power, whether by incorporation or by maintaining independence, as well as how the older and newer forms will interact. If the past is anything to judge by, institutional change will come from layering and conversion rather than exhaustion and displacement, while underlying norms which reject separation of the economic from the social and ethical will persist.

9

External Dependencies and Shifting Global Contexts

Japan's path to a new economy will not be entirely of its own making. A further set of influences on the building of Japan's new economy is external; much will depend on how the country navigates increasingly turbulent geopolitical currents and its external dependencies. These present Japan with both threats and opportunities and will take the country in directions as yet unforeseen. Chapter 9 highlights Japan's shifting global and regional contexts, its rising security concerns, and how it is addressing these through strategic diplomacy and 'economic statecraft'. Japan is itself being changed by these responses, making security and hence the role of the government more central in its digital and green transformation.

The discussion of state–market and organization–technology dyads in the Introduction concluded that we are at a major historical juncture in terms of: (a) a Polanyian shift in state-market relations, or 're-embedding' of markets; (b) an analogous shift in embedding of disruptive digital technologies; and (c) the geopolitical context of these dyads is in the throes of change. Far-reaching change is happening at all three levels simultaneously, and through their interaction. Geopolitical tensions are changing state–market relations, and at the core of these tensions are new technologies.

Since the Global Financial Crisis, and especially since 2016, a succession of events has led many to proclaim the end of globalization, at least in its current form. They include Brexit, Trump, the US–China trade and technology war, Covid-19 pandemic, Russia's invasion of Ukraine and the climate crisis. Vulnerabilities arising from the globalization of value chains have been exposed, and governments, including Japan, have introduced incentives for reshoring or 'friendshoring'. Yet in industries as complex as electronics and automobiles, this is no easy task, for reasons discussed in Chapter 5.

Interdependence is real but is increasingly prone to 'weaponization'. As Gertz and Evers (2020: 117) put it:

Building a New Economy. D. Hugh Whittaker, Oxford University Press. © D. Hugh Whittaker (2024).
DOI: 10.1093/oso/9780198893394.003.0010

Geopolitical competition increasingly takes place not on the battle-field but in a tightly networked global economy. As distinctions between economic and national security collapse, governments are embracing economic statecraft as a vital element in their foreign policy toolkits. They are learning how to weaponize the interdependencies produced by economic globalization and how to leverage their positions in networks to manipulate and coerce other states.

Economic statecraft is the use of economic means by states to pursue foreign policy goals or to incentivize or sanction businesses in pursuit of those goals. The US–China trade and technology war, Russia's invasion of Ukraine, and the ensuing Western sanctions are obvious examples. In the broad sense of a fusion of economic with political and military interests, this might even be called neo-mercantilism.[1] Although this is typically seen in geopolitical or geoeconomic terms, the nature of digital technology itself has been an important factor in bringing about the fusion. Technologies developed in small firms far from any battlefield can have important military significance, making cybersecurity and economic security a joint state and company concern.

For all but the biggest powers, however, and for especially Japan, ideas of statecraft and neomercantilism need to be anchored in a further perspective, which may be called resource dependence. Influential in organization studies, resource dependence theory can be applied at the national level as well. It holds that organizations—or here, countries—must secure resources from their environment, and this dependence plays an important role in shaping internal strategies, structures, and processes.[2] It does not happen in a mechanistic way; how the environment is perceived—constructed even—matters a great deal to goal achievement. Japan's external resource dependencies are manifold, and the changing nature of the dependencies, as well as its pursuit of geoeconomic interests, are bringing about changes within the Japanese state and economy. Thus the word 'security' appears many times in this chapter—economic security, energy security, food security, data security, and climate security.

The over-arching issue for Japan is how to achieve security and stability amidst geopolitical turbulence, especially vis-à-vis its postwar protector and ally the US on the one hand, and its biggest trading partner China on the other, amidst an increasingly fractious US–China relationship. China's

---

[1] Cf. M. Mueller (2021), 'Why We Need to Start Talking About Neo-mercantilism', https://www.internetgovernance.org/2021/08/04/why-we-need-to-start-talking-about-neo-mercantilism/ (accessed 28 May 2022).

[2] The seminal work was Pfeffer and Salancik, 1978.

growing assertiveness in Asia, backed by its military build-up, provides cause for the strengthening of US–Japan relations. On the other hand, domestic political turbulence within the US and uncertainties over future US commitments indicate a need for caution against over-identification with US policy. Both point to a need for Japan to greatly enhance its own defensive capabilities, but this conflicts with Article 9 of the postwar Constitution, (self-imposed) defence spending limits and other constraints. Arguably, Japan has dealt with these combined constraints deftly to date. In doing so, however, the Japanese state is being changed, as are state–market relations. To date Society 5.0 writing has shown little inclination to engage with this.

From a different perspective, Japan is also being influenced by its relations with emerging economies, particularly in Asia. At the height of its economic rise in the 1980s it was possible for Japan to see itself as the lead goose of a flying goose formation of emerging economies in East Asia. Some followers flew a little too fast, however, and began to challenge Japan's leadership in important industries, creating a Red Queen effect. One goose became a giant, and the formation lost its shape. But Japan has found new ways to maintain a leadership role vis-à-vis emerging Asia and beyond as far as Africa, linking its own digital and green transformation with countries in those regions, and upgrading its exports from goods to systems, services, and know-how. Smart cities are one example (Chapter 4), decarbonization is another (Chapter 3).

At the same time Japan looks to Europe—as Europe looks to Japan and Asia—finding overlapping interests not just in trade, but in digital and green transformation. The Japan–EU Economic Partnership Agreement (EPA), Strategic Partnership Agreement (SPA), data agreement and Green Alliance provide Japan with a further axis of security and stability which complements that of the US. By and large both Japan and the EU share a cautious approach to neoliberal market ideology and seek to balance state, market, and civil society relations. Their agreements focus less on free trade and tariff reductions, and more on technology, digital, green, strategic, and defence collaborations. If multilateralism gave way to a 'noodle bowl' of bilateral and minilateral agreements in the 2000s and first half of the 2010s, building a new digital and green economy requires Japan to prepare a new menu for its noodles.

Chapter 9 is structured as follows. The first section starts with a brief overview of trends in Japan's trade and overseas investments, its role in GVCs, and the challenges and responses to 'weaponized interdependence', one of which is 'friendshoring'. The case of semiconductors is particularly relevant. The second section extends this discussion to consider economic security and changes it is bringing within the Japanese state and its governance.

The third section considers Japan's energy dependencies, which have been brought into sharp relief by Russia's invasion of Ukraine. Japan's reliance on imported fossil fuels increased after Fukushima nuclear disaster in 2011 and the closure of the country's nuclear reactors. Russia's invasion of Ukraine posed another challenge, namely severing imports of Russian coal and oil as part of the country's package of sanctions. Ironically, Japan had increased its imports from Russia to reduce the risk of over-reliance on Middle East energy sources. Meanwhile, economic growth elsewhere in Asia is also increasing rather than decreasing demand for fossil fuels, and Japan hopes to become a leader in Asian decarbonization through its Asia Energy Transition Initiative and Asia Zero Emissions Community. This is now expressed as 'co-creation', avoiding the terminology of flying geese.

The fourth section considers food security, also problematized by Russia's invasion of Ukraine. Japan's policy of maintaining the postwar food system, including agricultural protection, arguably had the perverse effect of diminishing food self-sufficiency and security. Policy has begun to change, however, and Japan is seeking to leverage this change in Southeast Asia. The final section turns to Japan's evolving relations with the EU, encompassing climate security and data security. Linking with the previous section, it begins with geographic indications (GI) and growing areas of overlap, before turning to the EU–Japan EPA and SPA, partnership on infrastructure projects in third countries, and Green Alliance. The discussion of its external dependencies and security challenges which Japan is attempting to navigate is thus overlaid onto a geographic and geopolitical progression, from US–China tensions, to Russia, Asia, and Europe.

Changing Economic Interdependence

Few contemporaries could have foreseen the changes that would be unleashed by the visits of Richard Nixon and Tanaka Kakuei to China in 1972, or the Open Door policy announced by Deng Xiaoping in 1978, in terms of future trade, investment, production systems and geopolitics; changes which would accelerate in the 1990s, and yet further in the 2000s, leading to intense friction and rivalry between China and the US by the mid 2010s. Close relations with the US were paramount for Japan's postwar security and economic growth; the US was easily Japan's largest trading partner, and remained so into the twenty-first century. In 2002, however, imports from China overtook those of the US, and in 2009 China became Japan's largest export destination (Tables 9.1 and 9.2).[3] Good relations with both the US and China are thus critical to Japan, which must walk a tightrope in the trade and technology war between the two countries in view of these trade dependencies.

Next, Japan has consistently run a surplus in its balance of payments current account, but the trade surplus virtually disappeared after 2010, while primary income (profits, interest, and dividends from overseas investments) surged, indicating a qualitative shift in how Japan relates to other countries economically. In 2021 Japan's primary income was 12 times the trade surplus, and in 2022 the latter plunged into deficit.[4] In terms of foreign direct investment (FDI), the US has easily maintained its position as Japan's leading destination (Table 9.3), but Japan's investments in mainland China are nonetheless significant, especially because they are highly profitable, returning close to 15 per cent annually, as against a rate closer to 6 per cent for the

Table 9.1 Japan's top five trading partners for imports 2000, 2010, 2020 (%)

2000		2010		2020	
US	19.0	China	22.1	China	25.7
China	14.5	US	9.7	US	11.0
S. Korea	5.4	Australia	6.5	Australia	5.6
Taiwan	4.7	Saudi Arabia	5.2	Taiwan	4.2
Indonesia	4.3	U.A.E.	4.2	S. Korea	4.2

Source: Japanese customs data, https://www.customs.go.jp/toukei/suii/html/data/y5.pdf (accessed 15 May 2022).

Table 9.2 Japan's top five trading partners for exports 2000, 2010, 2020 (%)

2000		2010		2020	
US	29.7	China	19.4	China	22.1
Taiwan	7.5	US	15.4	US	18.4
S. Korea	6.4	S. Korea	8.1	S. Korea	7.0
China	6.3	Taiwan	6.8	Taiwan	6.9
Hong Kong	5.7	Hong Kong	5.5	Hong Kong	5.0

Source: Japanese customs data, https://www.customs.go.jp/toukei/suii/html/data/y4.pdf (accessed 15 May 2022).

---

[3] The US topped China in 2019, but in 2020 China was once again Japan's leading export destination.
[4] Nikkei Asia, 27 May 2022 ('Helped by Weak Yen, Japan Remains Top Creditor Nation with Record Net External Assets').

Table 9.3 Japan's top FDI destinations in 2000, 2010, 2020 (US$ billion, stock)

2000		2010		2020	
US	132.2	US	251.8	US	591.5
Asian NIES	23.2	Latin Am.	107.0	Asian NIES	197.5
UK	21.8	Netherlands	76.0	U.K	174.0
Latin Am.	21.0	Asian NIES	68.4	Netherlands	154.9
Netherlands	16.7	China	66.5	ASEAN 4	152.7
ASEAN 4	15.6	ASEAN 4	58.4	China	143.5
China	8.7	Australia	39.9	Latin Am.	128.1

Source: JETRO, https://www.jetro.go.jp/world/japan/stats/fdi.html (accessed 15 May 2022).
Note: Includes country groupings: Asian NIES (Hong Kong, Taiwan, S. Korea, Singapore);
ASEAN 4 (Thailand, Indonesia, Malaysia, Philippines); Latin Am. = Central and South
America (including—or especially—Cayman Islands, etc.). Calculation methods were
changed in 2014, so figures before and after this date are not directly comparable.

US and Europe, with the rest of Asia and Latin America in between (JETRO,
2021: 26).

Trade and investment figures, furthermore, are insufficient to grasp the
extent of economic dependence—or interdependence—and its changes over
time, as they don't fully account for trade in intermediate goods which
contribute a significant share of the value added of many exports. A more
nuanced picture comes from trade in value added (TIVA) indicators of forward and backward participation in GVCs, the former showing the share
of export value incorporated in the products and services subsequently
exported from receiving countries, and the latter conversely showing the
share of imported intermediate goods and services which are incorporated
into exports. Japan had the highest forward participation ratio in 2011, when
a third of its exports were incorporated into receiving countries' exports. Its
'decline' as an exporting nation, then, may better be understood as a shift to
a less visible but nonetheless important role in world trade, in addition to
its overseas investments. By the same token, its dependence on a stable and
rules-based trading order has become even more pronounced.[5]

This order has been thoroughly shaken in recent years. Speculation that
the age of globalization was over following the Global Financial Crisis proved
premature, but escalating US–China trade and technology friction, followed
by Covid-19 and Russia's invasion of Ukraine have shaken the neoliberal global trading order. Reactions include 'reshoring' and 'friendshoring'.
Already in the years leading up to Covid-19 Japanese companies had been

---

[5] Whittaker et al., 2020: 114–119; Katada, 2020.

diversifying their supply chains in response to rising labour costs in China, as well as risk hedging—the so-called 'China plus one' strategy. In the pandemic this diversification became more compelling, and the Japanese government set aside ¥240 billion for supply chain re-organization, including reshoring production back to Japan. The first to be granted what became known as a 'China-exit subsidy' was Iris Ohyama, a producer of face masks. As the value of the yen dropped in 2022, moreover, more companies announced plans to relocate production back in Japan. Yet reshoring is not without its challenges; waiting for these companies were high energy costs, and a shortage of labour.

Covid-19 and a mix of contingent factors created a shortage of semiconductors, just as demand for them was surging. Concentration of production in Taiwan and South Korea was also a strategic concern. As a US White House report put it:

> US companies, including major fabless semiconductor companies, depend on foreign sources for semiconductors, especially in Asia, creating a supply chain risk. Many of the materials, tools, and equipment used in the manufacture of semiconductors are available from limited sources, semiconductor manufacturing is geographically concentrated, and the production of leading-edge semiconductors requires multi-billion dollar investments.
>
> **(The White House, 2021: 24)**

From this assessment came the Chips Act, with $52 billion of federal funding to rebuild the US semiconductor industry. The Japanese government, too, introduced a support package of ¥774 billion (then $7 billion), later raised to ¥2 trillion, which enticed investment from leading Taiwanese, US, European, and Korean companies (Chapter 5). The Biden administration set up the formation of the Indo-Pacific Economic Forum (IPEF) in 2022, not so much as a conventional trading bloc, but officially to enhance supply chain resilience, and to promote digitalization, decarbonization, and clean energy. The unstated aim was to reduce supply chain reliance on China.

Economic Security and Defence

> Many Japanese companies that never considered their business or R&D to have national security implications have begun to realize that this is no longer the case. For instance, the drone swarm technology that allowed 1824 drones to create the shape of the Earth during the opening ceremony of the Tokyo 2020 Olympic Games

can be used by UAVs for combat. There are many other examples, such as 3D print-ing, biotechnology, or artificial intelligence, that are being researched by Japanese companies that don't fully realize the technology's military potential.

(Igata and Glosserman, 2021: 26)

Japan's digital and green transformation (DX, GX) will be increasingly influ-enced by issues related to security, in its many forms. DX in particular creates new vulnerabilities, which expand and change conventional secu-rity concerns. We touched on this in Chapter 2, noting that Japan has been scrambling to respond to these new vulnerabilities, which are compounded by geopolitical tensions. The tensions are often posed as a conflict between liberal and illiberal political-economic systems, but responding to them itself poses a challenge to the former, as the state assumes more powers to monitor and tighten security.

China's rise, its increasingly assertive stance on a range of issues including territorial disputes, and its rivalry with the US, is at the core of the geopo-litical tensions. The giant on its doorstep presents numerous challenges for Japan, from a territorial dispute over the Senkaku Islands and maritime secu-rity, to its heavy dependence on rare earths, highlighted by China's export embargo during the Senkaku confrontation, providing a lesson for Japan in the 'weaponization of interdependence'.

Japan's response to such tensions has included, first, a more assertive diplomacy, deploying 'strategic communication' to this end (Pugliese and Patalano, 2020). The Abe administration coined the notion of 'Free and Open Indo-Pacific' (FOIP) as a rallying cry to contain China and its Silk Road initiatives without explicitly naming them, and to appeal to its alternative credentials of democracy and the 'rule of law'. The US Trump and Biden administrations adopted the concept, and in May 2022 at a meeting of the Quad grouping of the US, Australia, India, and Japan hosted by Japan, IPEF was inaugurated. Japan, the US, and Australia also created a Blue Dot Net-work for assessment and certification of infrastructure projects, which was subsequently taken up by the OECD.

A second response has been a major shift in Japan's stance towards defence, and military spending, especially following Russia's invasion of Ukraine and fears that mainland China might invade Taiwan. The national security and defence strategies announced in December 2022 will see a substantial rise in defence spending, and the development of counterstrike capabilities. The US, South Korea, and Japan reactivated their 'extended (nuclear) deterrence capabilities' to respond to potential threats from China, North Korea, and Russia. Japan signed a Reciprocal Access Agreements with Australia and the UK, with whom it also agreed to develop a new fighter jet, together with Italy, the first such deal outside the US in the postwar era. And it loosened restrictions on exports of such fighter jets and missiles to countries it has signed security agreements with, hoping to defray weaponry development costs.[6] It has increased its cooperation with the 'Five Eyes' intelligence grouping of the US, UK, Canada, Australia, and New Zealand. The list could continue.

Third, there has been a tightening of economic security. Japan's relationship with the US remains central, both in defence and economic terms, which increasingly overlap. In 2021 the two countries signed the US–Japan Competitiveness and Resilience (CoRe) Partnership, which includes cooperation in R&D in a range of cutting-edge technologies and activities, including:

- 5G Networks, including Open Radio Access Networks (O-RAN)
- Next generation networks (Beyond 5G, or 6G), to which the US committed $2.5 billion and Japan $2 billion
- Global Digital Connectivity Partnership
- ICT global standard setting
- Sensitive supply chains, including semiconductors
- Biotechnology, including genome sequencing
- Quantum information science and technology

The US–Japan CoRe Partnership is an example of what Tyson and Guile (2021) call 'innovation for economic security', in the dual senses of innovation within a context of economic security (international R&D collaboration among friends), and innovation contributing to economic security. As its collaborations with the US become ever stronger, Japan is under pressure to tighten up on its domestic economic security, to prevent sensitive technologies from leaching to China. In 2022 the Japanese Diet passed the Economic Security Law, which had four main provisions:

- Government ability to vet procurement, equipment and cybersecurity in 14 key industries, including energy, water, IT, finance, and transportation;
- Subsidies to strengthen sensitive supply chains, especially in semiconductors, to make them less vulnerable to disruption;

---

[6] The countries include the US, UK, Germany, France, Italy, Vietnam, Thailand, Indonesia, Malaysia, the Philippines, India, and Australia. *Nikkei Asia*, 27 May 2022 ('Japan to Enable Fighter Jet and Missile Exports to 12 Nations').

- Government support for R&D in key technologies deemed important for economic security, and the promotion of public-private cooperation for this;
- Secret patents for technologies which could be used by other countries for military purposes, with fines or imprisonment for leaking such patent information.[7]

Japan plans to introduce a security clearance system with different levels of clearance in 2024 for government and private-sector workers with access to sensitive information, modelled after systems in the US and Europe.

Fourth, these diplomatic, defence, and economic security developments increasingly have cyber dimensions, or cyber parallels. Japan is planning to make around a thousand companies and organizations meet US cybersecurity guidelines in 2024, to protect potentially sensitive information. Fujitsu clearly failed to do so when its cloud-based internet service, which is used by government agencies and corporations, was hacked in 2021 and 2022, forcing government intervention.

Analogous to FOIP, Japan proposed 'Data Free Flow with Trust' (DFFT) at the G20 Summit in 2019. It signed a digital trade agreement with the US, and a data movement agreement with the EU in 2019. DFFT was in part a move to counter to China's Digital Silk Road, which was added to its Belt and Road initiatives in 2015 and has become increasingly linked to state objectives. Quite separately, Singapore, Chile, and New Zealand created a Digital Economy Partnership Agreement (DEPA) in 2019. These are three of the four countries which originally set in motion the Trans Pacific Partnership (the fourth was Brunei), which Japan joined and assumed leadership of when the Trump Administration withdrew from it.[8] Digital noodle bowls are beginning to form, and will be shaped by geopolitics.

Finally, these changes in Japan's external relations, and particularly the increased importance of economic security, have brought about changes in Japan's internal state governance. Under the National Security Council (itself established only in 2013; Figure 2.1), the National Security Secretariat added an economic division to its existing six divisions in 2020. By 2022 it had become the largest of the divisions. These all operate under the *Kantei* (OPMC), which has become the 'control tower' of the new Japanese state.

---

[7] Cf. Glosserman, 'New Economic Security Bill Lays the Foundation for Real National Security', *The Japan Times*, 17 May 2022; also 'Japan Passes Economic Security Bill to Guard Sensitive Technology', *The Japan Times*, 11 May 2022.

[8] China applied to join DEPA in 2021. It also applied to join the CPTPP (successor to TPP), as did Taiwan. The UK was admitted in 2023.

Table 9.4 Japan's fossil fuel imports by country of origin (2019, %)

Coal		Oil		LNG	
Australia	68.0	Saudi Arabia	34.1	Australia	39.2
Indonesia	12.4	U.A.E.	32.7	Malaysia	13.0
Russia	11.9	Qatar	9.3	Russia	8.3
US	3.7	Kuwait	8.9	Brunei	5.6
Canada	2.9	Russia	4.9	US	5.4
Share in electricity generation					
	32		7		37

Source: Agency for Natural Resources and Energy (ANRE) Energy White Paper 2021; https://www.enecho.meti.go.jp/about/whitepaper/2021/html/2-1-3.html (accessed 15 May 2022). Share of electricity generation figures as for Figure 3.1.

This control tower is linked closely with various ministries and agencies, such as an Economic Security Policy Division in MOFA, Economic Security Division in METI, and Economic Security Information Planning post at the Ministry of Defence (Igata and Glosserman, 2021). External security, as well as economic statecraft, will undoubtedly influence Japan's path towards Society 5.0.

Energy Security and Decarbonization

Japan has other security concerns as well, especially in the field of energy. With few natural energy resources of its own, Japan relies greatly on imported fossil fuels. Coal and LNG each generate a third of the country's electricity. Much of the coal comes from Australia, oil from the Middle East, and LNG from a variety of sources, especially Australia (Table 9.4). Nuclear reactors which had generated over a quarter of the nation's electricity were closed after the Fukushima nuclear disaster, and by early 2022 only ten of the 33 operable reactors had met new standards, with five actually in operation. Renewables had edged up to 20 per cent, but on the eve of the Russian invasion of Ukraine, fossil fuels still accounted for three-quarters of the total energy mix.

Previously, as Japan attempted to phase out older coal plants, LNG presented a less-polluting transition alternative. Japan became the world's biggest importer of LNG, until it was overtaken by China in 2021. In its quest to secure stable long-term supplies, Japan turned to Russia, and especially to nearby Sakhalin island. The solution became a nightmare when Russia invaded Ukraine. Joining the coalition of countries imposing sanctions, Japan announced that it would stop importing Russian coal, and that it would phase out Russian oil imports over time. LNG, less polluting than the other two, presented a more painful dilemma.

The dilemma focused on the Sakhalin 2 field, in which Mitsui & Co. held a 12.5 per cent stake and Mitsubishi Corp. a 10 per cent stake, with Japan importing 60 per cent of the output. If Japan were to pull out, not only would it lose a significant, somewhat cleaner, fuel source, but other countries—probably China—would be only too happy to take its place, benefiting from cheaper prices as Japan's energy costs soared. Russian President Putin turned the screw by announcing that the project's assets would be transferred to a new operating company, and investors would have to declare within a month whether they would stay in, with an uncertain share, or sell, with the proceeds kept in Russia. There was additional uncertainty about the purchase contracts. In the end, the two companies kept their stakes in the new operator.

The long-term effects of Russia's invasion of Ukraine on Japanese energy policy remain to be seen, but they appear to have pushed Japan more decisively along the path of GX, described in Chapter 3. This includes investments in new technologies for hydrogen and ammonia production, for example, and carbon capture, utilization, and storage (CCUS). And here, while its own dependence on external sources of energy poses severe challenges in terms of energy security, Japan also sees an opportunity—to apply its own experience and technologies in energy transition and decarbonization to Asian countries navigating their own transitions—just as it does for smart cities and digital transformation.

In Southeast Asia, energy demand is projected to grow 60 per cent by 2040, with 80 per cent of overall energy demand met by fossil fuels, including 70 per cent for electricity generation (METI, 2021b: 13). Japan launched the Asia Energy Transition Initiative (AETI) at the ASEAN–Japan Business Week in 2021 to support the development of energy transition roadmaps, and to promote of an 'Asian version' of transition finance, with $10 billion in funding to support energy efficiency and renewable energy, and access to Japan's Green Innovation Fund for technology development and deployment. 'We will continue to deepen our dialogue with ASEAN countries and extend our views on the need for a realistic transition to the international community', METI's press release stated.[9]

AETI, AZEC (Asia Zero Emissions Community, launched 2022) and other international GX initiatives encourage Japan's private sector companies to scale up their green efforts. Here too, the underlying stance is that growth and green are compatible, and that each country must determine its own

---

[9] https://www.meti.go.jp/english/press/2021/0528_002.html (accessed 20 May 2022).

combination in line with the principles of 3E+S (energy security, economic efficiency, environmental protection, and safety).

Food Security and Agriculture Revival

Parallels can be seen in food and agriculture. Russia's invasion of Ukraine revived another security concern for Japan: food. The country's vulnerability to food import interruptions was shown during the spike in global food prices in 2007–08, and earlier with the 1973 US embargo on soy bean exports. On those two occasions, Japan's giant trading companies acquired tracts of land overseas with ODA support, and made substantial investments in food chains, first into Japan, and then into China and elsewhere in Asia.[10] Nonetheless, once again a debate erupted over Japan's declining 'self sufficiency ratio.'

According to the calorie measure preferred by the Ministry of Agriculture, Forestry and Fisheries (MAFF), Japan's self sufficiency ratio dropped from 80 per cent in 1960 to 70 per cent in 1970, and continued to fall, to 40 per cent in 2000. Despite MAFF's declared determination to raise it to 45 per cent ever since, the ratio in fact continued to decline, reaching 37 per cent in 2020. During this time the area of cultivated land declined by roughly 40 per cent from its peak of roughly 6 million hectares in 1961, and with it, agriculture production also fell.

Yamashita (2022), a former MAFF official and now trenchant critic, attributes the fall and 2022 scare to policy failure, pointing out that acreage control and associated policies perversely maintained the over-production of rice through high prices despite declining demand, and conversely failed to stimulate wheat production despite rising demand because of an over-reliance on cheaper imports. (In 2010 household expenditure on bread surpassed rice, and by the early 2020s it looked like the same might happen with noodles.)

Yet change has come to Japanese agriculture. Despite fierce opposition to Japan joining the (then) TPP negotiations amidst claims that it would decimate the sector, and with it the soul of Japan, Abe succeeded in both joining the TPP grouping and eventually leading the formation of the Comprehensive and Progressive Agreement for Trans-Pacific Partnership (CPTPP), as well as changing the agriculture narrative. Placing it in his third

[10] Cf. Hall, 2015; Whittaker and Scollay, 2019.

arrow, he set up a 'Vitality Creation Headquarters of Agriculture, Forestry, Fisheries and Rural Regions' in 2013, tasking it with doubling agriculture exports to ¥1 trillion by 2020. The figure was achieved in 2021 (without accounting for imports of intermediate goods used), ironically, not just from exports of sake to China, but beef to the US.[11] The goal was increased to ¥5 trillion by 2030.

'Agriculture on the front foot' (*seme no nōgyō*) accelerated farmland consolidation and brought new actors into Japanese agriculture and food chains. Manufacturers, including almost all the major electronics companies, set up farm divisions, while Toyota applied its kaizen practices to rice, aiming to reduce costs to ¥100/kg.[12] The hope is that these technologies can be exported to Asia, for example to Dà Lat, Vietnam, with much greater access to land, and appealing the Japanese manufacturing reputation for quality to a growing Asian middle class.

Growing EU–Japan collaboration

Abe's attempt to put ailing Japanese agriculture on the front foot saw Japan adopt a sui generis geographical indication (GI) certification system in 2015, replacing its earlier trademark system. By January 2021, 105 products had been certified, with a high number of fresh, unprocessed foods (kaki persimmon, nashi pears, etc.) and bovine meats (nine certifications) in the total.[13] The system was adopted in the context of the EU–Japan Economic Partnership Agreement (EPA) negotiations, which specified mutual protection of GI products.[14] In fact Feuer (2019) argues that the EU promoted GI policies in Asia more generally with a view to shoring up its own position on IP rights for agri-food vis-à-vis the US in the (ultimately unsuccessful) Transatlantic Trade and Investment Partnership (TTIP) negotiations.

Despite intense trade friction in the past, the EU and Japan have found common interest, not just in protecting small-scale agriculture and small-scale businesses, but in an increasing range of areas, including digital and green transformation. The EU–Japan EPA was eventually signed and came

---

[11] https://english.kyodonews.net/news/2021/12/c0f11ce9a471-update1-japans-agricultural-exports-exceed-1-tril-yen-for-1st-time.html (accessed 21 May 2022).
[12] A separate, agro-ecological current of change has seen young urbanites returning to the land with government incentives and the prospect of a more family- and environmentally friendly way of living. Tourism, temporarily interrupted by the Covid-19 pandemic, has become a new source of off-farm supplementary income.
[13] Kimura and Rigolot, 2021. The law is administered by MAFF, and not the Patent Office, 'which essentially adds GI to the portfolio of rural support mechanisms in Japan' (Feuer, 2019: 43).
[14] Ibid.

into force in 2019. More than just a framework and schedule for the reduction of tariffs, it covered labour rights, environmental protection, state-owned enterprises, public procurement, intellectual property, and data protection. It was the first EU trade agreement to include specific reference to the Paris Agreement.

A Strategic Partnership Agreement (SPA) was signed at the same time, and although full implementation required the ratification of all EU member states, parts of it were implemented soon after. Whereas EU SPAs have mostly been expressions of good intent, this one also had legal provisions, a joint coordinating committee and a dispute settlement procedure. With Trump's 'America First' and pulling back from international agreements, as well as US–China tensions, the EPA and SPA assumed a new importance for both parties. Subtitled 'A partnership to promote shared values', the SPA as presented to the European Parliament stated:

> The EU and Japan share the same basic values, including on democracy, market economy, human rights, human dignity, freedom, equality, and the rule of law. Against a background of increasingly assertive neighbours, they are also putting emphasis on security issues... The SPA represents a framework strengthening the overall partnership, by promoting political and sectoral cooperation and joint actions in more than 40 areas of common interest... The agreement will facilitate joint EU-Japan efforts to promote shared values such as human rights and rule of law, a rules-based international system, and peace and stability across the world. It will allow EU-Japan security cooperation to reach its full potential.[15]

The 40 areas included tackling crime, climate change and environmental protection, space, culture, disaster management, sustainable development, and poverty eradication, reform of the United Nations, and cooperation in culture, science, technology, and industry.

A third agreement was signed in early 2019 regarding data flows. On the day that Abe proposed 'data free flow with trust' (DFFT) to the World Economic Forum, Japan became the first non-EU country to be recognized under the EU's General Data Protection Regulation (GDPR) adequacy provisions, and the EU became the first to be recognized under the Japanese Act on the Protection of Personal Information (APPI). Although it only covered the private sector (as data in Japan's public sector is not supervised by an independent authority), it was significant given the recent 'transatlantic data war'. This erupted in 2015 when the European Court of Justice struck down the Safe Harbour agreement that allowed data flows between the EU and US on

---

[15] https://www.europarl.europa.eu/RegData/etudes/BRIE/2018/630,323/EPRS_BRI(2018)630323_EN.pdf (accessed 22 May 2022).

the grounds that the privacy of EU citizens' data could not be guaranteed in the US.[16] The EU–Japan data agreement created the 'world's largest area of safe data transfer' with a 'high degree of convergence between the two systems', the joint statement enthused.

Cooperation in Aid, Infrastructure, and GX

The EU and Japan also signed a Partnership on Sustainable Connectivity and Quality Infrastructure in 2019. Aimed at deepening cooperation over aid and development, it covered trade and transport infrastructure, energy platforms, digital infrastructure and services, and human aspects.[17] Then in 2021 they formed a Green Alliance. In addition to encouraging mutual green investment, here too an objective was collaboration in GX projects in third countries.

It is notable that Japan sought closer alignment with the EU over data protection and the environment, and closer relations with the US, Quad, and AUKUS over security, at least until the advent of the Biden administration. The Inflation Reduction Act of 2022 marked a major change in US climate policy, as well as an attempt to rebuild the middle class in the US, while the EU (and NATO) has moved closer to Japan in terms of security in East Asia. These evolving relationships not only relieve Japan's insecurities and dependencies, but act as mechanisms to stimulate change within Japan as well. This is something we will return to in the concluding chapter.

Concluding Comments

Japan's path to Society 5.0 through digital and green transformation will not be entirely of its own making. This chapter has highlighted some of Japan's external dependencies, as well as its strategic diplomacy and communication which has sought to mitigate vulnerabilities to those dependencies. This has been situated against a backdrop of rising geopolitical tensions and has hastened the recalibration of state–market relations. Arguably Japan has steered an astute path through these choppy waters to date.

---

[16] Whereas EU countries had developed comprehensive rules around data collection and processing overseen by independent regulatory authorities, the US continued to rely on a patchwork of specific, and sometimes dated, rules governing different sectors (Farrell and Newman, 2016). However, Miyashita (2021) also points to different philosophical approaches emphasizing 'dignity' in the EU (Article 1 of the EU Charter of Fundamental Rights is titled 'Human Dignity') and (negative) freedom in the US.

[17] The EU's 'sustainable connectivity' emphasized connections between countries to achieve the SDGs, while Japan's 'quality infrastructure' emphasized social and environmental impact, debt sustainability, safety, etc. in an implicit contrast with China's Belt and Road infrastructure projects: Söderberg, 2021.

Geopolitically, Japan's biggest challenge has been how to navigate the growing rivalry between the US and China, its two biggest trading partners, one providing its postwar security umbrella, market access and access to new technologies and ideas, the other a close neighbour and historical source of much of Japan's culture. Both are crucial to Japan, but there are dangers as well. Japan also faces the challenge of being eclipsed in terms of influence, trade, and investment in Southeast Asia and elsewhere. It has responded by pursuing 'rules-based order' diplomacy and a 'free and open Indo-Pacific' to counter to China's growing attempts, and ability, to re-shape the regional and international order around its own interests. This has provided a rationale for new alliances, which extend beyond ASEAN to India and Africa, and to Australia and the Pacific island nations. And to Europe, where ties have deepened markedly in recent years.

New abrupt and disruptive challenges such as Covid-19 and the war in Ukraine have highlighted Japan's external vulnerabilities. Society 5.0 initially expressed a vision for internal economic and social transformation, but Japan is now having to factor in these external dependency challenges as it moves along the path towards that vision. Managing these interdependencies, as well as its domestic DX, GX, Society 5.0, and new capitalism agenda, is bringing changes to the Japanese state. We touched briefly on these in terms of changes to the OPMC—the Japan's new 'control tower'—and emanating from there, changes in bureaucracies and the business community. How might we characterize this new state? Are there potential lessons to be learned by other countries? If so, which ones? These are some of the questions that will be addressed in the concluding chapter.

10

Conclusion

Controlled Dis-equilibrium

Society 5.0, DX, GX, sustainable capitalism, new form of capitalism, digital garden city nation, rebuilding the middle class.... What are we to make of the flurry of initiatives to rebuild the Japanese economy, most with a target date of 2030 or 2030s? Do they add up to something coherent or are they just a lot of noise? The preceding chapters seem to add to the questions raised in the Introduction rather than answering them. Closer inspection, however, yields some unexpected answers, and interpretations, which will be presented in this chapter.

Japan has had two major periods of upheaval and institutional change in its recent history: the 1860s–80s, in the 'Meiji Restoration', and following the country's defeat in the Second World War. Much speculation has been expended on the possibility of a third major re-orientation (or 're-opening'), triggered variously by Japan's asset bubble burst (1989–1990); the Asian Financial Crisis and Japan's own financial crisis (1997–2000); the Global Financial Crisis (2008); 3:11 (2011).... Yet none of these has produced institutional change on a level of the two previous episodes. And rather than dealing with upheaval, the underlying concern has been how to escape from the gravitational pull of institutional stasis. This is the backdrop to the interpretations which follow.

There has been change; in fact quite a lot of it. The first task of this chapter, then, is to see what if anything can be said about the combined effects of the changes. I will venture, first, that there are three clusters of ongoing institutional change, and identify each with a 'spirit' of capitalism. They are, respectively, financialized capitalism, the new, adaptive developmental state (or state capitalism), and communitarian capitalism. Second, that these three 'spirits' are not simply grouping characterizations. On the one hand they contain contradictory currents. On the other hand, the tensions in their interactions produce change, which may be to some degree intentional rather than random. Third, this may be called *controlled dis-equilibrium*, an

Building a New Economy. D. Hugh Whittaker, Oxford University Press. © D. Hugh Whittaker (2024).
DOI: 10.1093/oso/9780198893394.003.0011

underlying 'trinity' (to borrow the term from Chapter 7) propelling Japan towards a new economy. The trinity is not entirely new, but its particular characteristics are.

Relatedly, rather than simply dismissing the vociferous 'fundamental' 'root and branch' reform, 'last chance' pronouncements as empty hyperbole, and targets such as increasing the number of startups and funding for them 'tenfold' as fantasy, we might rather see them as a rhetorical device, or *strategic hyperbole*, which like the three spirits, is intended to combat institutional stasis, although it does risk rhetorical inflation with diminishing returns. These primarily concern the state–market dyad and are discussed in the first section.

In the second section we turn to the organization–technology dyad. Here, too, there appear to be inconsistencies in industrial and innovation policy, namely between a competitive technology-push approach, and the social innovation approach advocated by the CSTI when it proposed Society 5.0. These respective approaches, in turn, manifest a further ambivalence, between situating Japan as lagging and in need of catch-up, a stance which motivated Japan for a hundred years, and post-catch-up, which sees Japan as having to forge its own path through DX and GX to Society 5.0. As well, we will consider the growing influence of security concerns on innovation, as a nascent third current. These very loosely map onto the three 'spirits' of Japanese capitalism.

The third section addresses the claims that Society 5.0 and new capitalism will put people at the heart of Japan's future economic model. It does so first in terms of the 'social investment state', second in terms of an 'anthropogenic' mode of development and third in terms of 'digital democracy'. Although not a model in normative terms, the addition of new capitalism and related initiatives discussed in the second half of the book give more credence to the human-centric claims than Society 5.0 and related initiatives considered in the first half. Together, to adopt the cart metaphor, they constitute a cart with wheels travelling along a path between oligopolistic Big Tech and an overbearing state.

Although there are contradictions, the significance of Japan's efforts may ultimately lie less in achieving institutional coherence, than in how it is grappling with complexity and contradictions. This is because, one way or another, most economies are also facing similar challenges, especially when it comes to the climate crisis, and in some cases demographics. This is an optimistic interpretation, of course; others are possible. We conclude by returning to the four scenarios of the Introduction.

Overcoming Institutional Stasis: Three Spirits of Japanese Capitalism

The developments described in the preceding chapters do not always point in the same direction. Institutionally and ideationally there are contradictions. For example, ongoing reforms under the influence of the Financial Services Agency and Tokyo Stock Exchange are intended to make corporate governance more responsive to shareholder interests, while Keidanren's 'sustainable capitalism' insists on a stakeholder orientation. Underneath the rhetoric of shared investor and manager interests in raising 'corporate value' and ESG, there are in fact conflicting interests. Kishida's 'new capitalism' calls for a doubling of *investment* income, while also seeking to reduce social polarization and inequality. The trinity labour market reforms are premised on compatibility between investment in human resources and increased labour mobility....

There is no single institutional logic in Japan's attempt to build a new economy. In fact, it is possible to divide them into *three* institutional logics, of varying strength. Drawing liberally on Boltanski and Chiapello's (1997/2005) *The New Spirit of Capitalism*, we may call them three 'spirits' of contemporary Japanese capitalism.[1] The first is *financialized capitalism*. This may seem odd, as conventional 'varieties of capitalism' typologies have placed Japanese capitalism in polarized opposition to financialized capitalism, although some have argued that Japan has defected from this camp. Here I will argue that it plays a role in upsetting stasis and is accepted as long as it is balanced by the other two spirits. As such, it is a variation on the theme of using foreign ideas to challenge and change Japanese practices and institutions.

The second and third spirits are sometimes presented as one. Anchordoguy, for example, defines 'communitarian capitalism' as:

> an economic system characterized by an activist state and a number of private sector organizations that manage markets to promote development and national autonomy in the context of broader goals of social stability, predictability, and order.... (C)ommunity is the basic organizational logic that guides state, corporate, and individual behaviour in Japan.
>
> (Anchordoguy, 2005: 6)

---

[1] Boltanski and Chiapello argue that socio-economies are produced by multiple cités or orders—civic, market, inspired, fame, industrial, domestic—the combination of which changes historically, producing a different 'spirit' of capitalism. In the nineteenth century it was familial capitalism, followed by managerial capitalism, and then a new spirit which they tentatively identified as global and project-oriented. The adaptation here proposes contemporaneous 'spirits' in a single economy.

Here we will differentiate between the 'activist state' part on the one hand, and a communitarian logic on the other. The former is related to the resurrection of Japan's famed developmental state, albeit in a modified form, with different tools. The latter is related to a more horizontal ethos and institutions, which can be at odds with the designs of the state, but also with financialized capitalism, as we saw in Chapter 8. I propose that the three spirits, *broadly* corresponding to market, state and civil society, interact in a state of tension and cooperation, to produce change within bounds. The label 'controlled dis-equilibrium' describes this. It has implications for our understanding of institutional change and coherence. Let us look at the three 'spirits' in turn.

Financialized Capitalism

Designating financialized capitalism as one of Japan's three spirits is unusual, to say the least, as it is typically associated with the liberal market Anglophone countries, as opposed to coordinated market capitalism, in whose camp Japan firmly sits. But that is only because of the influence of monolithic national labels, in which anything that does not fit is treated as an anomaly, an invasive force, or is ignored. Some observers, however, have argued that Japan has partly adopted neoliberalism and financialized capitalism, and its institutions have become hybridized (e.g. Aoki, 2008), while Dore (2009) went further and argued, polemically, that Japan dropped its resistance and in fact converted to neoliberalism and financialized capitalism. The argument here is somewhat different. It is not about hybridization or conversion, but instrumentalization of different logics, based on a tolerance of ambiguity and contradiction.

There is no simple definition of financialization or financialized capitalism. It is frequently linked to the growing influence of shareholder interests in corporate governance and hence corporate behaviour.[2] As we saw in Chapter 6, this has occurred in Japan through the Stewardship and Corporate Governance Codes, TSE listing requirements, and measures to make Tokyo more friendly to international investors. Rising returns to investors indicate that these have produced tangible results. Activists can now make a case to be heard rather than being shut down peremptorily, although they must be

---

[2] Krippner's definition of financialization was given at the end of Chapter 1. Epstein (2005: 3) defines it as 'the increasing role of financial motives, financial markets, financial actors and financial institutions in the operation of domestic and international economies'.

careful to justify their demands in terms of corporate value and not just shareholder property rights.

An expansive view of financialization links it with its 'twin'—marketization (Dore, 2008). As such we can see its influence in broad areas of the economy, including a growing market for corporations and parts of them through M&A and carve-outs. The rationale is that this will accelerate the allocation of resources to where they can create most value. Said METI's official responsible for the Fair Acquisitions Study Group: 'We are eager to compile guidelines from the logic of financialization that would make sense to people in capital markets.'[3]

The 'new trinity' reforms seek to activate labour markets, and labour mobility, again to improve allocative efficiency and hence, it is assumed, productivity. The associated campaign for wage system reform is intended to establish price signals as the means to achieve it. The appeal to individual career advancement across corporate boundaries is very different from the postwar company-centric system of lifetime employment, but consistent with individualist neoliberal assumptions. In education the GIGA-related initiatives have opened the door to private sector ed-tech and content companies. The growth of venture capital and its role in promoting high growth startups, and in turn the growing role of these startups in commercializing innovation, is a similar manifestation in the second dyad.

When it comes to capital markets themselves, however, financialization is partial at best. The postwar bank-centred system, which delivered credit to loan-hungry, growth-oriented corporations with spectacular results, had more or less run its course by the mid 1980s. Many assumed that market-based finance would follow. That ran out of steam, however, and ¥1 quadrillion of household savings remained in banks, while bank loans to corporations declined. Banks turned to buying government bonds and building up reserves at the Bank of Japan. The Kishida administration promised to engineer a shift to direct finance with a pledge to double investment income, but its rather timid expansion of Nippon Individual Savings Accounts (NISA) is hardly a game changer. If and when significant reforms to financial markets do come, they are likely to accelerate financialization.

---

[3] There was, however, criticism that activist investors were not represented on the Study Group, and fears that the 'corporate value' card could be used to block takeover bids *The Japan Times*, 18 April 2023 ('Japan's Powerful METI "Eager" for Guidelines that Spur M&A, Official Says').

New Developmental State

Globalization may be faltering in terms of global value chains, but global-ized finance is not. At the same time, the 'Big State' has been rehabilitated to deal with financial crises and the impacts of war, security, pandemics, and global warming. As the label 'state capitalism' is typically applied to coun-tries like China, its manifestation in Japan might more naturally be called the 'new developmental state', or following Whittaker et al. (2020), the 'adaptive developmental state'. The term 'developmental state' was originally coined by Johnson (1982) in reference to Japan, but as we have seen (Chapter 1), it came under attack from both the US and domestic reformers from the 1980s. Industrial policy was scaled back, and public financing institutions were placed under 'market discipline'. But the developmental state institu-tions were never fully dismantled, and industrial policy made a comeback after the Global Financial Crisis in Japan as elsewhere. Public financing insti-tutions were given new tasks, such as DX and GX, and the Fiscal Investment and Loan Programme was boosted to deal with the Covid pandemic.[4]

Japan's new developmental state is no carbon copy of the old one, which is not surprising, since the political economy has evolved. While new cap-italism's revised Action Plan (2023) does call for renewed emphasis on manufacturing, industrial policy has been re-modelled, in part with lessons drawn from outside Japan, such as from DARPA (US) and Horizon 2020 (EU; Chapter 2). Direct 'administrative guidance' is replaced by codes and guide-lines. Public financing institutions have become investors, and organizers of mezzanine finance. And the government is providing new services, such as supercomputing facilities for businesses developing generative AI.

Relatedly, Society 5.0, DX, GX, 'new capitalism', etc. may be seen as moonshot-like mission-oriented programmes (Mazzucato, 2021) or mission-oriented innovation policy (Arimoto, 2023) to tackle the major challenges Japan faces. These aim at broad socio-economic transformation, require extensive joined up policy making, and are built on public–private sector collaboration. In fact, these programmes themselves have become so com-plex and intertwined that a major state task is now coordinating them. This is done from the OPMC

Finally, the OPMC has additionally assumed the urgent roles of orchestrat-ing and integrating defence into the workings of the economy. Here the divid-ing line between the civilian and defence economies, and between traditional

---

[4] FILP's assets dropped from three quarters of Japan's GDP in 2000 to one quarter in 2019. Its annual loans in the 2010s ranged between ¥15 and ¥20 trillion, but during the pandemic they were increased to ¥67 trillion in 2020 and ¥41 trillion in 2021: MOF, 2020, 2021.

defence, cyber-security, and economic security, has become blurred and multidimensional. That is why the mainly public Japan Investment Corporation (JIC) launched a ¥1 trillion ($7 billion) bid in 2023 to acquire JSR, which supplies 30 per cent of the world's semiconductor photoresist market. If cleared by antitrust authorities, it will be delisted. The bid was made on the grounds of national economic security.[5] Japan is also planning to set up its own DARPA to fund civilian technologies with military applications in areas such as drones and AI, and has identified some 200 startups with potential defence-related technologies, which it aims to support.[6] This includes startups targeting space, which is emerging as an increasingly important theatre for defence.[7] The state's role in Japan's capitalism will strengthen accordingly, and moreover, it is likely to become more security and defence-oriented with the deepening of the digital economy.

Communitarian Capitalism

The third spirit is called 'communitarian capitalism', having separated out the 'activist state' in Anchordoguy's depiction to highlight the 'horizontal' dimensions, although in reality the distinction is blurred. As the economy is supposed to be morally embedded, so too for polity. A slogan of the Digital Garden City Nation vision is 'no-one left behind', referring to regional disparities, while the 'growth and distribution' cycle of new capitalism seeks to shrink income disparities. The distinction is not meaningless, however. The social and solidarity economy (SSE) in Japan has a long history, and the roots of cooperatism run deep (Chapter 8). Although cooperatives face the challenge of renewal, they still matter.[8] In fact, new shoots of cooperatism emerged after the Hanshin–Awaji earthquake in 1995 in NPOs, and again after the 2011 triple disaster. One reconstruction worker depicted the milieu as 'social capital-ism'. This extends to the spheres of DX, to what Aizuwakamatsu City calls a 'digital mutual support society', and where networks have formed to build a participative digital democracy, such as Code for Japan.

---

[5] *Nikkei Asia*, 24 June 2023 ('Japan State-backed Fund Looks to Buy Top Photoresist Maker JSR')

[6] *Nikkei Asia*, 20 October 2022 ('Japan Eyes US-Style Defence Research Agency as Tech Race Heats Up'); *Nikkei Asia*, 7 September 2023 ('Robot Suits, Long-Haul Drones: Japan Eyes Defence Tech Startups').

[7] See, for example, the Space Development Strategy Headquarters' 'Space Security Initiative' (2023: 13): https://www8.cao.go.jp/space/english/anpo/kaitei_fy05/enganpo_fy05_gaiyou.pdf (accessed 14 October, 2023).

[8] The task may be bigger for labour unions, which not only face the challenges of structural change, de-industrialization and generational renewal, but labour market reforms (membership- to job-based employment) which threaten their organizational basis.

Within companies, too, many managers seek to maintain 'company-as-community' practices. It is not just movements like *satoyama* capitalism which hold that Japan has shifted too far towards financialized shareholder capitalism; Keidanren itself agrees, and advocates rebuilding the middle class.[9] As Schaede (2020) argues, moreover, even the behaviour of would-be financialization agents like Private Equity is bent towards prevailing business norms.

A recent but largely unheralded aspect of communitarian norms is coordination around wage and price increases. As inflationary pressures from Russia's invasion of Ukraine spread in the economy, it was feared that large firms would raise their prices, and wages, but prevent small firm suppliers from raising theirs, exacerbating the price squeeze on small firms, and expanding wage differentials. This was even as the government was attempting to orchestrate above-inflation wage increases, including the minimum wage—extraordinary from the perspective of the UK government trying to reduce inflation by *suppressing* wage increases—and breathe new life into the spring wage negotiations. A response was the 'partnership construction declaration' (*Partnership kōchiku sengen*), signed by 22,000 companies by early 2023 who promised to negotiate with their suppliers over price increases. (In fact in late 2022 13 well-known companies were named and shamed by the Fair Trade Commission for refusing to do so.)

Controlled Dis-equilibrium

What, then, are we to say about these three spirits of Japanese capitalism? First, we could select the spirit(s) and associated institutional changes which interest us, such as the revival of the (adaptive) developmental state or the ongoing march of financialization, and then ignore those pieces that don't fit our argument. Or we could emphasize the contradictions and tensions and argue that they are indicative of the randomness of the reform efforts with no over-arching, integrative concept or ideology, and that they will inevitably compromise Japan's attempts to build its new economy, pulling it in different directions. That there are contradictions is not surprising, as proposed in Scenario 2 (Maturity) in the Introduction, and that policies are sometimes hurriedly introduced to shore up government approval ratings, with little internal or external coherence, is also undeniable.

---

[9] Gotoh (2020) goes so far as to claim that Keidanren is 'anti-capitalist', by which he means it rejects the norms of financialization, marketization, and shareholder interest maximization.

Yet there is another possible interpretation, namely that the different spirits and their associated institutions are not merely tolerated, but that they are played off against each other. As many writers have noted, Japan's interlocking institutions and strong social norms, combined with the success of the postwar productionist system in delivering relatively egalitarian economic growth, created rigidities which were difficult to change. Institutional change was 'slowed by a combination of highly coordinated and thus time-intensive adjustment processes paired with relatively limited adjustment pressure from the micro level' (Witt, 2006: 7). The downside has been perceived as *institutional stasis*, amplified after Japan's neoliberal flirtation, whereby the government generally pursued policies of 'security and safety' (*anshin anzen*, or peace of mind), generalizing the over-riding preference for stability.

Japan now faces the need to overcome inertia to accelerate DX and GX towards Society 5.0. To do so, the state may enact policies which favour financialization and marketization. Or it may seek to support cooperative norms, NPOs, and 'free, trustworthy and credible norms' in smart cities to counterbalance the disruptive effects of financialization and marketization. The balance of these add up to *controlled dis-equilibrium*, or the manufacture of change while maintaining overall stability (Table 10.1). We could go even further and argue that this is a state capability. Japan has a long history of leveraging outside pressures to overcome internal blockages to change. While it is possible to see financialization as something imposed on Japan, it is also possible to see it as the latest wave of this strategy. Financialized capitalism is not an unconditional importation, however, and it must be seen together

Table 10.1 Controlled dis-equilibrium and the three spirits of Japanese capitalism

	Financialized capitalism (FC)	New developmental state	Communitarian capitalism
Features	ROE, P/B ratio, share buybacks; influence on corporate governance—key institutional nexus; M&A; venture capital; marketization, DX; competition	New industrial policy; MOIP; intervention in corporate governance; economic security, cybersecurity; role of Kantei; economic statecraft	Cooperatives; SSE; moral economy norms; NPOs; social capitalism; digital mutual support society; public interest; generally non-confrontational
Role in controlled disequilibrium	Inject virus of change, overcome inertia	Set direction, incentives for change	Counterbalance FC; maintain 'Japanese' norms, stability

with the other two 'spirits', which act as balancing or countervailing forces. Similarly, financialization (market) and communitarian norms may counter the tendency towards an overbearing state.

Rhetoric and Reality

A further observation can be made in connection to overcoming institutional stasis. We have noted in various places the use of strong rhetoric in government—and company—pronouncements. Japan faces the need for 'fundamental' 'root and branch' reform. This is its 'last chance to reverse digital defeat', it is 'now or never' for decisive childbirth and childrearing policies. Japan must welcome rather than reject 'disruptive innovation'.... Unrealistic targets for startups, or training 450,000 IT specialists annually by March 2025, can be included here.

It is easy to dismiss this—and people often do—as wishful thinking. However, we might also see it as an attempt to get from *a* to *b* by aiming for *c*. As a large company executive put it: 'We point to what X [counterpart in the US] is doing, and say we need a change of magnitude 100. After all the internal negotiations, we will end up at about 50, which is probably closer to where we want to be.' The strategy risks rhetorical inflation and diminishing returns on the rhetoric, but there is a logic to it in situations such as in Japan where the amplitude of change is typically muted. In other words, like the three spirits, *strategic hyperbole* may be a device to combat institutional stasis.

The Innovation Dilemma

Figure 10.1 reproduces Figure 0.1, with some extra detail. Broadly speaking, the three 'spirits' correspond to the norms, institutions, and influence of markets, state, and civil society of the upper dyad respectively. Japan's shift from states to markets (liberalizing and dis-embedding dynamics) was muted; Japan stepped back from aggressive de-regulation and privatization when social divisions became a political problem in the mid 2000s. Subsequent fiscal policies aiming at stability no doubt helped to temper social and political polarization, but at the cost of rising government debt.

When it comes to institutional stasis, though, we also need to consider the second, organization–technology dyad. Here, too, Japan's evolutionary dynamic has been muted. While Silicon Valley startups backed by venture capital pioneered their disrupting digital technologies and revolutionizing

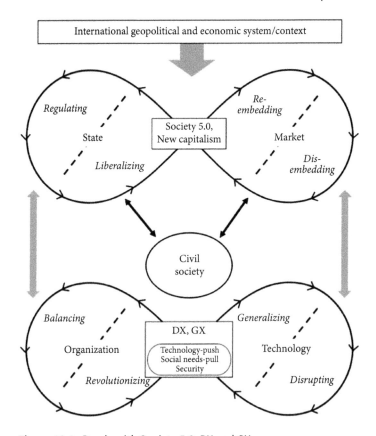

Figure 10.1 Dyads with Society 5.0, DX and GX

network and platform means of organizing them, Japan's productionist system centred on large firms remained largely intact. This is not altogether surprising, since the Silicon Valley innovation model is itself financialized while Japan's financialization has been partial, and second, Japan's innovation strengths may well lie less in the disrupting and revolutionizing phases of the second dyad than in the generalizing and balancing phases. Although there are pre-regulatory 'sandbox' experiments in Japan, the precautionary principle prevails, in stark contrast to the 'permissionless innovation' practiced Silicon Valley, where:

> The credo of digital innovation quickly turned into the language of disruption and an obsession with speed, its campaigns conducted under the flag of 'creative destruction'. That famous, fateful phrase coined by the evolutionary economist Joseph Schumpeter was seized upon as a way to legitimize what Silicon Valley euphemistically calls 'permissionless innovation'.
>
> (Zuboff, 2019: 50)

This 'abandon(s) the organic reciprocities with people that have long been a mark of capitalism' and 'formally rescinds any remaining reciprocities with its societies' (Zuboff, 2019: 499). In contrast, as we have seen there is a historical reluctance in Japan to treat the economic and social spheres as separate. This applies to technology and society as well. Japan has tended to keep technological innovation within the bounds of existing social relations rather than fundamentally challenging them. As a result, large established firms are still in the driving seat in many industries, including those undergoing technological innovation, and even in new industries. Until very recently, however, many preferred to build up their internal reserves and increase their shareholder dividends when they restored their profitability in the 2000s and 2010s rather than increase capital expenditure or invest in innovation. In Porter's (1990) words, they reached their 'wealth-driven' stage of development, in which the incentives for innovation dim and business leaders become stewards of existing resources rather than innovators.

Two Innovation (Policy) Logics: Catch-up and Post Catch-up

This created a dilemma for policy makers. Should revived industrial and innovation policy focus on large companies which have resources, and encourage them to raise their capital expenditure and investments in R&D, or should it place its bets on universities and startups, emulating Silicon Valley (minus its 'permissionless innovation')? Policy makers went for both, characteristically not posing it as a dilemma, and enlisting large firms to support startups with corporate venture capital through tax incentives. Startups feature in Keidanren's 'new growth strategy' and 'sustainable capitalism', as they do, prominently, in 'new capitalism'. They are celebrated in national awards, attended by the Prime Minister.

A further dilemma lies in the underlying rationale for innovation. Should policy target emerging technologies and their commercialization for competitive purposes or innovation for social needs? With its Society 5.0 proposal, the 2015 Council for Science, Technology and Innovation advocated a fundamental shift from a technology-driven policy approach to 'a more society-centred and challenge-driven innovation policy', one which recognized the need to prepare for an 'unpredictable and unforeseeable near future' (Carraz and Harayama, 2019: 40). Lechevalier and Laugier (2019) contrast the approaches as neo-Schumpeterian creative destruction versus non-Schumpeterian, social-needs, and stakeholder-oriented innovation. The former enriches the entrepreneurs and their financial backers, the latter the community.

Again policy makers have opted for both, and their combination. Keidanren's report 'Society 5.0 for SDGs: An Economic Analysis of Future Created' cites 57 emerging technologies which would grow the nominal GDP from ¥531 trillion to ¥900 trillion by 2030 (Chapter 6). The Green Growth Strategy focuses on green technologies, and the GX Realization Basic Plan on greening existing as well as emerging industries. Figure 3.4 shows that a large share of planned capital expenditure in 2022–2023 was targeted at DX and GX, a trend which seems set to continue. And a requirement for government funding overseen or influenced by METI, such as smart cities and GX, is that funded projects are competitive, and exportable, especially to Southeast Asia. At a more fine-grained level, however, *within* DX and GX, the distinction matters. Of particular concern to Japan, with demographic ageing and the prospect of a declining workforce, is technologies for social care, especially social care robots. Here studies have shown the dominance of technology-push funding, despite evidence that it often does not work, and often provides a poor return on investment (Wright, 2023).

Behind these two approaches, in turn, there is a further dilemma, namely a 'catch-up' stance versus a 'post catch-up' one. There was a growing sense in the 1980s that Japan had finally achieved its long-held goal of catching up to the advanced Western countries, and henceforth would have to navigate its own path (Chapter 1). In fact there was a certain amount of hubris at having not just caught up, but at having *surpassed* those it had formerly chased. This confidence disappeared in the 1990s, however, and recent years have seen a revival of 'Japan is lagging, and needs to catch up—quickly!' rhetoric—in digital technologies especially, but also in academic research, competitiveness, raising unicorns.... Ubiquitous rankings developed by international organizations and business schools, some of dubious worth, are used uncritically to drive home the point. In policy proposal preambles, the language almost by default slips back into 'catch-up' justification. On the other hand, the more cross-cutting 'mission-oriented' programmes, including Society 5.0 (most of the time), are presented in terms of social needs and transformation.

So we could say that there are *two spirits in the Japanese innovation system* as well, one adopting the language of competitiveness and catch-up, and the other of post-catch-up social needs. As a generalization, the first spirit inhabits the digital and IT sector, where the threat of getting left behind is never far away; DX is like a sword, hanging over the head of Damocles. GX is more varied. From the policy and the corporate point of view, the possibilities are much more open, and often require multi-stakeholder engagement. Specific technologies do matter, but they tend to play to Japan's strengths in materials, components, and processes. And although criticized by some for over-reliance on carrots, the comprehensiveness of the GX Realization Basic Plan attests to its attractiveness in combining these two spirits in pursuit of broader social ends.

Into this schematic, however, we must now add security, defence, military and dual use technology and innovation. With the escalation of geopolitical tensions, and growing cybersecurity and economic security concerns, a *third spirit* may be unleashed in Japan, with state power and security added to commercial and social orientations. (These would *broadly* correspond with the three spirits of Japanese capitalism—adaptive developmental state, financialization and communitarian—respectively.) Just how this will evolve will depend a lot on geopolitics, and developments outside Japan's borders (Chapter 9).

People-centred Society 5.0?

In the early postwar years a concern for policy makers was how to feed the burgeoning population, and whether there would be enough jobs for the baby boomers as they entered the labour market. Now the baby boomers have retired, the question is: who will fill the jobs to keep the economy going? People have become a scarce resource. It is little wonder that Society 5.0 aims to be 'people-centred' and that 'investment in human capital is at the heart of the growth strategy' of the Kishida administration.

We have summarized the spirits of Japan's (new) capitalism, as well as innovation, but not where they are taking the country. Are they really taking Japan towards a people-centred Society 5.0? This section returns to issues raised in Chapter 7, including the 'new trinity' labour market reforms and rebuilding the middle class, and relatedly, the 'social investment state'. It then touches on Boyer's (2019) 'anthropogenic' model of development, and Bodrožić and Adler's (2022) digital democracy.

Towards a Social Investment State

Human resources were a strength of the postwar productionist system. Companies benefited from an education system which produced literate and numerate school leavers and provided on-job-training to their youthful production workers. In response to their challenges in the late 1980s and 1990s, however, companies cut back on their investments in people, tried performance-based-pay to motivate their now-university-educated white collar regular workers, and became increasingly reliant on 'disposable' non-regular workers. Japan's strengths in human resources were eroded.

There is no going back to the postwar model. It was a male bread-winner model built on homogeneity, which is increasingly incompatible with expanding the workforce, and with work–life and work–family balance (which in turn is a prerequisite to raising the birthrate—social sustainability in other words) as well as the growing tide of diversity, equity and inclusion (DE&I). What will replace that model, however, is less clear. Abe's work-style reforms and Kishida's new trinity reforms point towards a model which is less encompassing for regular employees and more open. Strong social ties of 'company-as-community' will be replaced by Granovetter's (1973) 'strength of weak ties', in theory at least.

That not only requires dismantling the institutions associated with 'membership-type' employment but poses a strong challenge to the orga-nization principles of labour unions and requires a re-balancing of private and public sector commitments to vocational education and training (VET). It also calls for a much more determined effort to break down the barri-ers between regular and non-regular employment. To be compatible with rebuilding the middle class, it would have to be done through levelling up, and stemming the tide of levelling down. The social implications of wel-coming large numbers non-Japanese workers on a permanent basis are far-reaching. The challenges Japan has set itself should not be under-estimated.

The direction of travel is towards a 'social investment state', which sit-uates human capital and the labour market as central to individual and social well being. It requires substantial investment in public VET and active labour market policies to match supply and demand of skills. It probably also requires a commitment to 'decent jobs', about which there are currently plati-tudes in place of policies. The interaction of its three spirits of capitalism will obviously preclude Japan from becoming a Nordic-style social investment state, but it may end up with a 'Japanese-style' intermediate version.

'Anthropogenic' Mode of Development

Japan's direction of travel may also offer support to Boyer's (2019) 'anthro-pogenic' mode of development, a new institutional configuration succeeding the financialization regime of accumulation under neoliberalism, character-ized by increased employment and economic activity concentrated in educa-tion, healthcare, and leisure (or culture), and linked to non-Schumpeterian social innovation, referred to above. Noting that Japan invented an alternate version of production to Fordism, Boyer offers Japan as a candidate for this new mode of development, contrasting it with the US on a number of social indicators. One indicator on which Japan fares badly, however, is its low birth rate, indicative of the unequal economic status of men and women. This also suggests a muted version of the model, but 'provides the point of departure for a reconfiguration of the Japanese economy and society taken as a whole' (Boyer, 2019: 115).

Countering this, however, is the strengthening of the investor relations and corporate governance axis as the key institutional nexus, and Japan's determination to maintain manufacturing as central to the economy, expressed in a 2022 policy document from Keidanren titled 'Challenging Again to Become an Industry and Technology Power'. The document warns that this is Japan's last chance (of course), not to revive the past, but to build on its remaining strengths to invest in and challenge the future vision of Society 5.0, which is to be built by 2030–2040 through digital and green technologies, as well as biotechnology and materials. It calls for increased public spending and calls on its members to shift from 'select and focus', which creates vulnerabilities to disruptive technologies, to 'strategy and emergence/creation' to achieve disruptive innovation. It also calls on them to create *dejima*-type organizations which are both open to the outside and open to internal disruption, and for co-creation (*kyōsō*) with stakeholders.[10] It sounds very much like controlled dis-equilibrium. The view is echoed in 'new capitalism's' revised Action Plan (2023). Japan's future will be decided as much on the battlefields of automobiles and mobility as in nurseries, universities, and care homes.

Digital Democracy

Finally, we return to Bodrožić and Adler on whose evolutionary technoeconomic framework the second dyad draws. The authors have subsequently explored trajectories of digital transformation, based on two sets of variables (Bodrožić and Adler, 2022). The first is (macro-level) public policy regimes, which they divide into neoliberal laissez faire versus proactive system building. The second is (company level) management models, which they divide into business process versus 'community and collaboration' (Figure 10.2).

Their 2×2 matrix gives four ideal types, namely digital oligarchy (which they associate with the US), digital authoritarianism (China and Singapore),

[10] Dejima was an island off Nagasaki where trading with the Portuguese and Dutch was allowed during Japan's Tokugawa period of official isolation. On Dejima in business, see https://www.nri.com/en/journal/2020/0128 (accessed 24 October 2022).

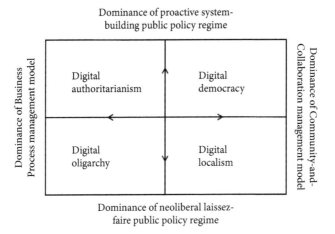

Figure 10.2 Four scenarios for the digital transformation

Source: Bodrožić, and Adler, 2022: 120, Zlatko Bodrožić and Paul S. Adler (2022) 'Alternative Futures for the Digital Transformation: A Macro-Level Schumpeterian Perspective', *Organization Science* 33(1): 105–125. https://doi.org/10.1287/orsc.2021.1558.

digital localism (Barcelona, but more likely to be a patchwork), and finally digital democracy, an empty quadrant which combines 'proactive system-building' public policy and 'community-and-collaboration' management. They conclude:

> Notwithstanding the fact that no major country has thus far embraced a digital democracy scenario, macro-Schumpeterians like Perez (2009) and Mazzucato (2018) argue that this is the most likely path to deployment success, given the historical record of previous revolutions, where deployment was stimulated by the combination of a system-building policy regime and a paradigm-balancing management model. The other three scenarios seem less likely to tap the digital transformation's full potential.
>
> **(2022: 120)**

Perhaps the authors did not look closely enough at Japan's efforts, and strengths in the balancing phases of technological innovation diffusion. Proactive system building characterizes adaptive developmental state efforts to build Society 5.0 through DX and GX, as well as a 'virtuous cycle of growth and distribution' with new capitalism. And Japan's management would be closer to a 'community and collaboration' pole than a business process one, even with the new trinity labour market reforms and job-based employment. The degree of genuine community participation might be debated, but Japan's fit with the digital democracy quadrant is much better than with any of the other three. It may take time to tap DX's full potential, but in these terms at least Japan may be a good candidate for a new socio-economic model, dependent of course on its geopolitical context and how far Japan's macro- and micro-level institutions are shaped by security issues.

A New Model?

Japan's new economy is a work in progress. It is not a 'model' either in the sense of a whole comprised of mutually supporting or coherent parts, or a normative example which other should follow. But we should not expect institutional coherence in what is clearly a set of unfolding changes. As Boyer (2005) notes, institutions come together through a process of trial and error and only appear *retrospectively* as coherent. The relevant question is whether the changes addressed in this book represent a continuation of the secular stagnation from the 1990s, or a turning point in the emergence of a new 'growth' model, and assuming the latter, whether there are lessons to be derived from Japan's experience.

First, the inconsistencies and contradictions in Japan's attempt to build a new economy can be debilitating or propulsive. Japan is betting on the latter through a combination of collaborative creation and competition, both represented by the homonym *kyōsō*, but written with different Chinese characters. Or *controlled dis-equilibrium*. And it is possible that as a new 'frontier of control' in which the state is also keenly invested, investor relations/ corporate governance tensions may be resolved as creatively as were employment relations in the postwar period. It is not for the purity of its model that Japan merits attention, but on the contrary, how Japan combines the different spirits, which to varying extents and in different combinations all countries have.

Second, the sequencing of Japan's reforms is significant. Initially there was an emphasis on innovation policy, as depicted in the first half of this book. It is likely, however, that the government and Keidanren realized the limitations of innovation policy alone and grasped the additional need to reform Japanese capitalism in order to create a 'virtuous cycle of growth and distribution', as depicted in the second half of the book. If the claim to be people-centred was to be credible, both were necessary. The unfolding of the reforms appears to represent a learning process, which others might also learn from.

As for being a normative example, if institutional scholars have learned anything in recent decades, it is that institutions can seldom be borrowed *in toto* and need to be adapted to the specific circumstances of the borrowers. If the Society 5.0 vision was initially influenced by Germany's Industrie 4.0, coming a full circle the EU has now proposed Industry 5.0. In remarkably similar language to Society 5.0 this:

> provides a vision of industry that aims beyond efficiency and productivity as the sole goals, and reinforces the role and the contribution of industry to society. It places the wellbeing of the worker at the centre of the production process and uses new technologies to provide prosperity beyond jobs and growth while respecting the production limits of the planet. It complements the existing 'Industry 4.0' approach by specifically putting research and innovation at the service of the transition to a **sustainable, human-centric** and **resilient European industry** [emphasis in original].[11]

Others, too, may be similarly inspired. The challenge will be in implementation.

Finally, let us return to the four scenarios proposed in the Introduction: Renewal, Maturity, Conversion and Imitation, and Decline. The focus has been on the plausibility of the Renewal scenario, tempered by a combination of the others. I remain cautiously optimistic, but for somewhat different reasons than originally set out—it is less in the clarity of Japan's transformative vision, but rather in its ability to entertain complexity and contradiction and to use social processes to work through them. The downsides of this proclivity were apparent during Japan's 'lost decades', but recent attempts to build a new economy have shown an upside as well. Future research will show whether this optimism is justified, and whether Japan has indeed harnessed its three spirits of capitalism, and melded catch-up and post-catch-up innovation, manufacturing, and post-industrialism, in controlled dis-equilibrium.

---

[11] https://research-and-innovation.ec.europa.eu/research-area/industrial-research-and-innovation/industry-50_en (accessed 24 October 2022).

References

Abegglen, J. and G. Stalk (1985), *Kaisha: The Japanese Corporation*, New York: Basic Books.

Akimoto, N. (2019), 'Urban Redesigns for the Networked Polycentric Compact City in Japan', paper presented to IGU Urban Commission Annual Meeting (Urban Challenges in a Complex World), Luxembourg, 4–9 August.

Albert, M. (1991), *Capitalisme contre Capitalisme*, Paris, Edition du Seuil; English edition *Capitalism against Capitalism*, London: Whurr Publishers, 1993.

Altura, T., Y. Hashimoto, S. Jacoby, K. Kanai, and K. Saguchi (2021), 'Japan Meets the Sharing Economy: Contending Frames', *Social Science Japan Journal*, 24(1): 137–161.

Amable B. (2003), *The Diversity of Modern Capitalism*, Oxford: Oxford University Press.

Amano, I. (2011), *The Origins of Japanese Credentialism*, Melbourne: Trans Pacific Press (orig. in Japanese, 1982).

Anchordoguy, M. (2005), *Reprogramming Japan: The High Tech Crisis under Communitarian Capitalism*, Ithaca: Cornell University Press.

ANRE (Agency for Natural Resources and Energy)—see Shigen enerugīchō.

Aoki, M. (2008), 'Conclusion: Whither Japan's Corporate Governance', in M. Aoki, G. Jackson, and H. Miyajima (eds), *Corporate Governance in Japan: Institutional Change and Organizational Diversity*, Oxford: Oxford University Press, 427–448.

Arai, N. (2018), *AI vs kyōkasho ga yomenai kodomotachi* (AI vs Children Who Can't Read Textbooks), Tokyo: Toyo keizai.

Arai, N. and M. Sato (2021), 'Chōjō taiketsu: Wareware wa dō ikinokoruka' (Summit Talk: How Will We Survive?), *Shūkan shinshō*, 8 April, 86–90.

Arimoto, T. (2023), 'SIP-adus and Mission-Oriented STI Policy', in SIP-adus Final Results Editorial Committee ed., *SIP 2nd Phase: Automated Driving for Universal Services, Final Results Report (2018–2022)*, Cabinet Office, Tokyo.

Atarashii shihonshugi jitsugen kaigi (ed.) (2023) 'Dai 16kai: Sanmi ittai rōdō shijō kaikaku no ronten'an' (New Form of Capitalism Realization Council, Meeting No.16: Draft of Issues in Trinity Labour Market Reforms), Tokyo.

Avenell, S. (2009), 'Civil Society and the New Civic Movements in Contemporary Japan: Convergence, Collaboration and Transformation', *Journal of Japanese Studies*, 35(2): 247–283.

Baldwin, Y. and K. Clark (2000), *Design Rules: The Power of Modularity*, Cambridge MA: MIT Press.

Bank of Japan (BoJ) (2019), 'Financial System Report Annex: Ginkō, shinyō kinkō ni kansuru dijitrizēshon e no taiō jōkyō—ankēto chōsa kekka kara' (Financial System Report Annex: Results of a Questionnaire of Banks' and Trust Banks' Response to Digitalization), Tokyo BoJ.

Bank of Japan (BoJ) (2021), 'Bank of Japan Review: Digital Transformation of Japanese Banks', Paper 2021-E 2, Tokyo: BoJ.

Barrett, B., A. DeWit, and M. Yarime (2021), 'Japanese Smart Cities and Communities: Integrating Technological and Institutional Innovation for Society 5.0', in H-M. Kim, S. Sabri and A. Kent (eds), *Smart Cities for Technological and Social Innovation: Case Studies, Current Trends and Future Steps*, London: Academic Press, 73–94.

Bartlett, B. (2018), 'Government as Facilitator: How Japan is Building its Cybersecurity Market', *Journal of Cyber Policy*, 3(3): 327–343.

Batty, M., K. Axhausen, F. Giannotti, A. Pozdnoukhov, A. Bazzani, M. Wachowitz, G. Ouzounis, and Y. Portugali (2012), 'Smart Cities of the Future', *The European Physical Journal Special Topics*, 214: 481–518.

Belloc, F. (2013), 'Law, Finance and Innovation: The Dark Side of Shareholder Protection', *Cambridge Journal of Economics*, 37(4): 863–888.

Best, M. (1990), The New Competition: Institutions of Industrial Restructuring, Cambridge: Polity Press.

Block, F. and M. Somers (2014), *The Power of Market Fundamentalism: Karl Polanyi's Critique*, Cambridge MA: Harvard University Press.

Bodrožić, Z. and P. Adler (2017), 'The Evolution of Management Models: A Neo-Schumpeterian Theory', *Administrative Science Quarterly*, 63(1): 85–129.

Bodrožić, Z. and P. Adler (2022), 'Alternative Futures for the Digital Transformation: A Macro-Level Schumpeterian Perspective', *Organisation Science*, 33(1): 105–125.

Boltanski, L. and E. Chiapello (2005), *The New Spirit of Capitalism*, London: Verso (orig. *Le nouvel esprit du capitalism*, Editions Gallimard, 1999).

Boston Consulting Group and Semiconductor Industry Association (BCG and SIA) (2021), *Strengthening the Semiconductor Supply Chain in an Uncertain Age*, Boston MA: BCG and SIA.

Boyer, R. (2005), 'Complementarity in Regulation Theory', in 'Dialogue on "Institutional Complementarity and Political Economy"', *Socio-Economic Review*, 3: 359–382.

Boyer, R. (2019), 'How Scientific Breakthroughs and Social Innovations Shape the Evolution of the Healthcare Sector', in S. Lechevalier (ed.), *Innovation Beyond Technology: Science for Society and Interdisciplinary Approaches*, Singapore: Springer, 89–119.

Braudel, F. (1982), *The Wheels of Commerce*, New York: Harper and Row.

Brown, C. and G. Linden (2009), *Chips and Change: How Crisis Reshapes the Semiconductor Industry*, Cambridge MA: MIT Press.

Buchanan, J., D. Chai and S. Deakin (2012), *Hedge Fund Activism in Japan: The Limits of Shareholder Primacy*, Cambridge: Cambridge University Press.

Bytheway, S. and M. Metzler (2016), *Central Banks and Gold: How Tokyo, London, and New York Shaped the Modern World*, Ithaca: Cornell University Press.

Cabinet Office (2022) 'Japan's Smart Cities: Solving Global Issues such as SDGs, etc. Through Society 5.0', Tokyo.

Caragliu, A., C. Del Bo, and P. Nijkamp (2009), 'Smart Cities in Europe', *Journal of Urban Technology*, 18(2): 65–82.

Carraz, R. and Y. Harayama (2019). 'Japan's Innovation Systems at the Crossroads: Society 5.0', *Panorama: Insights Into Asian and European Affairs*, January 1, pp.33–45.

Champy, J. and M. Hammer (1993), *Reengineering the Corporation: A Manifesto for Business Revolution*, New York: HarperBusiness.

Chiapello, E. and A. Engels (2021), 'The Fabrication of Environmental Intangibles as a Questionable Response to Environmental Problems', *Journal of Cultural Economy*, 14(5): 517–532.

Chiavacci, D. and C. Hommerich (2017), 'Re-assembling the Pieces: The Big Picture of Inequality in Japan', in D. Chiavacci and C. Hommerich (eds), *Social Inequality in Post-Growth Japan: Transformation During Economic and Demographic Stagnation*, London: Routledge.

Chūshō kigyōchō (2021) *Chūshō kigyō hakusho* (SME White Paper), Tokyo.

Clark, R. (1979), *The Japanese Company*, New Haven: Yale University Press.

Cole, R. (2006), 'The Telecommunication Industry: A Turnaround in Japan's Global Presence', in D.H. Whittaker and R. Cole (eds), *Recovering from Success: Innovation and Technology Management in Japan*, Oxford: Oxford University Press.

Cole, R. and S. Fushimi (2020), 'Sekyuritei manejimento no nichibei kigyō hikaku: soshikiron no kanten kara' ('Comparison of Information Security Management in the US and Japan: An Organizational Perspective') in IPA *Jōhō sekyuritei hakusho* 2020 (Information Security White Paper, 2020), pp. 198–203.

Cole, R. and Y. Nakata (2014), 'The Japanese Software Industry: What Went Wrong, and What Can We Learn from It?' *California Management Review*, 57(1): 16–43.

Cole, R. and D.H. Whittaker (2006), 'Introduction', in D.H. Whittaker and R. Cole (eds), *Recovering from Success: Innovation and Technology Management in Japan*, Oxford: Oxford University Press, 1–28.

Council for Science, Technology and Innovation (CSTI) (2015), 'Report on the 5th Science and Technology Basic Plan', Tokyo: Cabinet Office.

Cusumano, M. (1991), *Japan's Software Factories: A Challenge to US Management*, New York: Oxford University Press.

Cusumano, M. (1989), '"Scientific Industry" Strategy, Technology and Entrepreneurship in Prewar Japan', in W. Wray ed. *Managing Industrial Enterprise: Cases From Japan's Prewar Experience*, Cambridge MA: Harvard University Press, 269–315.

Dalton, E. (2017) 'Womenomics, "Equality" and Abe's Neo-liberal Strategy to Make Japanese Women Shine', in *Social Science Japan Journal*, 20(1): 95–105.

Datta, A. and A. Shaban (eds.) (2017), *Mega-Urbanization in the Global South: Fast Cities and the New Urban Utopias of the Postcolonial State*, London: Routledge.

Deguchi, A. (2020), 'From Smart City to Society 5.0', in Hitachi-UTokyo Laboratory (ed.), *Society 5.0: A People-centric Super-smart Society*, Singapore: Springer Open, 43–65.

Development Bank of Japan (DBJ) (2022), '2022 nendo setsubi tōshi keikaku chōsa: kekka gaiyō' (f2022 Capital Investment Plan Survey: Summary of Results), DBJ: Tokyo.

DeWit, A. (2018), 'Japan's Smart Communities as Industrial Policy', in W. Clark (ed.), *Sustainable Cities and Communities Design Handbook: Green Engineering, Architecture and Technology*, 2nd edn, Oxford: Butterworth-Heinemann.

DeWit, A. (2019), 'National Solutions at Local Levels: Case of Japan', in W. Clark II (ed.), *Climate Preservation in Urban Communities Case Studies*, Kidlington: Elsevier, 421–452.

DeWit, A. (2020), 'Is Japan a Climate Leader? Synergistic Integration of the 2030 Agenda', *The Asia-Pacific Journal/ Japan Focus*, 18(2): 1–21.

DeWit, A. and R. Shaw (2022), 'Society 5.0 and Inclusive Resilience', in R. Shaw (ed.), *Handbook on Climate Change and Disasters*, Cheltenham: Edward Elgar, 594–604.

Dillinger, W. (1994), 'Decentralization and Its Implications for Service Delivery', UNDP/ UNCHS/ World Bank Urban Delivery Programme, Urban Management and Municipal Finance Paper 16, Washington DC: The World Bank.

Dore, R. (1965), *Education in Tokugawa Japan*, London: Routledge and Kegan Paul.

Dore, R. (1973), *British Factory—Japanese Factory: The Origins of National Diversity in Industrial Relations*, Berkeley: University of California Press.

Dore, R. (1983), 'Goodwill and the Spirit of Market Capitalism', *British Journal of Sociology*, 34(4): 459–482.

Dore, R. (1987), *Taking Japan Seriously: A Confucian Perspective on Leading Economic Issues*, London: Athlone and Stanford: Stanford University Press.

Dore, R. (2000), *Stock Market Capitalism, Welfare Capitalism: Japan and Germany versus the Anglo-Saxons*, Oxford: Oxford University Press.

Dore, R. (2008), 'Financialization of the Global Economy', *Industrial and Corporate Change*, 17(6), 1097–1112.

Dore, R. (2009), 'Japan's Conversion to Investor Capitalism', in D. H. Whittaker and S. Deakin (eds), *Corporate Governance and Managerial Reform in Japan*, Oxford: Oxford University Press, 134–162.

Eccles, R., M. Krzus, and C. Solano (2019), 'A Comparative Analysis of Integrated Reporting in Ten Countries', SSRN Research Paper 3345590.

Emmott, B. (2020), *Japan's Far More Female Future: Increasing Gender Equality and Reducing Workplace Insecurity Will Make Japan Stronger*, Oxford: Oxford University Press.

Epstein, G. (2005), 'Introduction' in G. Epstein ed., *Financialization and the World Economy*, Cheltenham: Edward Elgar.

Ericson, S. (1989), 'Railroads in Crisis: The Financing and Management of Japanese Railway Companies During the Panic of 1890,' in W. Wray ed., *Managing Industrial Enterprise: Cases From Japan's Prewar Experience*, Cambridge MA: Harvard University Press.

Etzioni, A. (1988), *The Moral Dimension: Toward a New Economics*, New York: Free Press.

Farrell, H. and A. Newman (2016), 'The Transatlantic Data War: The EU Fights Back against the NSA', in *Foreign Affairs*, 95(1): 124–133.

Feuer, H. (2019), 'Geographical Indications Out of Context and In Vogue: The Awkward Embrace of European Heritage Agricultural Protections in Asia', in A. Bonnano, K. Sekine, and H. Feuer (eds), *Geographical Indication and Global Agri-Food: Development and Democratization*, London: Routledge, 39–53.

Filatotchev, I. and G. Lanzolla (2023), '"Open Source" Corporate Governance in the Era of Digital Transformation', in C. Cennamo, G. Dagnino, and F. Zhu (eds), *Elgar Handbook of Research on Digital Strategy*, Cheltenham: Edward Elgar, 309–323.

Financial Services Agency (FSA) (2021), 'Attention to Sustainability and ESG', Tokyo: FSA.

Francks, P. (2016), *Japan and the Great Divergence: A Short Guide*, London: Palgrave.

Frenkenberger, B. (2021), 'Convincing in the Tokyo Start-up Village: Possibilities of Malleable Structure', DPhil thesis, University of Oxford.

Friede, G., T. Busch, and A. Bassen (2015), 'ESG and Financial Performance: Aggregated Evidence from More than 2000 Empirical Studies', *Journal of Sustainable Finance and Investment*, 5(4): 210–233.

Gerlach, M. (1992), *Alliance Capitalism: The Social Organization of Japanese Business*, Berkeley CA: University of California Press.

Gertz, G. and M. Evers (2020), 'Geoeconomic Competition: Will State Capitalism Win?', *The Washington Quarterly*, 43(2): 117–136.

Global Wind Energy Council (2022), 'Global Offshore Wind Report 2022', Brussels: GWEC.

Glosserman, B. (2019), *Peak Japan: The End of Great Ambitions*: Washington DC: Georgetown University Press.

Gollin, D., R. Jedwab and D. Vollrath (2016), 'Urbanization With and Without Industrialization' in *Journal of Economic Growth*, 21, 35–70.

Goodrich, C. (1920), *The Frontier of Control: A Study in British Workshop Politics*, New York: Harcourt, Brace and Howe.

Gordon, A. (1985), *The Evolution of Labour Relations in Japan: Heavy industry, 1853–1955*, Cambridge, MA: Harvard University Press.

Gotoh, F. (2020), *Japanese Resistance to American Financial Hegemony: Global versus Domestic Social Norms*, London: Routledge.

Government Pension Investment Fund (2020), 'ESG Report, 2019', Tokyo: GPIF.

Government Pension Investment Fund (2022), 'Stewardship Activities Report, 2021–2022', Tokyo: GPIF.

Granovetter, M. (1973), 'The Strength of Weak Ties', *American Journal of Sociology*, 78(6): 1360–1380.

Green Alliance Japan (GAJ) (2020), 'Green Watch: A Civil Society Environmental White Paper 2020', Tokyo.

Greiner, L. (1998), 'Evolution and Revolution as Organizations Grow', *Harvard Business Review*, 76(3): 1–11.

Guttman, R. (2002), 'Money and Credit in Régulation Theory', in R. Boyer and Y. Salliard (eds), *Régulation Theory: The State of the Art*, London: Routledge, 57–63.

Hall, D. (2015), 'The Role of Japan's General Trading Companies (Sōgō Shōsha) in the Global Land Grab', paper presented to Land-grabbing, conflict and agrarian-environmental transformations: Perspectives from East and Southeast Asia conference, Chiang Mai University, 5-6 June.

Hall, P. and D. Soskice (eds) (2001), *Varieties of Capitalism: The International Foundations of Comparative Advantage*, Oxford: Oxford University Press.

Hamaguchi, K. (2009), *Atarashii kōyō shakai: rōdō shisutemu no saikōchiku e* (A New Employment Society: Rebuilding the Labour System), Tokyo: Iwanami shoten.

Hara, J. (2009), *Atarashii shihonshugi: Kibō no taikoku, Nihon no kanōsei* (New Capitalism: Country of Hope, Possibilities for Japan), Tokyo: PHP.

Hara, J. (2017), *Kōeki shihonshugi: Eibeigata shihonshugi no shūen* (Public Interest Capitalism: The End of UK-US-style Capitalism, Tokyo: Bungei shunjū.

Hatch, W. and K. Yamamura (1996), *Asia in Japan's Embrace: Building a Regional Production Alliance*, Cambridge: Cambridge University Press.

Hayakawa, M. and D. H. Whittaker (2009), 'Takeovers and Corporate Governance: Three Years of Tensions', in D. H. Whittaker and S. Deakin (eds), *Corporate Governance and Managerial Reform in Japan*, Oxford: Oxford University Press, 70–92.

Hayami, A. (2015), *Japan's Industrious Revolution: Economic and Social Transformation in the Early Modern Period*, London: Springer.

Hiroi, Y. (2019), 'Science as Care: Science and Innovation in Post-growth Society', in S. Lechevalier ed., *Innovation Beyond Technology: Science for Society and Interdisciplinary Approaches*, Singapore: Springer, 301–324.

Hirsch, F. (1976), *Social Limits to Growth*, Cambridge MA: Harvard University Press.

Hitachi-UTokyo Laboratory (2020), *Society 5.0: A People-Centric Super-Smart Society*, Singapore: Springer.

Hodgson, G. (2001), 'The Evolution of Capitalism from the Prespective of Institutional and Evolutionary Economics', in G. Hodgson, M. Itoh, and N. Yokokawa (eds), *Capitalism in Evolution: Global Contentions East and West*, Cheltenham: Edward Elgar, 63–82.

Holroyd, C. (2018), *Green Japan: Environmental Technologies, Innovation Policy, and the Pursuit of Green Growth*, Toronto: University of Toronto Press.

Huddle, N., M. Reich, and N. Stiskin (1975), *Island of Dreams: Environmental Crisis in Japan*, New York: Autumn Books.

Ibata-Arens, K. (2009), *Innovation and Entrepreneurship in Japan*, Cambridge: Cambridge University Press.

Igata, A. and B. Glosserman (2021), 'Japan's New Economic Statecraft', *The Washington Quarterly*, 44(3): 25–42.

Iijima, H. and E. Yamaguchi (2015), 'Decrease in the Number of Journal Articles in Physics in Japan: Correlation between the Number of Articles and Doctoral Students', *Journal of Integrated Creative Studies*, 009-a: 1–20.

Inagami, T. and Whittaker, D. H. (2005), *The New Community Firm: Employment, Governance and Management Reform in Japan*, Cambridge: Cambridge University Press.

International Energy Agency (IEA) (2021), 'Japan 2021: Energy Policy Review', Paris.

International Institute for Strategic Studies (IISS) (2021), 'Cyber Capabilities and National Power: A Net Assessment', IISS: London.

International Integrated Reporting Council (2013), *An International "IR" Framework*, IIRC: London.

Iriye, A. (1989), 'Japan's Drive to Great Power Status', in M. Jansen (ed.), *The Cambridge History of Japan, Volume 5, The Nineteenth Century*, Cambridge: Cambridge University Press, 721–782.

Itami, H. (1987), *Jinponshugi kigyō: Kawaru keiei kawaranu genri* (Human Capitalism: Changing Management, Unchanging Principles), Tokyo: Chikuma shobō.

Ito, K. and others (2014), 'The ITO Review of Competitiveness and Incentives for Sustainable Growth—Building Favourable Relationships between Companies and Investors: Final report', Tokyo.

Ito, K. and others (2017), 'Itō repōto 2.0: shizokuteki seichō ni muketa chōki tōshi' (Ito Report 2.0: Long-term Investment for Sustained Growth), Tokyo.

Ito, T. and T. Hoshi (2020), *The Japanese Economy*, 2nd edition, Cambridge MA: MIT Press.

Jacoby, S. (2005), *The Embedded Corporation: Corporate Governance and Employment Relations in Japan and the United States*, Princeton: Princeton University Press.

Jacoby, S. (2009), 'Foreign Investors and Corporate Governance in Japan' in D. H. Whittaker and S. Deakin (eds), *Corporate Governance and Managerial Reform in Japan*, Oxford: Oxford University Press, 93–133.

Japan Cooperative Alliance (JCA) see *Nihon kyōdō kumiai renkei kikō*.

Japan Exchange Group (JPX) and Tokyo Stock Exchange (TSE) (2020), 'Practical Handbook for ESG Disclosure', Tokyo: JPX and TSE.

Japan External Trade Organization (JETRO) (2021), *JETRO Global Trade and Investment Report 2021: Overview*, Tokyo: JETRO.

Japan Institute for Labour, Policy and Training (JILPT) (2017), *Japanese Working Life Profile 2016–17*, Tokyo: JILPT.

Jentsch, H. (2021), *Harvesting State Support: Institutional Change and Local Agency in Japanese Agriculture*, Toronto: University of Toronto Press.

Johnson, C. (1982), *MITI and the Japanese Miracle: The Growth of Industrial Policy, 1925–1975*, Stanford: Stanford University Press.

Jones, R. and H. Seitani (2019), 'Labour Market Reform in Japan to Cope with a Shrinking and Ageing Population', OECD Economics Department Working Paper 1568, Paris: OECD.

Kagawa, T. (1936), *Brotherly Economics*, New York: Harper and Brothers.

Kallender, P. and C. Hughes (2017), 'Japan's Emerging Trajectory as a "Cyber Power": From Securitization to Militarization of Cyberspace', *Journal of Strategic Studies*, 40(1–2): 118–145.

Kamakura, N. (2022), 'From Globalizing to Regionalizing to Reshoring Value Chains? The Case of Japan's Semiconductor Industry', *Cambridge Journal of Regions, Economy and Society*, 15(2), 261–277.

Kamimura, Y. (2021), 'Hataraku koto no imi to hogo: Jizokukanō na deisento uaku no kōsō' (The meanings and Protection of Work: Making Decent Work Sustainable), *Nihon rōdō kenkyū zasshi*, No. 736: 77–86.

Kankyōshō (MoE) (2021), '2019 nendō (reiwa gannendō) no onshitsu kōka gasu haishutsuryō (kakuhōne) ni tsuite' (About the volume of GHG emitted in fiscal 2019 (confirmed data)), Tokyo.

Kapturkiewicz, A. (2021), 'An Institutional Perspective on Entrepreneurial Ecosystems: Variation, Evolution, Agency in and across Organizational Fields', D.Phil thesis, University of Oxford.

Karatani K. (2021), *Niyū asoshiēshonisto sengen* (New Associationist Manifesto), Tokyo: Sakuhinsha.

Kariya, T. (2012), *Education Reform and Social Class in Japan: The Emerging Incentive Divide*, London: Routledge.

Kariya, T. (2020), 'Japan's Catch-up Modernity: Educational Transformation and Its Unintended Consequences', in H. Takeda and M. Williams (eds), *Routledge Handbook of Contemporary Japan*, London: Routledge.

Kariya, T. and Rappleye (2020), *Education, Equality, and Meritocracy in a Global Age: The Japanese Approach*, New York: Teachers College Press.

Katada, S. (2020), *Japan's New Regional Identity: Geoeconomic Strategy in the Asia-Pacific*, New York: Columbia University Press.

Katz, R. (2021a), 'Why Nobody Invests in Japan: Tokyo's Failure to Welcome Foreign Capital Is Hobbling Its Economy', *Foreign Affairs*, 13 October.

Katz, R. (2021b), 'The Essence of Japan's Plight: A Failure to Realize That This Is Not Your Father's Economy', *International Economy*, Winter, 48–51.

Katz, R. (2021c), 'New Business Lobby Pushes Japan Decarbonization', *Tokyo Business Today*, 26 February.

Keidanren (2023), 'Sasuteinaburu shihonshugi ni muketa kōjunkan no jitsugen: Buatsui chūkansō no keisei ni muketa kentō kaigi hōkoku' (Achieving a Virtuous Cycle towards Sustainable Capitalism: Report of the Deliberation Group on Building a Broad Middle Class), Tokyo.

Keidanren (2022), 'Sangyō gijutsu rikkoku e no saichōsen' (Challenging Again to Become an Industry and Technology Power), Tokyo.

Keidanren (2020), *Shin seichō senryaku* (New Growth Strategy), Tokyo.

Keidanren (2018), 'Society 5.0: Co-creating the Future', Tokyo: Keidanren.

Keidanren (2017), 'Revitalizing Japan by Realizing Society 5.0: Action Plan for Creating the Society of the Future', Tokyo: Keidanren.

Keidanren, Tokyo University and GPIF (2020), 'The Evolution of ESG Investment, Realization of Society 5.0, and Achievement of SDGs: Promotion of Investment in Problem-Solving Innovation'.

Keizai Koho Centre (2018), *Japan and the World 2018/19*, Tokyo.

Keizai sangyōshō (2018), 'DX repōto : IT shisutemu "2025 gake" no kuppuku to DX no honkakuteki na tenkai' (Report on DX [Digital Transformation]: Overcoming the "2025 Digital Cliff" Involving Digital systems and Full-Fledged Development Efforts for DX', Tokyo.

Keizai sangyōshō (2019), '"DX suishin shihyō" to sono gaidansu' ('"DX Promotion Indicators" and Guidance'), Tokyo.

Kimura, J. and C. Rigolot (2021), 'The Potential of Geographical Indications (GI) to Enhance Sustainable Development Goals (SDGs) in Japan: Overview and Insights from Japan GI Mishima Potato,' in *sustainability*, https://doi.org/10.3390/su13020961.

Kingston, J. (ed.) (2012), *Natural Disaster and Nuclear Crisis in Japan: Response and Recovery after Japan's 3.11*, London: Routledge.

Kinzley, D. (1991), *Industrial Harmony in Modern Japan: The Invention of a Tradition*, New York: Routledge.

Kishida, F. (2021), *Kishida bijon: Bundan kara kara kyōchō e* (The Kishida Vision: From Division to Cooperation), Tokyo: Kodansha.

Kita, T. (2006), 'Electronic Government in Japan: Towards Harmony Between Technology Solutions and Administrative Systems', in D. H. Whittaker and R. Cole (eds), *Recovering from Success: Innovation and Technology Management in Japan*, Oxford: Oxford University Press, 286–297.

Knight, C. (2010), 'The Discourse of "Encultured Nature" in Japan: The Concept of Satoyama and Its Role in 21st-Century Nature Conservation', *Asian Studies Review*, 34 (4): 421–441.

Koike, K. (1981), *Nihon no jukuren* (Skills in Japan), Tokyo: Yuhikaku.

Kojima, S. and K. Asakawa (2021), 'Expectations for Carbon Pricing in Japan in the Global Climate Policy Context', in T. Arimura and S. Matsumoto (eds), *Carbon Pricing in Japan*, Singapore: Springer, 1–22.

Kōsei Rōdōshō (2018), *Heisei 30 nen ban Rōdō hakusho* (2018 White Paper on Labour), Tokyo.

Konishi, S. (2013), *Anarchist Modernity: Cooperatism and Japanese-Russian Intellectual Relations in Modern Japan*, Cambridge MA: Harvard University Asia Centre.

Kotosaka, M. and M. Sako (2016), 'The Evolution of the ICT Start-Up Eco-System in Japan: From Corporate Logic to Venture Logic?', in T. Nakano (ed.), *Japanese Management in Evolution: New Directions, Breaks, and Emerging Practices*, Routledge, 237–261.

KPMG (2022), 'Survey of Integrated Reporting in Japan 2020', Tokyo: KPMG.

Krippner, G. (2005), 'The Financialization of the American Economy', *Socio-Economic Review*, 3, 173–208.

Kriss, P., H. Miki-Imoto, H. Nishimaki, and T. Riku (2021), 'Toyama City Compact City Development', Washington DC: IBRD and The World Bank.

Kurimoto, A. (2020), 'Consumer Cooperatives Model in Japan', in M. Altman, A. Jensen, A. Kurimoto, R. Tulus, Y. Dongre, and S-K. Jang (eds), *Waking the Asian Pacific Co- operative Potential*, London: Academic Press, 235–244.

Kurimoto, A. and T. Koseki (2019), '*Rokin Banks: 70 Years of Efforts to Build an Inclusive Society in Japan Through Enhancing Workers' Access to Finance*,' (edited by V. Breda), Geneva: ILO Social Finance.

Kurosawa, Y. (2020), 'Nihon keizai: Teitai no 30 nen no gen'in—chōwa ga torenai baburu hōkaigo no keizai no shikumi' ('The Japanese Economy: Causes of 30 Years of Stagnation'), in Toshika kenkyū kōshitsu *Rondan*, Vol. 12: 1–8.

Kusuda, E. and M. Moriguchi (2020), Zukai de hayawakari MaaS, Tokyo Sōtek sha.

Larrue, P. (2021), 'The Design and Implementation of Mission-oriented Innovation Policies: A New Systemic Policy Approach to Address Societal Challenges', OECD Science, Technology and Industry Papers, No. 100, Paris.

Lazonick, W. (2014), 'Profits without Prosperity: Stock Buybacks Manipulate the Market and Leave Most Americans Worse Off', *Harvard Business Review*, September, 11 pp.

Lechevalier, S. (2014), *The Great Transformation of Japanese Capitalism*, London: Routledge.

Lechevalier, S. (2024) forthcoming, Digitalization and Non-inclusive Growth in Japan: A Régulationist Perspective on Post-industrial Dynamics', in *Competition and Change*.

Lechevalier, S. and S. Laugier (2019), 'Innovation beyond Technology: Introduction', in S. Lechevalier (ed.), *Innovation beyond Technology: Science for Society and Interdisciplinary Approaches*, Singapore: Springer, 1–21.

Lechevalier, S. and B. Monfort (2018), 'Abenomics: Has It Worked? Will It Ultimately Fail?', *Japan Forum*, 30(2), 277–302.

Leoni, T. (2016), 'Social Investment as a Perspective on Welfare State Transformation in Europe', Intereconomics, 51(4): 194–200.

Lincoln, J. and M. Gerlach (2004), *Japan's Network Economy: Structure, Persistence, and Change*, Cambridge: Cambridge University Press.

Lollini, N. (2021), 'Becoming a Farmer in Contemporary Japan', DPhil thesis, University of Oxford.

Lucács, G. (2020), *Invisibility by Design: Women and Labour in Japan's Digital Economy*, Durham NC: Duke University Press.

Maclachlan, P. and K. Shimizu (2022), *Betting on the Farm: Institutional change in Japanese Agriculture*, Ithaca: Cornell University Press.

Macnaughton, H. (2015) 'Womenomics for Japan: Is the Abe Policy for Gendered Employment Viable in an Era of Precarity?', *The Asia Pacific Journal: Japan Focus*, 13(13): 1–19.

Manville, C. G. Cochrane, J. Cave, J. Millard, J. Pederson, R. Thaarup, A. Wik, R. Massink, and B. Kotterink (2014), 'Mapping Smart Cities in the EU', report commissioned for European Parliament, Strasbourg.

Matsumoto, K. (1991), *The Rise of the Japanese Corporate System: The Inside View of a MITI Official*, Cambridge: London: Kegan Paul International.

Matsushita, M. (1990), 'The Structural Impediments Initiative: An Example of Bilateral Trade Negotiation', *Michigan Journal of International Law*, 12(2): 436–449.

Mayer, C. (2018), *Prosperity: Better Business Makes the Greater Good*, Oxford: Oxford University Press.

Mazzucato, M. (2018), *The Value of Everything: Making and Taking in the Global Economy*, London: Allen Lane.

Mazzucato, M. (2021) *Mission Economy: A Moonshot Guide to Changing Capitalism*, London: Allen Lane.

McCormack, G. (1996), *The Emptiness of Japanese Affluence*, London: Routledge.

McKean, M. (1981), *Environmental Protest and Citizen Politics in Japan*, Berkeley: University of California Press.

Metzler, M. (2013), *Capital as Will and Imagination: Schumpeter's Guide to the Postwar Japanese Miracle*, Ithaca: Cornell University Press.

MEXT Minister's Meeting on Human Resource Development for Society 5.0 (2018), 'Human Resource Development for Society 5.0: Changes to Society, Changes to Learning (Summary)', Tokyo: MEXT. *See also Monbukagakushō*

Milberg, W. (2008), 'Shifting Sources and Uses of Profits: Sustaining US Financialization with Global Value Chains', in *Economy and Society* 37(3), 420–451.

Minami, R., K. Kim, F. Makino, and J-H Seo (1995), 'Japanese Experience in Technology: A Survey', in R. Minami, K. Kim, F. Makino, and J-H Seo (eds), *Acquiring, Adapting and Developing Technologies: Lessons from the Japanese Experience*, London: Macmillan, 1–28.

Ministry of Economy, Trade and Industry (METI) (2017), 'FinTech Vision: Summary', Tokyo.

Ministry of Economy, Trade and Industry (METI) (Study Group on New Governance Models in Society 5.0) (2020), 'Governance Innovation: Redesigning Law and Architecture for Society 5.0, Version 1.1' METI: Tokyo. *See also Keizai sangyōshō*,

Ministry of Economy, Trade and Industry (METI) (Study Group on New Governance Models in Society 5.0) (2021a), 'Governance Innovation 2.1: A Guide to Designing and Implementing Agile Governance', METI: Tokyo.

Ministry of Economy, Trade and Industry (METI) (2021b), 'Japan's Carbon Neutral Scenario and Asia Energy Transition Initiative', unpublished powerpoint resource.

Ministry of Education, Culture, Sorts, Science and Technology (MEXT) (2018), 'Special Feature: Grand Design for Higher Education toward 2040', Tokyo.

Ministry of Finance (MoF) (2020; 2021), 'Overview of Fiscal Investment and Loan Program', Tokyo: MoF. Ministry of Land, Infrastructure, Transport and Tourism (MLIT), *See Kokudo kōtsushō*.

Ministry of Land, Infrastructure and Transport (MLIT) – see Kokudo kōtsushō

Minsky, H. (1988), 'Schumpeter: Finance and Evolution', paper prepared for Evolution of Technology and Market Structure in an International Context' conference sponsored by the International Schumpeter Society and Universita degli Studi di Siena, Siena, 24–27 May.

Mitchener, K. Shizume, M., and Weidenmier, M. (2010), 'Why Did Countries Adopt the Gold Standard? Lessons from Japan', *The Journal of Economic History*, 70(1): 27–56.

Miura, M. (2012) *Welfare through Work: Conservative Ideas, Partisan Dynamics, and Social Protection in Japan*, Ithaca, NY: Cornell University Press.

Miyagawa, T. (2018), *Seisansei to wa nanika: Nihon keizai no katsuryoku o toinaosu* (What Is Productivity?: Reconsidering Japanese Economic Vitality), Tokyo: Chikuma shinsho.

Miyajima, H. and R. Ogawa (2022), 'Atarashiii shihonshugi to jishakabukai kisei' ('New Capitalism and Regulation of Share Buybacks'), RIETI Special Report https://www.rieti.go.jp/jp/special/special_report/169.html (accessed 17 July 2022).

Miyashita, H. (2021), *Puraibashī to iu kenri: Kojin jōhō wa naze mamorarerubekika* (The Right of Privacy: Why Must Individuals' Information be Protected?), Tokyo: Iwanami shoten.

Mogaki, M. (2019), *Understanding Governance in Contemporary Japan: Transformation and the Regulatory State*, Manchester: Manchester University Press.

Morel, N., B. Palier, and J. Palme (eds) (2011), *Towards a Social Investment Welfare State?: Ideas, Policies and Challenges*, Bristol: Policy Press.

Morikawa, H. (1989), 'The Increasing Power of Salaried Managers in Japan's Large Corporations', in W. Wray (ed.), *Managing Industrial Enterprise: Cases from Japan's Prewar Experience*, Cambridge MA: Harvard University Press, 27–51.

Morikawa, M. (2021), 'Work-from-home Productivity During the Covid-19 Pandemic: Evidence from Japan', *Economic Inquiry*, 60(2): 508–527.

Morishita, T. (2023), *Morishita Tadashi sensei ni yoru kumiai kasseika adobaisu* (Advice on Energizing Cooperative Associations from Professor Morishita Tadashi), Shiga: Chūshō kigyō Shiga (e-book).

Morris-Suzuki, T. (1989), *A History of Japanese Economic Thought*, London: Routledge.

Morris-Suzuki, T. (2020), *Japan's Living Politics: Grassroots Action and the Crises of Democracy*, Cambridge: Cambridge University Press.

Motani, K. and NHK Hiroshima Reporting Team (2013), *Satoyama shihonshugi: Nihon Keizai wa 'anshin no genri' de ugoku* (Satoyama Capitalism: Japan Moves by the 'Peace of Mind Principle'), Tokyo: Kadokawa.

Motani, K. and the Japan Times Satoyama Consortium (2020), *Shinka suru satoyama shihonshugi* (Evolving *Satoyama* capitalism), Tokyo, Japan Times Publishing.

Müller, L. and A. Miki, with H. Kagayama (2011), *Insular Insight: Where Art and Architecture Conspire with Nature*, Baden CH: Lars Müller Publishers.

Naikaku kanbō (Cabinet Secretariat) plus eight ministries and agencies (2021) '2050 nen kābon nyūtoraru ni tomonau gurīn seichō senryaku' (Green Growth Strategy through Achieving Carbon Neutrality in 2050), Tokyo.

Najita, T. (2009), *Ordinary Economics in Japan: A Historical Perspective, 1750–1950*, Berkeley CA: University of California Press.

Nakamura, H. (2022), 'The Potential of Renewable Energy Deployment in Japan', in *Japan Spotlight*, March/April, 26–30.

Nakamura, K. (2019), 'Rentai shakai no kanōsei' (Possibilities for a Solidarity Society), Tokyo: Zenrōsai kyōkai.

Nakamura, K. (2020), 'Jobu-gata jinji no honshitsu: Keidanren teigen "Society 5.0: sōzō shakai" no yōten o manabu' ('The Real Nature of Job-Type Personnel Management: Learning the Key Points of Keidanren's "Society 5.0: Creating Society"') https://www.mercer.co.jp/our-thinking/consultant-column/836.html (accessed 25 April 2022).

Nakamura, K. (2021), *Chiiki kara kaeru: Chiiki rōdō undo e no kitai* (Change from Below: Expectations for the Local Labour Movement), Tokyo: Shunposha.

Nakamura, T. (1988), 'Depression, Recovery, and War 1920–1945', in P. Duus (ed.), *The Cambridge History of Japan, Volume 6 The Twentieth Century*, Cambridge: Cambridge University Press, 451–493.

Nakane, C. (1970), *Japanese Society*, London: Weidenfeld and Nicholson.

Nakanishi, T. (2020), *CASE kakumei: MaaS jidai ni ikinokoru kuruma* (The CASE Revolution: Cars that Will Survive in the Age of MaaS), Tokyo: Nikkei BP.

Nakano, M. (2016), *Financial Crisis and Bank Management in Japan (1997–2016): Building a Stable Banking System*, London: Palgrave.

Nakata, Y. (2018), Nihon no sofutouea sangyō to gijutsusha no genjō o kokusaiteki ni hyōka suru (An International Evaluation of the Current State of the Japanese Software Industry and Engineers), *SEC Journal*, 13(4): 56–59.

Nakata, Y. (2023), '"Jobu-gata koyō" o chushin to suru koyō shisutemu no minaoshi no dōkō' (Trends in Revision of the Employment System, Centred on 'Job-based Employment') in Rengo Sōken (ed.), *Aratana jidai ni okeru keizai no kōjunkan jitsugen ni mukete* (Towards the Realization of a Virtuous Economic Cycle in a New Age), Tokyo: Rengo-RIALS, 192–195.

Nakata, Y. and S. Miyazaki (2011), 'The Labour Market for Japanese Scientists and Engineers: Is the Labour Market Externalized? What Has Happened at Their Workplace?', *Japan Labour Review*, 8(3): 95–117.

Neff, G. (2012), *Venture Labour: Work and the Burden of Risk in Innovative Industries*, Cambridge MA: MIT Press.

Nihon kyōdō kumiai renkei kikō (JCA) (2021), '2018 jigyō nendō kyōdō kumiai tōkeihyō' (2018 Cooperative Statistics), Tokyo.

Nihon kyōdō kumiai renkei kikō (JCA) (2018), 'Aratana renkei soshiki e no ikō ni tsuite' (About the New Alliance Organization), Tokyo.

Nihon setsubi tōshi ginkō (DBJ) (2022), '2022 nendo setsubi tōshi keikaku chōsa: kekka gaiyō' (FY2022 Capital Investment Plan Survey: Summary of Results), DBJ: Tokyo.

Nishimura, I. (2021), 'Working Conditions of Crowdworkers: How Working Conditions of Crowdworkers Vary by Job Content', *Japan Labour Issues* 5(32): 28–40.

Nishioka, Y. (2020), 'Connected Manufacturing Practices that Pioneer Future of Manufacturing', *Hitachi Review*, 69(1): 25–29.

Nishiyama, T. (1984), 'The Structure of Managerial Control: Who Owns and Controls Japanese Businesses?', in K. Sato and Y. Hoshino (eds), *The Anatomy of Japanese Business*, New York: Routledge, 33–77.

Noguchi, Y. (1992), *Baburu no keizaigaku* (Economics of the Bubble), Tokyo: Nihon keizai shinbunsha.

Noguchi, Y. (1998), 'The 1940 System: Japan under the Wartime Economy', *The American Economic Review*, 88(2): 404–416.

Nomura, K. (2020), 'Society 5.0 for SDGs: Sōzō suru mirai no Keizai hyōka' (Society 5.0 for SDGs: An Economic Analysis of Future Created), Tokyo: 21st Century Research Institute.

Nomura Research Institute (NRI) (2020), 'Financial Services in Japan, 2019/20', Tokyo: NRI.

Nonaka, I., A. Hirose, and T. Hirata (2014), *Jissen sōsharu inobēshon: komyunitei, kigyō, NPO* (Applied Social Innovation: Community, Company, NPO), Tokyo: Chikura shobō.

Norton, R. (2001), *Creating the New Economy: The Entrepreneur and the US Resurgence*, Cheltenham: Edward Elgar.

O'Sullivan, M. (2000), 'The Innovative Enterprise and Corporate Governance', *Cambridge Journal of Economics*, 24(4): 393–416.

Odagiri, H. and A. Goto (1996), *Technology and Industrial Development in Japan*, Oxford: Oxford University Press.

Odaka, K. (1941), *Shokugyō shakaigaku* (Occupational Sociology), Tokyo: Iwanami shoten.

OECD (2021), 'Effective Carbon Rates 2021', Paris: OECD.

Ogino, N. (2021), 'What Is Shuntō?', Japan Labour Issues, 5(28): 18–21.

Ohta, H. (2020), 'The Analysis of Japan's Energy and Climate Policy from the Aspect of Anticipatory Governance', MDPI Energies, 13: 1–22, doi:10.3390/en13195153.

Okazaki, T. and M. Okuno-Fujiwara (eds) (1999). The Japanese Economic System and Its Historical Origins. Oxford: Oxford University Press.

Okumura, H. (1984), Hōjin shihonshugi (Corporate Capitalism), Tokyo: Ochanomizu shōbō.

Ovsiannikov, K., K. Kotani, and H. Morita (2022), 'Online Productivity and Types of Assignments in a Japanese Workplace', Social Design Engineering Studies SDES-2022-5, Kochi University of Technology.

Palley, T.I. (2013), Financialization: The Macroeconomics of Finance Capital Domination, New York: Palgrave-Macmillan.

Pekkanen, R. (2000), 'Japan's New Politics: The Case of the NPO Law', The Journal of Japanese Studies, 26(1): 111–148.

Pempel, T. and K. Tsunekawa (1979), 'Corporatism without Labour? The Japanese Anomaly', in P. Schmitter and G. Lehmbruch (eds), Trends towards Corporatist Intermediation, London: Sage, 231–270.

Perez, C. (2002), Technological Revolutions and Financial Capital: The Dynamics of Bubbles and Golden Ages, Cheltenham: Edward Elgar.

Perez, C. (2009), 'The Double Bubble at the Turn of the Century: Technological Roots and Structural Implications', Cambridge Journal of Economics, 33(4): 779–805.

Pfeffer, J. and G. Salancik (1978), The External Control of Organizations: A Resource Dependence Perspective, New York: Harper and Row.

Plastic Waste Management Institute (2021), 'Purasuteku risaikuru no kisō chishiki' (An Introduction to Plastic Recycling), Tokyo: PWMI.

Polanyi, K. (1944), The Great Transformation: The Political and Economic Origins of Our Time, New York: Farrar and Rinehart.

Pomeranz, K. (2000), The Great Divergence: China, Europe, and the Making of the Modern World Economy, Princeton: Princeton University Press.

Porter, M. (1990) The Competitive Advantage of Nations, Basingstoke: Macmillan.

Pugliese, G. and A. Patalano (2020), 'Diplomatic and Security Practice under Abe Shinzō: The Case for Realpolitik Japan', Australian Journal of International Affairs, 74(6): 615–632.

Royal Society, The (2019), 'Explainable AI: The Basics', London.

Ruggie, J. (1982), 'International Regimes, Transactions, and Change: Embedded Liberalism in the Post-war Economic System', International Organization, 36(2), 379–415.

Saito, K. (2020), Hitoshinsei no 'Shihonron' ('Capital' of the Anthropocene), Tokyo: Shueisha.

Sakamoto, Y., W. Spinks, and Y. Shozugawa (2003), 'An Analysis of the MLIT Survey 2002: The Japanese Telework Population', paper presented to the 8th International Telework Workshop, Sao Paulo, 23–27 August.

Sako, M. (2007), 'Organizational Diversity and Institutional Change: Evidence From Financial and Labour Markets in Japan', in M. Aoki, G. Jackson, and H. Miyajima (eds), Corporate Governance in Japan: Institutional Change and Organizational Diversity, Oxford: Oxford University Press, 399–426.

Samuels, R. (1987), The Business of the Japanese State: Energy Markets in Comparative and Historical Perspective, Ithaca: Cornell University Press.

Samuels, R. (1994) Rich Nation, Strong Army, Ithaca: Cornell University Press.

Samuels, R. (2013), 3.11: Disaster and Change in Japan, Ithaca: Cornell University Press.

Sasada, H. (2013), The Evolution of the Japanese Developmental State: Institutions Locked in by Ideas, London: Routledge.

Saxenian, A. (1996), *Regional Advantage: Culture and Competition in Silicon Valley and Route 128*, Harvard: Harvard University Press.

Saxenian, A. (2007), *The New Argonauts: Regional Advantage in a Global Economy*, Cambridge MA: Harvard University Press.

Schaede, U. (2020), *The Business Reinvention of Japan: How to Make Sense of the New Japan and Why It Matters*, Stanford: Stanford University Press.

Shigen enerugīchō (2021), 'Enerugī kihon keikaku (sōan)' (Energy Basic Plan: Draft), Tokyo.

Söderberg, M. (2021), 'Policy Brief: EU-Japan Connectivity Promises', Robert Schuman Centre, EUI Global Governance Programme, Issue 2021/22.

Sonku, Y. (2020), 'Shisutemu o kanjōkei to gyōmukei ni kiriwake, ajairu kaihatsu de henka ni sokuo suru' (Separate Systems Into Reconciliation and Operations and Respond to Changes Rapidly Through Agile Development), in Japan IBM (ed.), The DX: dijitaru henkaku no shinzui (The DX: The Esssence of Digital Transformation), Tokyo.

Sorensen, A. and C. Funck (eds) (2009), *Living Cities in Japan: Citizens' Movements, Machizukuri and Local Environments*, London: Routledge.

Stalk, G. (1988), 'Time: The Next Source of Competitive Advantage', *Harvard Business Review*, 66: 41–51.

Stolz, R. (2014), *Bad Water: Nature, Pollution and Politics in Japan*, Durham NC: Duke University Press.

Streeck, W. (1997), 'Beneficial Constraints: On the Economic Limits of Rational Voluntarism', in R. Hollingsworth and R. Boyer (eds), *Contemporary Capitalism: The Embeddedness of Institutions*, Cambridge: Cambridge University Press, 197–219.

Streeck, W. (2001), 'Introduction: Explorations Into the Origins of Nonliberal Capitalism in Germany and Japan,' in W. Streeck and K. Yamamura eds, *The Origins of Nonliberal Capitalism: Germany and Japan*, Ithaca: Cornell University Press, 1–38.

Streeck, W. (2016), *How Will Capitalism End?* London: Verso.

Streeck, W. and K. Thelen (2005), *Beyond Continuity: Institutional Change in Advanced Political Economies*, Oxford University Press, Oxford

Sturgeon, T. (2002), 'Modular Production Networks: A New American Model of Industrial Organization', *Industrial and Corporate Change*, 11(3): 451–496.

Sturgeon, T. (2007) 'How Globalization Drives Institutional Diversity: The Japanese Electronics Industry's Response to Value Chain Modularity', *Journal of East Asian Studies*, 7(1): 1–34.

Sugeno, K. (1996) *Koyō shakai no hō* (Laws of Employment Society), Tokyo: Yuhikaku.

Takagi, S., H. Tanaka, M. Takemiya, and Y. Fujii (2017), 'Blockchain-Based Digital Currencies for Community Building', Glocom Discussion Paper Series, 17-004, International University of Japan.

Takemoto, S., N. Shibuya and K. Sakoda (2021), ''Learning from Megadisasters: A Decade of Lessons from the Great East Japan Earthquake', World Bank Report, New York.

Teece, D. (2018), 'Business Models and Dynamic Capabilities1', *Long Range Planning*, 51(1): 40–49.

Teece, D., G. Pisano, and A. Shuen (1997), 'Dynamic Capabilities and Strategic Management', *Strategic Management Journal*, 18(7): 509–533.

Terada, T., E. Ueda, H. Kishi, and A. Morii (2017), *Dare ga Nihon no rōdō ryoku o sasaerunoka* (Who Will Bolster Japan's Labour Force?) Tokyo: Toyo keizai.

Thelen, K. (2004), *How Institutions Evolve: The Political Economy of Skills in Germany, Britain, the United States, and Japan*, Cambridge: Cambridge University Press.

Thun, E., D. Taglioni, T. Sturgeon, and M. Dallas (2021), 'Massive Modularity: Why Reshoring Supply Chains Will Be Harder than You May Think', World Bank Blogs, https://blogs.

worldbank.org/developmenttalk/massive-modularity-why-reshoring-supply-chains-will-be-harder-you-may-think (accessed 1 July 2021).

Trencher, G. (2019), 'Towards the Smart City 2.0: Empirical Evidence of Using Smartness as a Tool for Tackling Social Challenges', *Technological Forecasting and Social Change*, 142: 117–128.

Tsujimura, Y. (2022), *Chūshō kigyō no machi Ota-ku kara hajimaru monozukuri Nihon saisei purojekuto* (Project to Re-boot Japanese Manufacturing Starting from the SME Ota-Ward), Toky: Daiyamondosha.

Tsutsui, W. (1998), *Manufacturing Ideology: Scientific Management in Twentieth-Century Japan*, Princeton: Princeton University Press.

Tyson, L. and B. Guile (2021), 'Innovation-based Economic Security', *Issues in Science and Technology*, 37(4): 1–12. https://issues.org/innovation-based-economic-security-tyson-guile/ (accessed 29 May 2022).

United Nations (2004), 'Who Cares Wins: Connecting Financial Markets to a Changing World', Swiss Federal Department of Foreign Affairs, International Finance Corporation and United Nations.

United Nations Environment Programme (2005), 'Innovative Financing for Sustainability: A Legal Framework for the Integration of Environmental, Social and Governance Issues into Institutional Investment', Nairobi: UNEP.

Utting, P. (2015), 'Introduction: The Challenge of Scaling up Social and Solidarity Economy', in P. Utting (ed.), *Social and Solidarity Economy: Beyond the Fringe*, London: UNRISD and Zed Books, 1–37.

Vogel, Stephen (2018), *Marketcraft: How Governments Make Markets Work*, Oxford: Oxford University Press.

Watanabe, T., M. Okuyama and K. Fukamachi (2012), 'A Review of Japan's Environmental Policies for *Satoyama* and *Satoumi* Landscape Restoration', *Global Environmental Research*, 16: 125–135.

White House, The (2021), 'Building Resilient Supply Chains, Revitalizing American Manufacturing, and Fostering Broad-based Economic Growth', June, Washington DC.

Whittaker, D. H. (1997), *Small Firms in the Japanese Economy*, Cambridge: Cambridge University Press.

Whittaker, D. H., with P. Byosiere, S. Momose, T. Morishita, T. Quince, and J. Higuchi (2009), *Comparative Entrepreneurship: The UK, Japan, and the Shadow of Silicon Valley*, Oxford: Oxford University Press.

Whittaker, D. H. and Y. Kurosawa (1998), 'Japan's Crisis: Evolution and Implications', *Cambridge Journal of Economics*, 22(6): 761–771.

Whittaker, D. H. and R. Scollay (2019), 'Japanese Agri-food in Transition', in G. Allaire and B. Daviron (eds), *Ecology, Capitalism and the New Agricultural Economy: The Second Great Transformation*, London: Routledge, 227–242.

Whittaker, D. H., T. Sturgeon, T. Okita, and T. Zhu (2020), *Compressed Development: Time and Timing in Economic and Social Development*, Oxford: Oxford University Press.

Witt, M. (2006), *Changing Japanese Capitalism: Societal Coordination and Institutional Adjustment*, Cambridge: Cambridge University Press.

World Bank (2020), 'Resilient Industries in Japan: Lessons Learned in Japan on Enhancing Competitive Industries in the Face of Disasters Caused by Natural Hazards', Washington DC.

World Business Council for Sustainable Development (2019), 'Corporate and Sustainability Reporting Trends in Japan', Geneva: WBCSD.

Wright, J. (2023), *Robots Won't Save Japan: An Ethnography of Eldercare Automation*, Ithaca: Cornell University Press.

Yamaguchi E. (2019), *Innovation Crisis: Successes, Pitfalls, and Solutions in Japan*, Singapore: Pan Stanford.

Yamaoka, H. (2022), 'Digital Currencies and the Future of Money', in M. Heckel and F. Waldenberger (eds), *The Future of Financial Systems in the Digital Age: Perspectives from Europe and Japan*, Singapore: Springer, 49–73.

Yamashita, K. (2022), 'Shokuryō jikyūritsu wa ageraremasu', ('The Self-Sufficiency Ratio Can Be Raised') in *Gurōbaru ekonomī*, https://cigs.canon/article/20220714_6871.html (accessed 14 July 2022).

Yunogami, T. (2006) 'Technology Management and Competitiveness in the Japanese Semiconductor Industry', in D. H. Whittaker and R. Cole (eds), *Recovering From Success: Innovation and Technology Management in Japan*, Oxford: Oxford University Press, 70–86.

Yunogami, T. (2021), 'Nihon no handōtai buumu wa "nisemono": Honki no saisei ni wa gakkō kyōiku no kaikaku ga hitsuyō da' (Japan's Semiconductor Boom Is Fake: For Real Recovery School Education Reform Is Needed), *EE Times Japan*, 22 June https://eetimes.itmedia.co.jp/ee/articles/2106/22/news042.html (accessed 1 July 2021).

Zou, F. (2023), 'An Emerging Labour Market Player: The Evolving Role of Employment Agencies in Japan and China,' DPhil thesis, University of Oxford.

Zuboff, S. (2019), *The Age of Surveillance Capitalism: The Fight for a Human Future at the New Frontier of Power*, London: Profile Books.

Index

For the benefit of digital users, indexed terms that span two pages (e.g., 52–53) may, on occasion, appear on only one of those pages.

.